Dr. Geyman connects [illegible] point that Ben Franklin feared, the point at which we are at risk [illegible] our democratic republic. He explains how the growth of corporate power—and the outsized ability of corporations to control elections and shape public policy to their liking—have led to this moment. He also explains what we must do to keep the democracy our founders gave us nearly two and a half centuries ago. I plan to give this sobering book to friends and family this election year, which arguably could be the most important in our nation's history.

—Wendell Potter, President of the Center for Health and Democracy and Business Leaders for Health Care Transformation, Founder of Tarbell, and author of *Deadly Spin: An Insurance Company Insider Speaks Out on How Corporate PR Is Killing Health Care and Deceiving Americans* (2010) and *Nation on the Take: How Big Money Corrupts Our Democracy* (2016)

Great book! Just what we need right now. It will help individuals get the issues clear in their minds and give them a pathway for activism so we can straighten up our nation's politics. I think that it is the kind of information resource that people are craving right now, or at least they should be.

—Don McCanne, M.D., family physician, senior health policy fellow and past president of Physicians for a National Health Program (PNHP)

How concentrated economic power fueled the rising authoritarianism that has made American democracy dysfunctional is told powerfully, smoothly, and in plain English by John Geyman, a country doctor turned professor of medicine at the University of Washington. *Corporate Power, and Oligarchy: How Our Democracy Can Prevail Over Authoritarinism and Fascism* prescribes the political medicine needed to restore our democracy to health. In his latest diagnosis of our national political ills, John Geyman explains powerfully and clearly how highly concentrated economic power makes our democracy dysfunctional and threatens to ruin our future.

—David Cay Johnston, Pulitzer Prize-winning investigative journalist and author of *The Fine Print: How Big Companies Use 'Plain English' to Rob You Blind*

Inflated corporate power and associated wealth inequality threaten our democracy. John Geyman, in his trademark logical and accessible style, describes how the U.S. has evolved in recent decades to a precarious top-heavy imbalance, how that has been exacerbated by the rise of the MAGA right, how recent elections offer hope for staving off the anti-democratic GOP, and how the looming 2024 elections are critical to our national well-being. John documents a powerful and scary reality, incorporating the insights of major thought-leaders. This book is an invaluable resource and inspiration for action.

—Jim Kahn, M.D., Professor Emeritus in the Institute for Health Policy Studies, University of California San Francisco and Editor of *Health Justice Monitor*

Dr. Geyman has long been an invaluable interpreter of what is wrong with the health care system in the U.S. today, and how to fix it. This book uses a wider lens, courageously and with his characteristic attention to evidence, showing how increasing concentrations of wealth and power are threatening, not just health care, but American democracy, itself. We ignore Dr. Geyman's warnings at our peril.

—Donald Berwick, M.D., health policy expert, President emeritus of the Institute for Healthcare Improvement, and former administrator of the Centers for Medicare Medicaid Services

In his latest work, Dr. John Geyman extensively researches the pervasive corporatization, commodification, and commercialization of American society, attributing economic and political failures to the growing dominance of large for-profit corporations and inappropriate use of market forces. He contends that the ongoing implosion of the healthcare system is a symptom of the broader underlying pathology within American capitalism, emphasizing the prioritization of shareholders' interests over the interests of all other stakeholders. His work exposes the 21st-century gold rush that is turning Medicine, a once-revered calling, into just another business. This trend has not only corrupted clinical decision-making and resource allocation in the American healthcare system but has also affected broader aspects of American society, including a just distribution of income and wealth. It's time to acknowledge and rectify this mistake in our pursuit of a more effective healthcare system and a fairer and more successful democracy.

—Phillip Caper, M.D., internist with long experience in health policy since the 1970s, and past chairman of the National Council on Health Planning and Development

CORPORATE POWER
and
OLIGARCHY

How Our Democracy Can Prevail Over Authoritarianism and Fascism

John Geyman, M.D.

CORPORATE POWER and OLIGARCHY
How Our Democracy Can Prevail
Over Authoritarianism and Fascism

John Geyman, M.D.

Copernicus Healthcare
Friday Harbor, WA

Ingram Edition

Cover image used under license from Istock/Getty Images
Author photo by Anne Sheridan

softcover: ISBN: 978-1-938218-42-2
eBook version: ISBN 978-1-938218-44-6
Library of Congress Control Number: 2023920877

Copernicus Healthcare
34 Oak Hill Drive
Friday Harbor, WA 98250

www.copernicus-healthcare.org

CORPORATE POWER and OLIGARCHY

How Our Democracy Can Prevail Over Authoritarianism and Fascism

PART III
HOW THE OLIGARCHY THREATENS FAIR ELECTIONS

PART IV
THE BATTLE AHEAD: DEMOCRACY UNDER ATTACK AND AT RISK

TABLES AND FIGURES

PREFACE

In the United States, long a supporter of both foreign autocracies and open societies, the struggle between illiberalism and democracy has become a central theme of American politics and a source of grave divisions in society. Four years of an authoritarian-style presidency cemented the GOP's abandonment of consensus politics and the norms and customs of democracy. The widening gap between the rhetoric, values, and methods of Democrats and Republicans poses difficult questions. What happens in a bipartisan system when one of two parties turns toward autocracy? What is the fate of a country in which right-wing extremist incidents are surging, as elsewhere in the world, but sales of guns to civilians have also reached record levels?

—Ruth Ben-Ghiat, Professor of History at New York University and author of the 2021 book, *Strongmen: Mussolini to the Present.*

The above observation captures a key question of where the U. S. finds itself after four years of the Trump presidency and a January 6, 2021 armed insurrection attack on our Capitol. Together, they came dangerously close to putting us in the abyss. We are now more aware of how far down the road of authoritarianism, corruption, and polarized division that we have come. Historians and political commentators are in agreement that we are now having to cope with the third major threat to our very union—the first having been the Civil War in the 1860s and the second during the Great Depression years in the 1930s. To a considerable extent, what we are seeing now in modern times is uncharted territory.

My 2022 book, *Are We the United States of America? Can We Hold Together as One Country?*, asked those two questions, which address this third major threat to our republic. They are relevant to such continuing questions as what will be the impact of the Final Report of the January 6 Select Committee, what the Department of Justice will do about indicting and prosecuting the former president, and what impact the GOP-controlled House of Representatives and rising tide of authoritarianism will have on the electorate as the 2024 election campaigns get underway.

Most of my previous books have dealt with one or another aspect of health care, but my interest and research in the excesses and negative impacts of the growing power of increasingly monopolistic U. S. corporations goes back more than 20 years.[2] Health care remains an important marker of broader corporate excesses today as then, as Americans know when they try to pay for many of PhRMA's drugs. Dr. Don Berwick, former administrator of the Centers for Medicare and Medicaid Services, has this to say about greed in our health care system that has larger societal impacts:

> *You cannot find a sector in healthcare in which greed is not just manifest, but I would claim even dominant. Greed right now effectively concentrates wealth in the United States; wealth concentrates political power and influence through the role of lobbying and political contribution, and that political contribution stops efforts to reign in or place constraint on greed.*[2]

This book has four goals: (1) to bring historical perspective to how corporate monopoly power, together with more recent changes in the Republican Party, have brought this country to the point of oligarchy and near-fascism; (2) to describe how oligarchs defend their power as it grows; (3) to consider how their Big Money strongly influences elections in their favor; and (4) to discuss the increasing stakes for the 2024 campaigns and to lay out steps that can enable our democracy to prevail over authoritarianism and fascism.

In the following opening chapter, we will trace some of the highlights of how oligarchy and authoritarianism have taken root in the Republican Party and led to its present mission to take our democracy apart under the banner of white supremacy.

***References*:**

1. Ben-Ghiat, R. *Strongmen: Mussolini to the Present.* New York. *W. W. Norton & Company*, 2021, p. 266.
2. Berwick, D. Lancet panel on investor-owned health care. *Health Justice Monitor*, October 3, 2023.

PART I

HOW CORPORATE POWER AND RULE BY THE FEW HAVE COME TO DOMINATE OUR COUNTRY

What America now faces, if we do not change the fundamental structures of the relationship of money to legislative power, is neither mob rule nor democracy, but oligarchy.[1]

—Zephyr Teachout, Associate Professor of Law at Fordham University and author of the 2014 book, *Corruption in America* and the 2020 book *BREAK 'EM UP: RECOVERING OUR FREEDOM* from *BIG AG, BIG TECH, and BIG MONEY.*

The danger we now face is of a passage from the politics of inevitability to the politics of eternity, from a naïve and flawed sort of democratic republic to a confused and cynical sort of fascist oligarchy.[2]

—Tim Snyder, Ph.D., Professor of History at Yale University and author of *On Tyranny: Twenty Lessons from the Twentieth Century*

References:

1. Teachout, Z. *Corruption in America: From Benjamin Franklin's Snuff Box to Citizens United.* Cambridge, MA. *Harvard University Press,* 2014, p. 16.
2. Snyder, T. *On Tyranny, Twenty Lessons from the Twentieth Century,* New York. *Tim Duggan Books,* 2017, p. 124.

CHAPTER 1

HISTORICAL PERSPECTIVE: AUTHORITARIANISM AND RULE BY THE FEW IN AMERICA

We must make our choice. We may have democracy, or we may have wealth concentrated in the hands of a few, but we can't have both.

—Louis Brandeis, Associate Justice, U.S. Supreme Court 1916-1939

We should be awake to the assault on democratic values that has gained strength in many countries abroad and that is dividing America at home. The temptation is powerful to close our eyes and wait for the worst to pass, but history tells us that for freedom to survive, it must be defended, and that if lies are to stop, they must be exposed.[1]

—Madeleine Albright, former Secretary of State, U. S. Ambassador to the United Nations, and author of the 2018 book, *Fascism: A Warning.*

In this opening chapter, I have just one overall goal—to bring some historical perspective to how rule by the few (oligarchy) and authoritarianism have come to pass in these United States. Before starting, we can set out with these definitions: *oligarchy*, defined as a form of government in which power is vested in a few, or in a dominant class; *authoritarianism*, defined as a political system wherein individual freedom is completely subordinate to the power or authority of the state; and *fascism*, an anti-democratic hierarchial form of government run by an all-powerful dictator.

How Did We Get to Oligarchy and Authoritarianism?

These nine events and trends coalesce to answer this important question, which on the surface, given the long-professed beliefs underlying this nation's heritage, would have seemed rude and unruly.

1. Rise of the Corporate State and Oligarchy

Early in the history of this country, this letter from John Adams to Thomas Jefferson gave us some warning of what has befallen us over the last 70 or so years:

> *Power always thinks it has a great Soul, and vast Views, beyond the Comprehension of the Weak, and that it is doing God's Service, when it is violating all his Laws.*[2]

"Neoliberalism" is a term developed by utopian economists in France and Western Europe during the mid-1900s with the hope that it could prevent the rise of fascism and communism in developed democracies. It called for privatizing most government functions, deregulating business, and letting the "magic of the marketplace" ensure an abundance of life, liberty and pursuit of happiness. It took root in the U. K in 1978 under Margaret Thatcher and in this country with the election of Ronald Reagan in 1980.[3]

In the 1980s, Reagan's policies of corporate growth, neoliberalism, and deregulation brought in these big changes that were good for big business and the financial industry. Here are some highlights since then that stand out as leading to the all- powerful corporate state in this country:

- "Corporate lobbying in Washington and the number of political action committees wildly increase, and the costs of congressional campaigns begin their doubling and tripling over the next thirty years.
- Federal enforcement of antitrust laws to rein in corporate power suddenly shrinks to a fraction of what it has been.
- The deregulation of business by government accelerates.

- Large, dominant companies start charging customers historically higher markups on the products they sell.
- Stock prices almost tripled (before almost quadrupling again during the 1990s.
- The long-standing federal prohibition on companies buying their own stock, meant to prevent share price manipulation, is repealed.
- The new "shareholder value" movement's redefinition of capitalism makes a company's current stock price essentially the only relevant measure of corporate performance.
- Leveraged buyouts, financial firms using excessive debt to take over and often ruin companies, becomes normalized and significant.
- Wall Street salaries increase by more than 25-percent before increasing another 50 percent in the 1990s."[4]

In his book, *The Hidden History of Neoliberalism: How Reaganism Gutted America,* Thom Hartmann described the premise and outcomes of neoliberalism whereby the "magic of the marketplace" would serve the public interest if most government functions and decisions were turned over to the most powerful economic stakeholders through privatization and deregulation.[5] As Hartmann has recently noted, however:

> *The (neoliberalism) experiment has been, to be charitable, a failure. In every country where it was tried inequality has exploded, workers have fallen behind, corporate monopolies have strangled competition and destroyed small businesses, and political systems have been corrupted by big money.*[6]

Dr. Noam Chomsky, Professor Emeritus of Linguistics at the Massachusetts Institute of Technology and author of the 2023 book, *Illegitimate Authority: Facing the Challenges of Our Time*, brings us this further perspective:

Class war never ceases. One participant, the business classes—the "masters of mankind" in Adam Smith's phrase—is constantly engaged in the conflict, with no little passion in a country like the US that has an unusually high level of business class consciousness. As Smith pointed out 250 years ago, they strive to control state policy and employ it for their own interests, commonly succeeding, though with occasional partial setbacks. If their victims are beaten down or retire from the struggle, they win enormous victories for themselves. We have just experienced that during the neoliberal regression, which undermined democracy along with the huge robbery. That's a basic factor in the surge of "illegitimate authority" in today's declining democracies, and in the pervasive anger, resentment, and distrust of authority.[7]

2. Decline of the middle class with rise of elitism

The middle-income group of Americans fell from 61 percent of all Americans to just 51 percent between 1971 and 2011. Those years were also associated with reductions of real hourly compensation in what economists labelled a wage-productivity gap or "the great wage slowdown of the 21st century" that depressed wages of low-income and middle-income workers.[8,9]

According to the Rand Institute, since 1975 some $50 trillion in wealth has been redistributed from the bottom 90% of our population to the top 1%, especially because corporate profits and CEO compensation have grown so much faster than the wages of average workers. Starting in the late 1970s, as recorded by the Economic Policy Institute, the growth of median wages diverged farther from that of the economy, as shown by Figure 1.1. By 2022, the three wealthiest people had more wealth than the bottom 50 percent.[10]

In his 2020 book, *The System: Who Rigged It: How We Fix It,* Robert Reich, Professor of Public Policy, the University of California Berkeley, noted this connection to oligarchy:

Figure 1.1

THE GROWING GAP BETWEEN PRODUCTIVITY AND PAY, 1948-2020

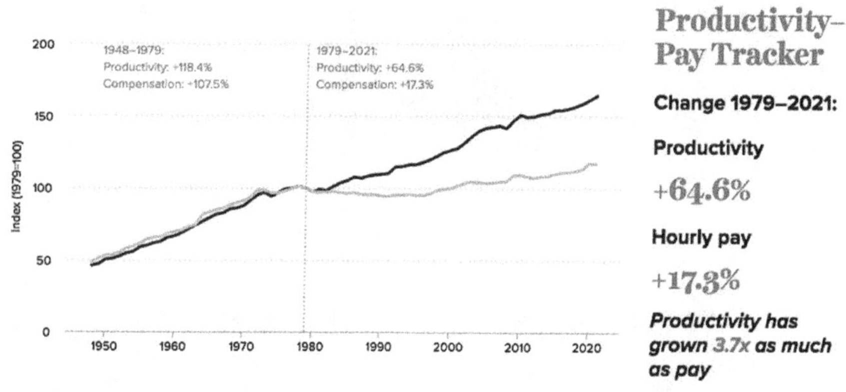

Source: Economic Policy Institute, Bureau of Labor Statistics, and Bureau of Economic Analysis

Even a system that calls itself a democracy can become an oligarchy if power becomes concentrated in the hands of a corporate and financial elite. Their power and wealth increase over time as they make laws that favor themselves, manipulate financial markets to their advantage, and create or exploit economic monopolies that put even more wealth into their own pockets.[11]

3. *Increasing diversity, projections of white minority by 2045, and growth of the white supremacy movement*

The 2020 Census report showed a diversifying country where the total white population shrank for the first time in its history. It is now less than 60 percent of the entire U. S. population. The Census Bureau further projects that the country will become "minority white" in 2045 with 49.7 percent of the population. Figure 1.2 shows the expected racial profile of the U. S. population at that time when Hispanics will comprise 24.6 percent, Blacks 13.1 percent, and Asians 7.9 percent of the population.[12]

FIGURE 1.2

RACIAL PROFILE OF U. S. POPULATION, 2045

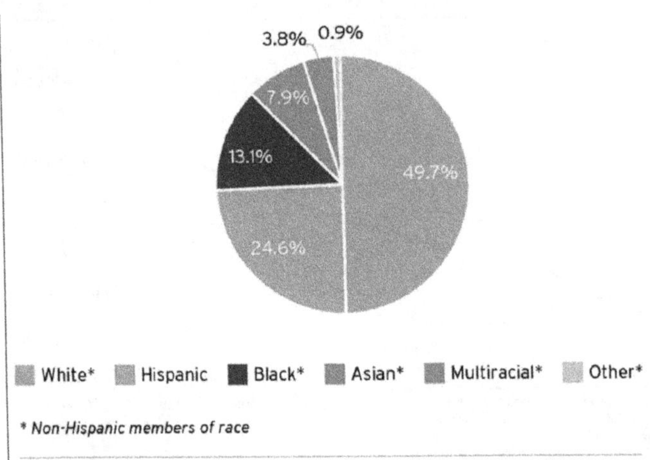

Source: William H Frey analysis of U.S. Census population projections released March 13, 2018 and revised September 6, 2018. Metropolitan Policy Program at Brookings.

That major change became associated with the *further* growth of the white supremacy movement, which had a long history, starting with the arrival of slave ships from Africa in the early 1600s. The plight of Blacks in this country did not improve much for centuries thereafter. As historian Jim Downs described in his 2012 book, *Sick from Freedom*, white leaders had fears that free and healthy African-Americans could upset their existing racial hierarchy.[13] The well-known Tuskegee experiment was a classic example of how Blacks were mistreated from 1932 to 1972, when a supposed "study" was conducted by the U. S. Public Health Service whereby Blacks were treated with a placebo for "bad blood" instead of penicillin for syphilis, leading to the deaths of more than 128 participants.[14]

The January 6, 2021 insurrection at the U. S. Capitol was a reminder that white supremacy remains as a persistent sickness in our society. Wesley Lowery, Pulitzer Prize-winning journalist and author of the new book, *American Whitelash: A Changing Nation and the Cost of Progress*, brings us this important historical insight:

> *On the night of his election in 2008, Barack Obama had declared his ascent as proof that the dreams of the founders remained alive in our time. A decade and a half later that dream has become a nightmare.*
>
> *The same battles that accompanied the black presidency—debates about who belongs, what speech is acceptable in our public square, and who is responsible when bigotry's bark eventually turns into a devastating bite—remain at the fore of discourse. Black Americans, immigrants and refugees continue to shape our culture, society and democracy, demanding not just equality under law but also equity of outcome. In the meantime, the country's white majority grows increasingly agitated and aggrieved, convinced that it's all gone too far. All the while, an emboldened white supremacist movement stands eager to convert these disaffected citizens into soldiers for its cause.*[15]

4. *Citizens United in 2010*

The U. S. Supreme Court advanced the power of corporations immeasurably in a single stroke in 2010 by giving corporations the political equivalence of personhood and allowing unmonitored campaign contributions by billionaires. These two observations call attention to some of the serious implications of that ruling on our democracy:

> *Corporatism, in reality, is the corporate state—a tyranny, greased by big money in elections—never envisioned by the framers of our Constitution when they started its preamble with "We the people."*[16]
>
> —Ralph Nader, longtime consumer advocate, attorney, founder of Public Citizen and of the Center for the Study of Responsive Law, and author of *Wrecking America: How Trump's Lawbreaking and Lies Betray All*

> *It is difficult to overstate the significance of the ideas that Milton Friedman launched in 1970, now compounded by the Citizens United decision and the power granted to make corporate values, already dominant, pervasive in every aspect of American life . . . Citizens United is to the expansion of corporate power what the big bang was to the beginning of the universe.*[17]
>
> —David Cay Johnston, Pulitzer Prize-winning investigative journalist and author of *The Fine Print: How Big Companies Use 'Plain English' to Rob You Blind*

5. *Trump elected without winning popular vote in 2016 election*

Trump's loss of the popular vote was the 7th time the Republicans have lost the popular vote for president since 1992.[18] As an authoritarian with a long history of lies and corruption, right off the bat he confused the words "company" and "country" in his first formal press conference as president-elect:

> *Tilting the country towards oligarchy requires confusing—as Trump did in his first press conference as president-elect—"company" and "country," making no distinction between the national interest and what he sees as his broader "family" interest . . . "Family" also includes those officials and employees from whom he demands obsequious loyalty, though unlike his actual family, these people can move in and out of favor at Trump's whim. This broader group also includes the very rich, who can prove their own loyalty through incessant financial favors: campaign donations, club memberships, hotel stays, condo purchases . . . The entire apparatus of government, the president argues almost every day, should serve his interests.*[19]

6. *Trump lost to Biden in 2020 election; results have been denied by the Big Lie and other disinformation*

Despite conclusive evidence that the outcome of the 2020 presidential election was fair without any widespread election fraud, former president Trump has continued to promulgate the Big Lie that it was stolen. It strains credibility how pervasive the Big Lie has become since adopted by so many in the Republican Party. A Reuters/Ipsos poll in May, 2021 found that 61 percent of Republican respondents believed that the 2020 election was "stolen" from Donald Trump, that more than one-half considered him the "true president" and did not consider him to be at least partly to blame for starting the deadly January 6 riot at the U. S. Capitol.[20]

7. Increasing Extremism of the Republican Party

The Republican Party in the runup to the 2022 midterms—many GOP candidates were election deniers, issuing anti-democratic, pro-fascist rhetoric as the party pursued a national strategy of putting secretaries of state in place who could swing the outcomes of electoral votes their way.

In his 2022 book, *Going Big: Biden's New Deal, and the Struggle to Save Democracy*, Robert Kuttner has this to say about the Republican Party:

> *The Republican Party has literally become the party of fear—of domestic terrorism, of hatred, of deceit, of division, and of ending the American experiment in democracy.*[21]

That observation is hardly new. As David Corn recounts in his new book, *American Psychosis: A Historical Investigation of How the Republican Party Went Crazy*, the Republican Party has a long history of fear mongering:

> *Since the 1950s, the GOP has repeatedly mined fear, resentment, prejudice, and grievance and played to extremist forces so the party could win elections . . . In the 1950s, the foe was Reds. In the 1960s (and beyond), it was Black people demanding social justice and societal change. In the 1970s, the New Right and the religious right claimed liberals and Democrats (and gays!) were plotting to destroy the nation. Tea Partiers asserted Obama headed a sinister cabal bent on turning the United States into a socialist hellhole . . .* [22]

> *[More recently] Under Trump's control, the Grand Old Party was consumed and conquered by the extremism, rage, and hatred it had long exploited. Born 168 years earlier to save the nation from the expansion of slavery, the Republican Party, now infected with a political madness, had become a threat to the Republic.*[23]

Paul Starr, Professor of Sociology and Public Affairs at Princeton University calls attention to three historic changes in the two major political parties in this country starting in the mid-20th century:

- "the racial and regional realignment that has made the Democratic Party the home of Black Americans and majorities of other people of color, while enabling the Republicans not only to capture most southern states but to become the majority party of white America."
- "An independent though related cultural shift, in which women, people with non-conforming gender identities, and the more secular, urban, and better-educated moved toward the Democrats, while the more religious, rural, and less-educated, particularly men, moved into the Republican Party."
- "Collapse of the center-right, the takeover of the Republican Party by its ethnonationalist right wing, and the resulting uncertainty as to whether Republicans can still be counted on to follow the basic rules of democratic government, like giving up power after losing an election."[24]

The hard right that has evolved in the Republican Party is based on exclusion and the construction of hierarchies, with a goal to revive an older social order of a white-dominated, patriarchal society with male supremacy and increasing authoritarianism.[25]

8. *Normalization of Extremism*

Jason Stanley, Ph.D., Professor of Philosophy at Yale University and author of the 2020 book, *How Fascism Works: The Politics of Us and Them*, brings us this important insight:

> *In the United States, we have seen normalization of extreme policies with the rapid development of racialized mass incarceration, which occurred in my lifetime. More recently, in the United States, we have seen the normalization of mass shootings. . . What normalization does is transform the morally extraordinary into the ordinary. . . Normalization means precisely that encroaching ideologically extreme conditions are not recognized as such because they have come to seem normal. The charge of fascism will always seem extreme; normalization means that the goalposts for the legitimate use of "extreme" terminology continually move . . . Fascist politics lures its audiences with the temptation of freedom from democratic norms while masking the fact that the alternative proposed is not a form of freedom that can sustain a stable nation state and can scarcely guarantee liberty.*[26]

Many wonder how Trump can keep as much support among his followers as he has. The 2020 book by John Dean and Bob Altemayer, *Authoritarian Nightmare: Trump and His Followers,* gives us a useful answer—authoritarianism requires an authoritarian *leader*, who demands complete obedience and denies individual freedom, and authoritarian *followers*, who submit too much to the authorities in their lives, despite the lies, bad decisions, immoral and outright unlawful acts that the "leader" performs.[27]

9. *Increasing violence*

The Great Replacement theory has been put forward in white nationalist circles claiming that non-white individuals are being brought into the U. S. to "replace" white voters and achieve political supremacy. This kind of fear-mongering, fed over the internet by conservative and Republican institutions, has incited mass shootings in churches, markets and other public places with the shooters inspired by this theory. One recent example took place in a Buffalo, New York supermarket, where 10 people were killed and 3 wounded, with 11 of the victims African American.[28.] Another recent example shows how lethal conspiracy theories can be, even within a family, when a father killed all members of his family over disagreement with this theory.[29]

Predictably, as a result of all this fear-mongering and conspiracy theories, the numbers of active anti-government and hate groups have grown markedly, as tracked by the Southern Poverty Law Center (Figure 1.3).[30] Many of these groups use flyers and banners in public places steeped in racism and misogyny to recruit new members.[31] Increasingly, members of these hate groups have disrupted and threatened poll workers, election officials, school boards and other public venues. As the Southern Poverty Law Center notes in its recent publication, *2022: The Year in Hate & Extremism*:

> *In the two years since the insurrection, the right has only increased the political temperature. Far-right activists have embraced ever more violent rhetoric, while Republican officials consistently fail to acknowledge that their words are contributing to an atmosphere that breeds political violence.*[32]

FIGURE 1.3

ACTIVE ANTIGOVERNMENT AND HATE GROUPS IN THE U. S. IN 2022

Source: Southern Poverty Law Center

The depth of alienation among Republicans is confirmed by the results of an August 2021 nationwide poll by Bright Line Watch/ You Gov Nationwide that found that 50 percent of respondents preferred secession to compromising with a Democratic administration. (Figure 1.4)[33]

FIGURE 1.4

SECESSIONIST SENTIMENT BY REGION

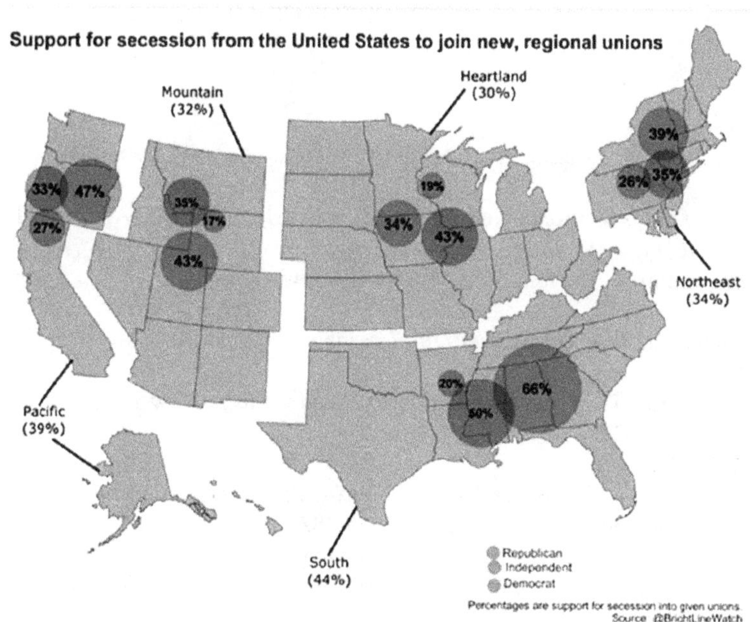

Source: Bright Line Watch/YouGov, August, 2021

Not surprisingly, gun sales in the U. S. have increased markedly, now with as many guns as our entire population,[34] while FBI data show rising numbers of hate crimes against Black Americans.[35] As Susan Corke, director of the Southern Poverty Law Center's Intelligence Project, observes:

> *The mainstreaming of hate and extremism threatens our people, our education system and democracy itself . . . The January 6 attack on the U. S. Capitol was the culmination of*

years of right-wing radicalization . . . The reactionary and racist beliefs that propelled a mob into the Capitol that day have not dissipated. Instead they've coalesced into a political movement that is now one of the most powerful forces shaping politics in the United States.[36]

Conclusion:

With that historical background, we are now better prepared to shift our attention to the next chapter to see how the corporate state has evolved to implant oligarchy and elitism in our society.

References:

1. Albright, M, *Fascism: A Warning*. New York. *HarperCollins*, 2018, pp. 252-253.
2. John Adams to Thomas Jefferson, with Postscript by Abigail Adams, February 2, 1816, https://founders.archives.gov/documents/Jefferson/03-09-02-0285.
3. Hartmann, T. The failure of neoliberalism. www.laprogressive.com, April 16, 2022.
4. Andersen, K. *Evil Geniuses: The Unmaking of America*. New York. *Penguin Random House*, 2020, p. 119.
5. Hartmann, T. *The Hidden History of Neoliberalism: How Reaganism Gutted America*, 2022.
6. Ibid # 3.
7. Chomsky, N. *Illegitimate Authority: Facing the Challenges of Our Time*. Chicago, IL. *Haymarket Books*, 2023, pp. 286-287.
8. Formisano, RP. *Plutocracy in America: How Increasing Inequality Destroys the Middle Class and Exploits the Poor*. Baltimore, MD, *John Hopkins University Press*, 2015, pp. 53, 62, 63.
9. Leonhardt, D. The great wage slowdown of the 21st Century. *New York Times*, October 7, 2014.
10. Kuttner, R. *Going Big: FDR's Legacy, Biden's New Deal, and the Struggle to Save Democracy*. New York. *The New Press*, 2022, p. 90.
11. Reich, R, *The System: Who Rigged It: How We Fix It*. New York. *Alfred A Knopf*. 2020, p. 14.
12. Frey, WH. The U. S. will become 'minority white' in 2045, Census projects. *Brookings*, March 14, 2018.
13. Downs, J. *Sick from Freedom*. New York. *Oxford University Press*, 2012, pp. 78-88.
14. Nix, E. The Tuskegee experiment: The infamous syphilis study. *National Archives*, December 15, 2020 (https://www.history.com/news/theinfamous-40-year-tuskegee-study).

15. Lowery, W. American *Whitelash: A Changing Nation and the Cost of Progress.* New York, Boston. *Mariner Books*, 2023, p. 237.
16. Nader, R. Corporate destruction of free markets rules us. In the Public Interest. *Common Dreams*, October 31, 2014.
17. Johnston, DC. *The Fine Print: How Big Companies Use 'Plain English' to Rob You Blind.* New York. *Penguin Group*, 2013, p. 26.
18. Starr, P. How American politics turned deadly: The explosive consequences of the realignment of the two major parties. *The American Prospect*, August 2022, p. 57.
19. Bernstein, A. *American Oligarchs: The Kushners, the Trumps, and the Marriage of Money and Power.* New York. *W. W. Norton & Company*, 2020, pp. 407-408.
20. Smoking gun. What Republicans believe. *The Progressive*, August 24, 2021, p. 17.
21. Kuttner, R. *Going Big: Biden's New Deal, and the Struggle to Save Democracy.* New York. *The New Press,* 2022, p. 192.
22. Corn, D. The elephant in the room. *Mother Jones*, September-October 2022, pp. 21, 66.
23. Corn, D. *American Psychosis: A Historical Investigation of How the Republican Party Went Crazy,* 2022, p. 337.
24. Ibid # 18.
25. Miller, C. Male supremacy is at the core of the hard right's agenda. Hate and extremism in 2023. Southern Poverty Law Center, 2023.
26. Stanley, J. *How Fascism Works: The Politics of Us and Them.* New York. *Random House,* 2020, p. 189-191.
27. Dean, JW, Altemeyer, B. *Authoritarian Nightmare: Trump and His Followers.* Brooklyn, NY. *Melville House*, 2020, p. 25.
28. Ryland, A. Senator Chris Murphy calls on GOP to condemn white nationalist "great replacement" theory. *Politicus USA*, May, 17, 2022.
29. Neiwert, D. Tragedy in small Michigan town once again demonstrates how lethal conspiracy theories can be. *Daily Kos*, September 12, 2022.
30. Hankes, K, Janik, R. *The Year in Hate and Extremism 2020. Southern Poverty Law Center*, 2021, pp. 2-16.
31. Ibid # 27, p. 11.
32. Miller, C, Kieffer, C. *Hate and extremism: In the Mainstream and on Main Street.* Southern Poverty Law Center, 2023.
33. Crowther, H. A confederacy of dunces? Once again, Dixie wants out. *The Progressive Populist*, 27:21, December 1, 2021: p. 1.
34. Wernau, J, Elinson, A. New buyers rush to acquire guns. *Wall Street Journal*, July 15, 2020: A 20.
35. Burch, ADS, Vander Ploeg, L. Surge in hate crimes against Black people is seen in FBI data. *Wall Street Journal*, May 17, 2022.
36. Corke, S. The SPLC identifies 733 hate groups, issues recommendations for protecting democracy. *SPLC Report* 52 (2): 1, 2022.

CHAPTER 2

CONSOLIDATION, MERGERS, AND MONOPOLY POWER IN CORPORATE AMERICA

In the capitalist society, the economy is the dominant sector. Here power and values flow from money to economic institutions that in turn shape the institutions of government and culture to align society's rules, values, and symbols with financial interests. The key to capitalism's power over society is its ability to maintain a materialistic culture that denies the spirit and constantly reinforces the idea that humanity's capacity for greed, competition, and violence exceeds its capacity for sharing, cooperation, and love.[1]

—David C. Korten, M.B.A., Ph.D., economist, business leader and author of the 2001 book *When Corporations Rule the World*

The very existence of a rapidly expanding billionaire class in the United States is a manifestation of an unjust system that promotes massive income and wealth inequality . . . It is also a manifestation of a corrupt political system, in which immense power over the lives of the great mass of Americans is concentrated in the hands of a small number of people who —through campaign finance arrangements that can only be described as legalized bribery—buy control of our elections and the policies that extend from them.[2]

—Bernie Sanders (I-VT), third term United States Senator, longest-tenured independent member of Congress in American history, and author of the 2023 book, *It's OK to Be Angry about Capitalism.*

Following up on the last chapter, here we have three goals: (1) to summarize the evolution of consolidation and mergers of U. S. corporations over the last 60 years; (2) to show how concentrated corporate monopoly power now dominates the U. S. economy; and (3) to briefly consider the impacts of this profound change on prices, compensation, and decline of the middle class.

I. The Uninterrupted Growth of Corporate Consolidation and Mergers in the U. S.

Free trade and globalization have been front and center of U. S. economic policy for more than five decades. Reagan's election in 1980 launched a merger wave similar to that of the 1890s. The new pressure on U. S. corporations became "buy or be bought" as an industry of arbitrageurs emerged to restructure corporate America.[2] Corporate takeovers became common with raiders pursuing a single goal of chasing profits for themselves and their shareholders.

Downsizing of the major corporations was also common in those years. Many had become global, with redistribution of factories around the world. A new social contract was being established whereby growth involved diffusion of jobs and products globally resulting in threats to living standards of many poor and lower-income people in both advanced and developing nations.[3] Between 1981 and 1985, as one example, GE cut more than one-quarter of its U.S. workforce while tripling its net income,[4] while it developed a large contract workforce outside of the U. S., often paid less than $2 a day and without benefits and without legal or union protections.[5]

William Greider, in his 1992 book, *Who Will Tell the People: The Betrayal of American Democracy,* had this to say about the political power of large corporations by that time:

> *Political events of the past two years have delivered a more profound and devastating message: American democracy has been conclusively conquered by American capitalism. Government has been disabled or captured by the formidable powers of private enterprise and concentrated wealth. Self-governing rights that representative democracy conferred*

on citizens are now usurped by the overbearing demands of corporate and financial interests. Collectively, the corporate sector has its arms around both political parties, the financing of political careers, the production of policy agendas and propaganda of influential think tanks, and control of most major media.

And further:

General Electric is a conglomerate that, in addition to its productive, profit-making activities, also functions as a ubiquitous political organization. With great sophistication and tenacity, GE represents its own interests in the political arena, as one would expect. But that is not what makes it so influential . . . GE has the resources to develop and promote new political ideas and to organize public opinion around its political agenda. It has the capacity to advise and intervene and sometimes veto. It has the power to punish political opponents.[6]

At the start of the 21st century, more than one-half of the 100 largest "economies" were corporations, not countries.[7]The largest corporations at that time included General Electric (GE), Ford, General Motors, and Exxon. GE had the broadest of interests, ranging from manufacturing of locomotives, jet engines, and industrial turbines to robotics and medical diagnostic equipment. It was also a media giant, with broadcast and cable television operations like NBC, CNBC, and MSNBC. As an active member of the Business Roundtable, which orchestrates the political agenda of Fortune 500 companies, it also sponsored the right-wing TV talk show, the *McLaughlin Group*.

By 2014, most markets for essential goods were covered by monopolies. As Zephyr Teachout, Ph.D., author of the book, *Corruption in America: From Benjamin Franklin's Snuff Box to Citizens United*, noted at that time:

Retail is governed by Walmart and Amazon, cable by Comcast, finance by four banks, and meat production by four companies.[8]

Matt Stoller, in his 2019 book, *Goliath: The 100-Year War Between Monopoly Power and Democracy*, brings us a counter-vailing view to the incessant overbearing power of corporate monopolies:

> *Nothing about monopolization is inevitable. Our increasingly dystopian and corrupt political apparatus was brought to us by people selling a fantasy of inevitability. Some of them sold us a right-wing fantasy of corporate monopolies and bigness as a sign of progress. Some of them sold us a left-wing fantasy of corporate monopolies as an unstoppable feature of capitalism. But these fantasies are, in the end, the same. They both are designed to sell you on the idea that you have no power, that you are nothing but a consumer . . . The real question is not whether commerce is good or bad. It is how we are to do commerce, to serve concentrated power or to free ourselves from concentrated power.*[9]

Beyond the question of *how* the power of the corporate state has enveloped America, another important question is *why* it has happened. For the answer we have only to go back to the opening quote of this chapter—unbridled greed by those leading the corporate charge. Here is how Bill Moyers brought home the implications of this big change 15 years ago:

> *So, it is contrary to what we have heard rhetorically for a generation now, the individualist, greed-driven, free market ideology is at odds with our history and with what most Americans really care about. More and more people agree that growing inequality is bad for the country, that corporations have too much power, that money in politics is corrupting democracy and that working and poor communities need and deserve help when the market system fails to generate shared prosperity. Indeed, the American public is committed to a set of values that almost perfectly contradicts the conservative agenda that has dominated politics for a generation now.*[10]

II. How Corporate Monopoly Power Dominates the U. S. Economy

When the top four firms account for 40 percent or more of sales, economists consider a domestic market to be monopolistic. Global markets are considered highly monopolistic when five firms control more than one-half of the market. By 1990, through a series of mergers and consolidations, the top four major appliance corporations in the U. S. controlled 92 percent of the U. S. appliance market,[11] while the top five durable consumer firms controlled almost 70 percent of the global market of that industry.[12] Today, out of almost 6 million corporations worldwide, 53 are among the world's largest economies. Walmart, for example, is larger than the economies of Israel and Greece together.[13]

Here are some examples of how extremely monopolized various parts of our economy are in this country now:

- *Retail*: Walmart controls 72 percent of warehouse clubs and super centers in the entire U. S.
- *Amazon:* Sells 74 percent of all e-books and 64 percent of all print books sold online; with the recent acquisition of One Medical, it has become a primary care middleman "clinic" with access to personal medical records that sacrifices patients' privacy by selling personal data.[15]
- *Food and farming:* Beef, pork, and poultry are all dominated by four giants at the national level.
- Two firms, Dean Foods and the Dairy Farmers of America, control as much as 80-90 percent of the milk supply chain in some states and have substantial influence across the entire industry.
- Grocery stores: Supermarket giant Kroger is finalizing an almost $25 billion deal to acquire its jumbo-size competitor Albertsons; the new megacorporation will combine more than 13 grocery chains, including Safeway, Fred Meyer, and others in 5,000 supermarket locations, likely to result in increased prices, worker layoffs, and lower wages.[16, 17]
- The top 3 hospitals and systems in the country account for 77 percent of all hospital admissions.

- The pending takeover of Rite Aid by Walgreen's would reduce the market to two giants, along with CVS.
- *Health insurers*: The announced plans of Aetna to merge with Humana, Anthems's agreement to purchase Cigna, and Centene's proposed merger with Healthnet, would leave 3 giant companies in dominant positions in the industry.
- *Defense contractors:* Since 1993, consolidation has reduced their numbers from 107 to 5.
- *Office supplies:* Office Depot and Office Max control 69 percent of the entire office supplies market.
- *Television advertising:* The top two agencies control more than 70 percent of television advertising.
- *Internet searches:* Google controls 64 percent of all desktop searches and 94 percent of all global and mobile tablet searches.
- *Semiconductors:* Intel controls some 98 percent of the microprocessor market in servers and about 93 percent in notebooks.
- *Airlines*: Recent mergers have left four carriers—American, United, Delta and Southwest—with control of over 80 percent of the market.
- *Travel search*: Recent purchases have Expedia and PriceLine as the only two independent travel search companies.[15]

III. Impacts of Corporate Monopolies on Prices, Compensation, and the Middle Class

The opening quote for this chapter by David Korten draws from the ancient Greek philosopher Aristotle (551-479 B.C) who used the term civil society to describe a civilized society of free or equal citizens who act in their civic roles with a mindful consciousness of the needs of both the individual and the whole. With the goal to transform the present decidedly uncivil global capitalist society into a global civil society, Korten offers us a view of how civic and capitalist societies differ (Figure 2.1). In a civic society, the power and values flow upward from the living spirit through people to culture and then to institutions, while financial markets in a capitalist society dominate spirit and set the values of society.[16] Figure 2.2 shows how the quest for money can then widen the gap between individuals, families and community, leading to increasing alienation within our society.[17]

FIGURE 2.1

CIVIL OR CAPITALIST SOCIETY?

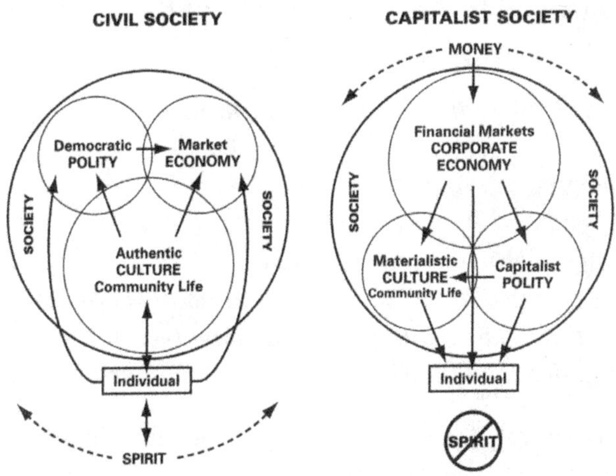

Source: Korten, DC. *When Corporations Rule the World. Kumarian Press, Inc,* Bloomfield, CT and *Berrett-Koehler Publishers, Inc*, San Francisco, CA, Second edition 2001, p. 331 (permissions pending)

FIGURE 2.2

DOWNWARD SPIRAL OF DEEPENING ALIENATION

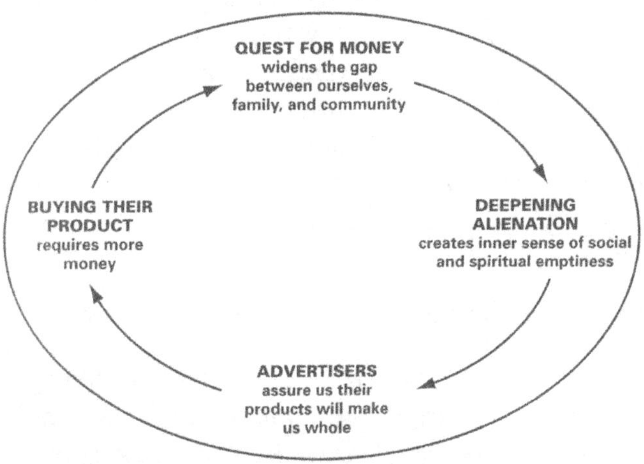

Source: As above, p. 239 (permissions pending)

Corporate profit gouging through monopolies:

Large corporate monopolies bent on profits above all use the power of their market dominance to set their own prices, with disregard of social responsibility. As Jim Hightower of the *Hightower Lowdown* has observed:

In the last 40 years or so, a handful of ever-bigger predators have:

- *Squeezed out and Bought out*
- *Merged and Purged*
- *Conglomerated and Integrated*
- *Undermined and Overpowered so many economic interests that America the Free has devolved into a corporate confederacy of anti-competitive, profiteering combines.*[18]

Mega corporations have themselves become big drivers of inflation, with some even admitting that "inflation is good for business." Rakeen Mabud, chief economist and managing director of policy and research at the Groundwork Collaborative, has compiled these findings based on analysis of profits of oil, motor vehicle, airline, and commercial real estate giants:

- *Chevron* made $11.6 billion in the second quarter of 2022 as its production actually decreased and as its CEO stated that its goal was focused on generating returns as he touted its most successful returns since 2008.
- *Driven Brands*, which runs auto shops and car repair services across the country, boasted that their essential services made it easier to take advantage of inflation since consumers have to have their services whatever the prices.
- *Four major airlines*—American, Delta, Southwest and United—each bragged about how they are constraining capacity on flights to drive up prices and generate higher profits.

Concerning those results, Mabud had this to say:

Big corporations are getting away with pushing up prices to fatten their profit margins, and families are quite literally paying the price. It's time to rein them in. Policymakers must address corporate profiteering as a driver of inflation by reining in mega corporations and addressing the unsustainably high prices facing families around the country.[19]

Big corporations continue to feed inflation by raising prices through their monopoly power because they can, to the point that their "greedflation" stalks the economy.[20] Even when questioned on this score, some of the largest corporations will continue that practice into the future. According to a new report—*Conspiring Against Competition*—large corporations, instead of competing with each other, often secretly conspire to set prices.[21] However, despite strong evidence that corporate monopolies play a large role in driving inflation through control of supply chains and price gouging, the Federal Reserve Board still looks the other way as it keeps raising short-term interest rates. Meanwhile, inflation continues to hit the purchasing power of middle-income families the hardest.[22]

CEO vs. worker compensation in large corporate monopolies

In their drive for higher net revenue, CEOs of large corporations are often incentivized to increase their own compensation, as well as that of shareholders through higher stock values, by raising prices for consumers. As one example of the impacts of this strategy, the U. S. House of Representatives recently completed a three-year investigation of the pricing and business practices of the pharmaceutical industry. These are some of its findings:

- Among the 12 drugs and 10 drug companies studied, prices increased by a median of almost 500% above the prices when the drugs were first brought to market; in one case, the price soared by more than 100,000% since it was launched.
- All 10 companies have senior executive compensation practices that link incentive payments to revenue and other financial targets, often for drug-specific targets.
- Between 2016 and 2020, the companies paid more than $2.2 billion to their top executives under these policies.
- With the goal to maintain high prices and block competition from generic-drug companies, the 10 companies obtained more than 600 patents that potentially expand their monopoly protection for a combined total of almost 300 years.[23]

As Senator Bernie Sanders observes:

> *Our struggle is against a system where the top twenty-five hedge fund managers in the United States pocket more money than 350,000 kindergarten teachers combined. When did we the people make that determination? When did we decide that a drug company executive at Moderna can collect a "golden parachute" valued at $926 million for not working, while EMT workers who work around the clock to save lives make as little as 40,000 a year?* [24]

These predatory practices of large corporations have led to increasing gaps between CEO and worker compensation as shown in Figure 2.3, which led to wide separation between these two groups from 1980 to 2016. (Figure 2.4) Between 1978 and 2021, CEO pay increased by 1,460 percent while that of ordinary workers rose by only 18.1 percent.[25] That separation continues to grow, with increasingly stark comparisons of CEO to worker pay. In 2023, the median CEO-to-worker pay ratio rose to 288-to-1, compared to 20-to-1 in 1965!

FIGURE 2.3

CEO-WORKER COMPENSATION RATIO, 1965-2012

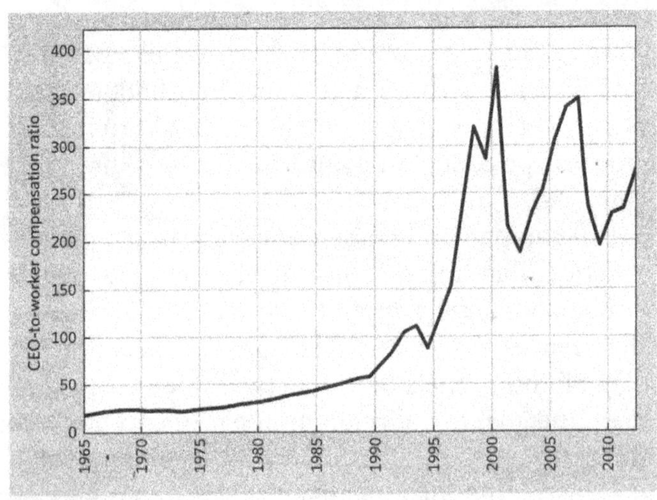

Source: Economic Policy Institute, December 20, 2013

FIGURE 2.4

RISE OF TOP 1% AND FALL OF BOTTOM 50%, 1980-2016

In 1980, 11 percent of national income was received by the top 1 percent in the United States, compared with 21 percent received by the bottom 50 percent. In 2016, 20 percent of national income was received by the top 1 percent in the United States, compared with 13 percent received by the bottom 50 percent.

Source: Facundo Alvaredo, Lucas Chancel, Thomas Piketty, and Emmanuel Saez, *World Inequality Report 2018* (Paris: World Inequality Lab, 2017). See https://wir2018.wid.world for data series and notes.

Interestingly, the skyrocketing inequality that occurred in compensation between senior management and workers did not happen in rich nations of Western Europe, as shown by Figure 2.5.[26]

FIGURE 2.5

CONTRASTING TRENDS OF THE TOP 1% AND BOTTOM 50% IN WESTERN EUROPE, 1940-2018

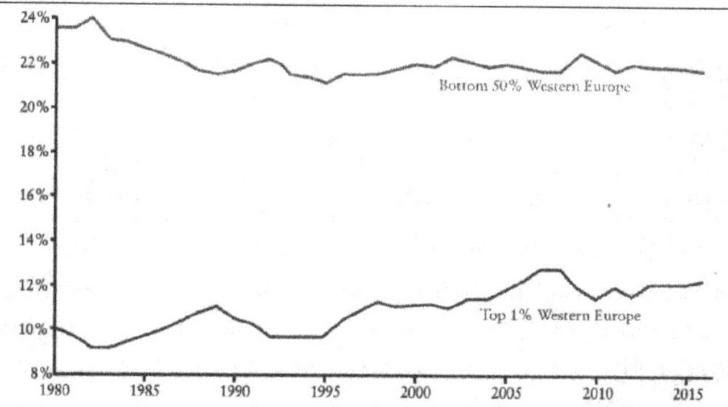

Source: *World Inequality Report*, See https: wir2018.wid.world for data and notes

In the 1940s, the salaries of the top CEOs the Fortune 300 largest companies were about 12 times that of average workers in their business. Today, that difference has soared to 300 or more times that difference. Incredibly, as Ralph Nader notes, the compensation package of Apple CEO Tom Cook comes to $833 a MINUTE or $50,000 an hour on a 40-hour week![27] Going back to Figure 2.1 (p. 27), this becomes an example of the supremacy of raw commercial power over civic values.

Dean Baker, co-director of the Center for Economic and Policy Research, questions whether the government should grant patent monopolies when it has already paid for research of new technologies. As one example, Moderna was paid $450 million to develop its COVID vaccine, followed by another $450 million for its phase 3 testing as required for FDA approval, and then was permitted to claim intellectual property in the vaccine that will likely involve tens of billions of dollars in future revenue. That approach led to at least five new Moderna billionaires and further widening of the gap in compensation between senior management and workers. With large amounts of money at stake from innovation—likely more than $1 trillion a year— Baker calls for discussion of alternative funding mechanisms.[28]

Decline of the middle class

Figures 2.3 and 2.4 have much to do with the decline of the middle class in this country and further documented by the resulting decline of middle-income wealth from 1983 to 2016 in this country. (Figure 2.6)[29]

Thom Hartmann, in his important book, *The Hidden History of Monopolies: How Big Business Destroyed the American Dream*, adds this further dimension of social injustice to the decline of the middle class in the U. S.:

> *While the monopolization of wealth and political power by giant corporations and the billionaires they create has reached crisis proportions in this country, the monopolization of middle-class wealth by white people—and particularly, white men—is also a crisis that keeps our country unequal and out of balance.*[30]

FIGURE 2.6

DECLINE OF MIDDLE-INCOME AGGREGATE WEALTH IN THE U. S., 1983-2016

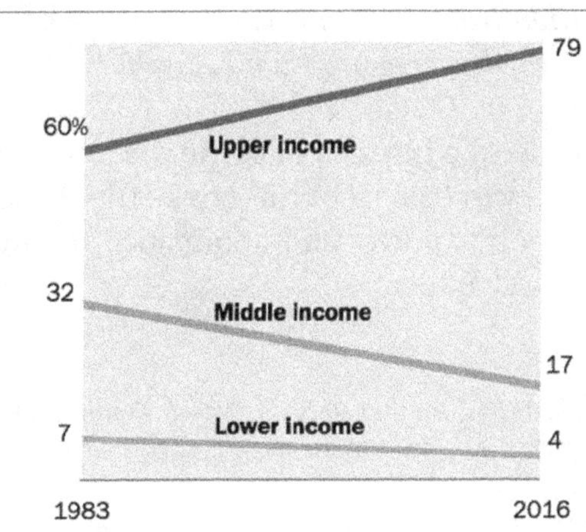

Source: Pew Research Center analysis of the Survey of Consumer Finances

Conclusion:

In defense of corporate behavior described above that has drawn widespread negative public reaction, the Business Roundtable in 2019 issued a re-definition of the purpose of a corporation that would promote "an economy that serves all Americans", not just its shareholders and CEOs. It was signed by 181 CEOs who declared their commitment to such a goal.[31] It appears to be window dressing, however, without observable change.

This wide inequality gap in American society has important political implications that have already led to extreme polarization between our two major political parties. In their 2020 book, *Let Them Eat Tweets: How the Right Rules in an Age of Extreme Inequality*, political scientists Jacob Hacker and Paul Pierson identify these three threats when inequality increases to extreme levels, as it already has: (1) power shifts to economic elites, (2) their interests diverge from those of their fellow citizens, and (3) they become more apprehensive about democracy. As they conclude at this point:

> *It would be foolish to rely on the enlightened self-interest of economic elites, or to expect that they will correct course out of some sense of noblesse oblige. As in the past—during when the New Deal and the reforms of the 1960s, or when Eisenhower rebuffed business conservatives because he knew voters were with him—moderation from economic elites is most likely to emerge in response to growing pressure from below.*[32]

We will consider the impacts of corporate power on self-governance and democracy in Part IV of this book. The challenges to bring reform against corporate power and dominance are immense, as we will see in following chapters.

References:

1. Korten, DC. *When Corporations Rule the World. Kumarian Press, Inc,* Bloomfield, CT and *Berrett-Koehler Publishers, Inc*, San Francisco, CA, Second edition 2001, pp. 330-331.
2. Sanders, B. *It's OK To Be Angry about Capitalism*. New York. *Penguin Random House LLC*, 2023, p. 97.
3. Stoller, M. *Goliath: The 100-Year-War between Monopoly Power and Democracy.* New York. *Simon & Schuster*, 2019, p. 380.
4. Derber, C. *Corporation Nation: How Corporations Are Taking Over Our Lives and What We Can Do About It*. New York. *St. Martin's Griffin*, 1998, p. 88.
5. Naisbitt, J. *Global Paradox*. New York. *William Morrow*, 1994.
6. Greider, *Who Will Tell the People: The Betrayal of American Democracy*. New York. *Touchstone, Simon & Schuster*, 1992, pp. 335-336.
7. Hartmann, T. *Unequal Protection: The Rise of Corporate Dominance and the Theft of Human Rights.* Emmaus, PA. *Rodale Press*, 2002, p. 378.
8. Teachout, Z. *Corruption in America: From Benjamin Franklin's Snuff Box to Citizens United.* Cambridge, MA. *Harvard University Press*, 2016, p. 301.
9. Ibid # 2, p. 456.
10. Moyers, B. A new story for America. *The Nation* 284:3, p. 17, 2007.
11. The age of consolidation. *Business Week*, October 14, 1991, pp. 86-94.
12. A survey of multinationals: Everybody's favorite monsters. *The Economist*, March 27, 1993 (special supplement, p. 17).
13. Donohoe, MT. Combating corporate control: Protecting education, media, legislation and health care. In Donohoe, MT (Ed). *Public Health and Social Justice*. San Francisco, CA. *Jossey-Bass*, 2013, p. 445.
14. Stoller, M. *The Smash and Grab of Kroger-Albertson's*, October 18, 2022. (act. demandprogress.org)
15. Anti-Monopoly Basics: Monopoly by the Numbers. *Open Markets Institute*, 2022.

16. Ibid # 1.
17. Ibid # 1, p. 239.
18. Hightower, J. Let's tackle monopoly power. *The Hightower Lowdown*, October 2021.
19. Mabud, R. As quoted by Stancil, K. 'Their price strategies are bearing fruit': Oil and coal profits surge 340 %. *Common Dreams*, September 30, 2022.
20. Kuttner, R. The Fed keeps throttling the economy. *The American Prospect*, December 14, 2022.
21. Reich, R. It's greedflation, stupid. RobertReich@substack.com, June 1, 2023.
22. Hilsenrath, J, Wolfe, R. Inflation takes biggest bite from the middle. *Wall Street Journal*, December 29, 2022.
23. Big PhRMA's "unjustified and unfair" business and pricing practices. Public Citizen Newsletter. *Citizens for the Future*, Summer 2022.
24. Sanders, B. *It's OK to Be Angry about Capitalism*, 2023, p. 106.
25. Johnson, J. As fed pushes to 'get wages down,' study shows CEO pay has soared by 1,460% since 1978. *Common Dreams*, October 4, 2022.
26. Formisano, RP. *Plutocracy in America: How Increasing Inequality Destroys the Middle Class and Exploits the Poor.* Baltimore, MD, *Johns Hopkins University Press*, 2015, p. 53.
27. Nader, R. Watch out for big corporations and dangerous politicians breaking our established norms. In the Public Interest, *The Progressive Populist*, September 15, 2022, p. 9.
28. Baker, D. Hey, if the government pays for the research, it doesn't have to grant patent monopolies. *The Progressive Populist*, October 15, October 15, 2022, p. 11.
29. Ibid # 26.
30. Hartmann, T. *The Hidden History of Monopolies: How Big Business Destroyed the American Dream*, 2020, p. 115. *ReadHowYouWan*t (October 26, 2020)
31. Statement on Purpose of a Corporation. *Business Roundtable*, August 19, 2019.
32. Hacker, JS, Pierson, P. *Let Them Eat Tweets: How the Right Rules in an Age of Extreme Inequality.* New York. *W. W. Norton, Inc.* 2020, p. 200-201.

CHAPTER 3

PROFITEERING, PRIVATIZATION AND CORRUPTION IN THE CORPORATE STATE

Corporate America has long looked at the government, not as an enemy, but as a source of profit. That's more true now than ever before, as corporate welfare expenditures grow larger and public money is being given to corporations tax free.[1]

—Joseph W. Cotchett, author of numerous books on law, ethics, corporate practices and civil rights

The theory of maximizing "shareholder value" was always BS. It was a smoke screen for bumping up stock prices, the better to enrich executives paid substantially in stock options. The maximize-shareholder-value school also became the justification for leveraged buyouts and hedge fund takeovers, whose entire business model was to screw stakeholders . . . Reform will come because the public demands it, and Congress passes something like Elizabeth Warren's Accountable Capitalism Act.[2]

—Robert Kuttner, co-founder of The American Prospect and author of the 1999 book, *Everything for Sale: The Virtues and Limits of Markets*

As we saw in the first chapter, growth of the corporate state has been proceeding apace for more than 40 years in this country in an era of deregulation established during the Reagan administration. Enlarging corporate monopolies with little accountability have also taken root, especially benefiting two major groups—stakeholders and shareholders—but in different ways.

Corporate *stakeholders* may range from manufacturers of products and their users to insurers and investment firms, all of which benefit from corporate growth, while *shareholders* are those investors holding stock in corporate investments who benefit when their successful investments are sold.

This chapter has two goals: (1) to describe today's corporate profiteering, privatization of public programs, and corruption/fraud; and (2) to consider the disconnect between monopolistic corporate goals and the public interest. As we go through this chapter, it is useful to distinguish between stakeholders and shareholders, both of which benefit from further growth of the corporate state, but in different ways.

I. Corporate Profiteering, Privatization, and Corruption/Fraud

Profiteering

These examples speak for themselves on how profiteering, benefitting the corporate elite and Wall Street stakeholders at the expense of the public interest, holds sway across a large part of the U. S. economy, even during the COVID pandemic:

1. Billionaire wealth surge during pandemic. By the end of the first pandemic year, the combined net worth of the richest Americans totaled $4 trillion, more than four times the price tag of the economic relief package being debated in Congress.[3]

2. Coronavirus relief funds siphoned off. More than $5 billion in coronavirus relief funds intended for small, independent businesses were re-directed to more than 600 portfolio companies owned or backed by private equity firms on Wall Street that already had almost a trillion dollars in cash reserves.[4]

***3. Prices* for COVID vaccines.** Prices charged by U. S. manufacturers of COVID-19 vaccines exceeded their production costs by 10-fold or more.[5] As the major manufacturers, Pfizer and Moderna had received government contracts for $1.95 billion and almost $1 billion, respectively, for research and development, and still could expect profit margins between 60 and 80 percent.[6,7] Moderna is considering pricing its COVID-19 vaccines between $110 and $130 per dose compared to earlier pricing in a federal supply contract at about $26 per dose. [8]

4. COVID. Early in the pandemic, Amazon hiked its prices for essential safety items, such as face masks and hand sanitizer, by up to 1,000 percent during a time of bidding wars.[9]

5. *Big PhRMA* raised the prices of 300 medications early in 2021, when there was less demand for prescription drugs due to reduced numbers of visits to physicians and when future legislation in Congress was anticipated requiring Medicare to negotiate drug prices.[10] More than one-half of new drugs coming onto the market today cost more than $220,000, while some cost more than $1 million.[11] Mirati Therapeutics Inc is charging $19,750 a month for Krazati, its new drug for lung cancer ($237,000 a year!); those prices are not affordable for most sick Americans, but Big PhRMA rolls on with its outrageous profiteering.[12]

6. Insulin Costs have increased by 6-fold over the last 20 years,[10] rendering this life-saving drug unavailable to many lower-income diabetic patients who cannot afford its monthly costs that can reach up to $1,200.[13,14] Eli Lilly recently announced its intent to cut some of its insulin costs to $35 per month, as imposed by the Inflation Reduction Act of 2022 under mounting public pressure, but there is no assurance that all of its insulin products will be so reduced or that future increases will not take place.[15]

7. Hospitals. As the pandemic spread rapidly across the country, the 100 most expensive hospitals in the U. S. jacked up their charges by as much as 18 times their costs.[16] HCA Healthcare owned and operated more than one-half of these hospitals, and their profits per patient increased by 10 percent despite a 4.7 percent drop in hospitalized patients during 2020.[17] In 2022, in U. S. hospitals, the average emergency room 'facility fee' (before the patient is even seen) was $1,201, while American hospitals were billing 10 to 20 times the rates for equivalent services in French hospitals.[18]

8. Nursing homes. 70% of nursing homes in the U. S. are corporate-owned and run by absentee executives who have little or no experience in nursing homes and long-term care. Their overall goal is profits for themselves and shareholders through emphasis on "efficiency" (translation—reduction of nursing staff and lower quality of care).[19]

9. Health Insurers. Financial analysis of 2022 statements of Big Insurance, including United Health Group, CVS/Aetna, Cigna, Elevance, Humana, Centene, and Molina, showed that their revenues reached $1.25 trillion with profits of $69.3 billion; revenue growth over the preceding 10 years was especially high in taxpayer-supported programs such as privatized Medicare Advantage and Medicaid, which grew 500%.[20] Medical directors for Cigna spend an average of just 1.2 seconds to review a claim before rejecting it! [21]

10. Big Oil. When Russia's invasion of Ukraine led to surging prices of oil and gasoline, Big Oil companies directed large profits to shareholders through increased dividends as they purchased back their own shares of that stock, retiring them and driving up the value of remaining shares.[22] Chevron took in its highest-ever annual profit of $35.5 billion in 2022 as it continued to give higher priority to shareholder returns over pumping oil and gas that could contain consumer costs at the pump.[23]

11. Wheat and food supplies. Commodity traders on Wall Street have been helping to fuel increasing prices (likely by 10 to 25%) of wheat and other food supplies, with profits of about $18 billion in 2022 for major world banks during a crisis of famine around the world.[24]

12. Aid to gun maker companies. As the economic impacts of the pandemic were becoming severe, gun maker companies took in $125 million in aid, including $3.1 million to the manufacturer of the assault rifle used by the shooter who killed 19 school children and 2 teachers in the Uvalde, Texas mass shooting.[25]

13. "Junk fees," especially credit card late fees, are fees for which Americans pay $12 billion a year; the industry average for these fees is $31, but the actual cost to banks is just $8. The Consumer Financial Protection Bureau under the Biden administration is moving to cut the late fee to $8, but Big Banks are opposing this reform.[26]

14. Defense contractors. A recent CBS News report found that defense contractors often overcharge the Department of Defense to boost profits by nearly 40%.[27]

Profiteering and widening economic inequality in this country are, of course, by no means new. A recent report by the nonpartisan Congressional Budget Office reveals the appalling impacts on family wealth in the U. S. from 1989 to 2019. During that period, while the total real wealth of American families tripled over those 30 years, that growth was very unequal. In 2019, families in the top 10% held more than one-third of total wealth, leaving families in the bottom one-half with just 2% of total wealth. This report led Bernie Sanders (D-VT) to this comment:

In the richest country on Earth, the time is long overdue for us to create a government and an economy that works for all of us, not just the 1% . . .The obscene level of income and wealth inequality in America is a profoundly moral issue that we cannot continue to ignore or sweep under the rug.[28]

Privatization of Public Programs

Advancing privatization in the U. S. has been a neoliberal long-term strategy from its beginning based on the theory, disproven by experience, that competition would provide more efficiency, controlled prices, and higher value to consumers. Instead, however, we have consistently seen pricing to what the traffic will bear, less value for consumers, more profiteering, and minimal oversight by government.

Privatization of public programs, such as Medicare and Medicaid, gives us solid examples of what happens over time that is detrimental to those on the receiving end while those on the front end prosper.

1. Privatized Medicare

Figure 3.1 shows the remarkable growth of privatized Medicare Advantage compared to traditional Medicare since 2006.

FIGURE 3.1

NATIONAL MEDICARE ENROLLMENT BY COVERAGE TYPE, SINCE 2006

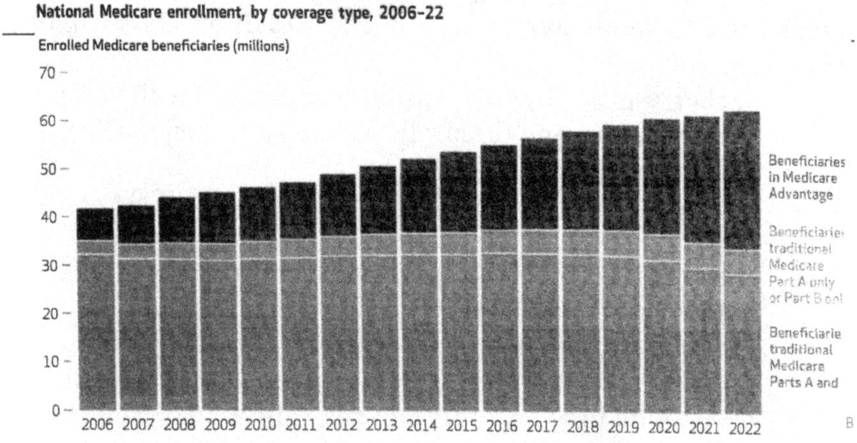

SOURCE Authors' analysis of data from the Centers for Medicare and Medicaid Services (CMS) Master Beneficiary Summary March 2006–20; the CMS monthly Medicare Advantage enrollment by contract-plan-state-county files, March 2021 and 2 and the CMS Medicare monthly enrollment file, 2021 and 2022.

Insurers have successfully lobbied Congress over the years for higher payments. They have also fraudulently increased these payments by up-coding diagnoses, whereby enrollees are claimed to be sicker than they are and billings are made for conditions for which treatment was not given. [29,30] The Affordable Care Act (ACA) of 2010 did nothing about this problem, and instead made it worse, with increased inflation of Medicare costs as shown by Figure 3.2. [31]

FIGURE 3.2

MEDICARE OVERPAYS PRIVATE PLANS,

Total Overpayments 2008-2016: $173.7 billion

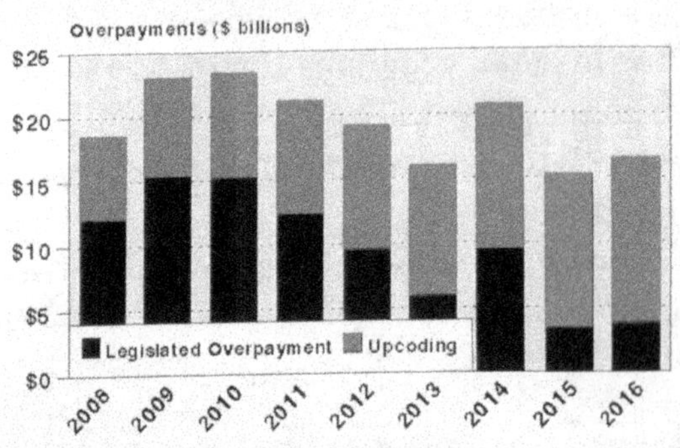

Source: PNHP Report 10/20/12 - based on data from MedPAC, *Comonwealth*

Medicare Advantage, the current version of privatized Medicare, should be more appropriately named Medicare *Disadvantage* for these reasons:

- It cherry-picks healthier enrollees at the start with deceptive marketing and disenrolls them if and when they get sicker and less profitable;[32]
- access to care is restricted through narrowing of networks that are also subject to change;[33]
- there is little competition in Medicare Advantage markets, with 97 percent of its markets in U. S. counties "highly concentrated;" [34] the so-called direct contracting entities payment system, which has replaced fee-for-service, has been found to be six times more expensive (and profitable to insurers) than its predecessor;[35] and
- it is less efficient and more bureaucratic than traditional Medicare, with administrative costs about six times higher.[36]

A report released by the Senate Finance Committee in November 2022 catalogued many fraudulent marketing practices of insurance brokers promoting Medicare Advantage plans, including signing up people without their knowledge, false assurances about their doctor being in network, and targeting people with cognitive impairment. Almost 40,000 complaints were filed in 2021 to the CMS (Centers for Medicare and Medicaid Services) which runs the programs.[37] In response, CMS issued 957 pages of new rules intended to address the many problems of Medicare Advantage, none of which were seen by experts as addressing the privatized plans' central problem—putting profits to insurers ahead of covering enrollees needing more expensive care.[38]

The Biden administration's plans to rein in Medicare Advantage overpayments prompted an aggressive lobbying campaign by insurers' lobbyists. As a result, the recommended changes will be phased in over three years. Representative Pramila Jayapal (D-WA), who chairs the Congressional Progressive Caucus, had this to say about this delay:

> *Sadly, health insurance companies used taxpayer dollars meant for medical care to instead buy Super Bowl commercials and desperately lobby to stop these changes that would cut down on their profiteering.*[39]

2. Privatized Medicaid

Private insurers make money from Medicaid by reducing the use of medical services, with inadequate physician networks, longer waits for care, and worse outcomes of care.[40] Elevance Health (formerly Anthem) is a giant health insurer with one of the highest denial rates among managed care organizations. It makes huge profits by denying coverage of medications and treatments ordered by physicians.[41] Overpayments to private Medicaid plans are endemic in more than 30 states, often with unnecessary or duplicative payments to providers.[42]

The cruelty of predatory corporate looting of the federal Medicaid budget is well captured by Donald Cohen and Allen Mikaelian in their 2021 book, *The Privatization of Everything: How the Plunder of Public Goods Transformed America and How We Can Fight Back*:

Making a profit from the most desperate is difficult, even when the government pays. Those fellow citizens who live on the margins, those in the lowest tenth in terms of income, spend some 35 percent of their pre-tax income on medical care. Those in the top 10 percent of income spend 3.5 percent. But that translates into $2,119 per year for those on the margins and $8,720 for those on the top. These stats speak to the rawness of our inequality; the level of care the top 10 percent enjoys is shockingly out of reach for the bottom 10 percent, who would have to more than quadruple what they spend to match what the upper echelons consider pocket change. Every time a politician hands public health care programs over to private-sector profiteering, it creates a greater burden on those least able to afford it. The obvious result is a group of people who are sicker and poorer, so it's convenient for politicians to do this in the name of the free market, efficiency, and consumerism. It absolves them. But it also gives wealthy corporations a license to radically transfer public funds from the most desperate citizens to their CEOs and shareholders, to push those who are down ever further down while using those pittances to gild the upper reaches of the plutocracy.[43]

Taken together, the federal government and we taxpayers have been overpaying private insurers for Medicare and Medicaid for years. Figure 3.3 shows how these two programs have been keeping private insurers afloat through subsidies and overpayments while the five largest insurers pocket increasing profits.[44,45] Despite these overpayments, privatized Medicare plans offer rural hospitals such low negotiated rates that many are forced to close their doors and leave their surrounding areas without any hospital care.[46]

Corruption, even Fraud

Corruption is widespread in our economy and public life, now being so common as to not be everyday news. Robert Reich, whom we met in Chapter 1, describes our predicament this way in his 2020 book, *The System: Who Rigged It, How We Fix It*:

FIGURE 3.3

MEDICARE AND MEDICAID KEEP PRIVATE INSURERS AFLOAT

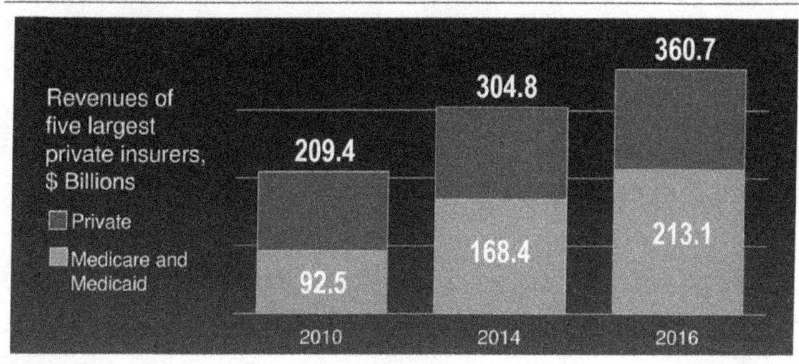

Source: *Health Affairs*; 36 (2):185, 2017

> *Corruption has become systemic, reaching deep into both political parties. While there are important differences between parties—Democratic members of Congress are far more socially liberal than Republicans and more concerned about poverty, climate change, guns, and the rights of women and minorities—neither party is committed to challenging the increasing concentration of wealth and power in America. Both have come to depend on that wealth, and therefore defer to that power.*[47]

As one example that flies under the radar, Public Citizen analyzed oil and gas corporations that filed the 25 largest bankruptcy cases between 2018 and 2020. During that period, 76 executives received a combined total of almost $200 million in cash bonuses, retention payments, and severance, with the largest single CEO payout of $14.5 million.[48]

Medicare Advantage, described previously, is another blatant example of fraud that pervades our society without igniting effective reform from an activated public or government itself. Tom Scully, as administrator of the Centers for Medicare & Medicaid in 2002, initiated major changes in privatized Medicare in order to compensate hospitals treating high-cost patients. He left CMS the next year to join a major private equity firm, where he profited immensely from those changes as Medicare Advantage games the system by overcharging more than $75 billion a year.[49]

Today, the government agency running Medicare is *promoting* Medicare Advantage over traditional Medicare despite all the evidence of corruption, even fraud among private insurers. A recent review by the *New York Times* of dozens of fraud lawsuits, inspector general audits and investigations by watchdogs has found that 8 of the largest 10 Medicare Advantage insurers, with more than two-thirds of the market, were submitting bills inflated by upcoding that led to at least $12 billion in overpayments in 2020.[50]

II. Disconnect between Monopolistic Corporate Goals and the Public Interest

Thom Hartmann, whom we met in the last chapter, identifies this central question of monopoly control by Big Business:

> *Big Business cares only about profit. With the rules that are currently in place, Big Business is encouraged to ruthlessly pursue profit at the expense of workers, communities, and the environment . . . Which raises a fundamental question, asked from the days of Plato to Adam Smith to Bernie Sanders: Is the economy here to serve the majority of the people, or are the majority of the people here to serve the economy and those few who own the largest parts of it?* [51]

As we saw in the last chapter, in an effort to respond to public resentment of corporate profiteering, the Business Roundtable released an updated statement on the purpose of a corporation in 2019. It declared this purpose of corporate CEOs:

> *. . . to lead their companies for the benefit of all stakeholders—customers, employees, suppliers, communities and shareholders . . . Each of our stakeholders is essential. We commit to deliver value to all of them, for the future success of our companies, our communities and our country.*[52]

Experience and track record since then, however, shows that the "re-definition of corporate purpose" is merely vacuous rhetoric as corporate crime goes on with impunity. The huge disconnect between the corporate world in the 1950s when Jonas Salk developed the polio vaccine and refused to patent it ("you can't patent the sun") and today's corporate profiteering of the COVID vaccine is a good example of the sea change that has enveloped us. Another such example is non-profit hospitals leaving poorer communities and markets, with higher numbers of patients on Medicaid, in order to boost system finances.[53]

Despite ongoing flagrant abuses of the public interest, they continue unchecked and are rarely prosecuted. The term "corporate crime" is verboten by the powers that be. Instead, newspapers and law schools tend to prefer "white collar crime," and corporate power reigns supreme. As Ralph Nader observes:

> *Despite the many books on corporate crooks, there have been no corporate crime reforms, no additional prosecutions of these CDOs, not even comprehensive congressional or state legislative hearings. The corporate crooks at the top of giant companies still get away with profiting from their corporate crime wave.*[54]

Iowa Law Professor Mihailis Diamantis and Michigan Business Professor Will Thomas, coauthors of an article titled *Branding Corporate Criminals*, in press for the Fordham Law Review, call attention to corporate punishment having a branding problem. As they propose:

> *Unsurprisingly, corporations view criminal charges as inconvenient economic uncertainties and criminal fines as mere costs of doing business. They propose that corporate criminal law disrupt this perverse dynamic by adopting a new sanction that would brand corporate criminals.*
>
> *This corporate criminal brand would stand as a 21st century reimagining of its medieval corporal punishment namesake. Lawmakers rightly rejected physical brands on individual criminals long ago. The criminal justice landscape is different for corporations, who feel no pain and have no dignity.*

Unlike monetary fines, corporate criminal branding would unambiguously signal a corporate's criminal status to outside observers. By forcibly integrating corporations' criminal identity into their public image, criminal law might finally have a way to recognize victims and to strike at what corporations value most[55]

Conclusion:

Assurances by the Business Roundtable and other corporate leaders ring hollow and are not to be believed based on experience. If the corporate excesses as described haven't impressed you as beyond the pale, you'll probably find that private equity in the next chapter likely will. We can expect that unrestrained corporate excess and malfeasance will continue to contribute to inflation, instability, and increased inequality in our society.

References:

1. Cotchett, J W. forward to *The Corporate Sabotage of America's Future: And What We Can Do About It.* By Weissman R., and Claybrook, J, Public Citizen. Washington D.C, 2023, p.2.
2. Kuttner, R. The Business Roundtable's strange outbreak of social conscience. *The Progressive Populist*, September 15, 2019, p. 18.
3. Ludwig, M. New report shows top billionaires' wealth skyrocketing during pandemic. *Truthout*, December 11, 2020.
4. Rosen, D. Billions in pandemic relief funds enriched investors, private equity. *Public Citizen* 41 (6): 1, November/December 2021.
5. Prabhala, A, Jayadev, Baker, D. Want vaccines fast? Suspend intellectual property rights. *New York Times*, December 7, 2020.
6. Hiltzik, M. Private firms keep stranglehold on COVID vaccines, though you paid for the research. *Los Angeles Times*, November 16, 2020.
7. Light, DW, Lexchin, J. The costs of coronavirus vaccines and their pricing. *J Royal Society of Medicine*, November 2021.
8. Loftus, P. Moderna to price COVID-19 shots at $110-$130. *Wall Street Journal*, January 10, 2023: A: 3.
9. Brown, E. Uncovering COVID-19 price gouging at Amazon. *Public Citizen News*, Nov/Dec, 2020, p. 6.
10. Stancil, K. Big PhRMA rings in the New Year by raising prices on 300 medications. *Truthout*, January 1, 2021.
11. Sanders, B, The greed of Big PhRMA cannot continue. *Fox News Channel*, June 23, 2023.
12. Loftus, P. New drugs hit market with hefty price tags. *Wall Street Journal*, March 10, 2023: A: 1.
13. Inskeep, S, Aubrey, A. Insulin costs increased 600% over the last 20 years. States aim to curb the price. *NPR*, September 12, 2022.

14. Martyn, A. States are trying to cap the price of insulin. Pharmaceutical companies are pushing back. *Fair Warning*, August 16, 2020.
15. Robbins, R. Eli Lilly says it will cut some of its insulin prices. *New York Times*, March 2, 2023, p. B:1.
16. Study finds hospitals hike their charges by up to 18 times costs. *Corporate Crime Reporter* 34 (45): p. 6, November 23, 2020.
17. Evans, M, Sebastian, D. HCA's profit increases despite fall in patients. *Wall Street Journal*, February 2, 2021.
18. Kuttner, R. Hospital billing is a crime against American patients. Portside, November 23, 2022. (https://portside.org/2022-11-23/hospital-billing-crime-against-american-patients).
19. Hightower, J. Would Wall Street kill your granny for a little more profit? *The Progressive Populist*, March 15 2023, p. 3.
20. Potter, W. Big Insurance 2022: Revenues reached $1.25 trillion thanks to sucking billions out of the pharmacy supply chain—and taxpayers' pockets. *Wendell Potter's Health Care un-covered*, February 27, 2023.
21. Cigna saves millions by having its doctors reject claims without reading them. *Corporate Crime Reporter* 37 (14): April 3, 2023, p. 5.
22. Zibel, A. Oil industry's war profiteers put shareholder cash over consumers. *Public Citizen News*, May-June, 2022, p. 1.
23. Eaton, C. Chevron rides high oil prices to record $35.5 billion annual profit. *Wall Street Journal*, January 27, 2023.
24. Johnson, J. Wall Street giants set to smash profit records off global hunger, energy crisis. *Common Dreams*, September 9, 2022.
25. Cowley, S, Koeze, E. Maker of gun used in massacre took in $3.1 million in aid. *New York Times*, May 27, 2022, B:4.
26. Reich, R. Inequality *Media Civil Action*, February 24, 2023.
27. 60 Minutes report on Pentagon price gouging. *Corporate Crime Reporter* 37 (22), May 29, 2023.
28. Wilkins, B. 'Obscene,' says Sanders after CBO reports richest 1% now owns over 1/3 of U. S. wealth. *Common Dreams*, September 28, 2022.
29. Schulte, F, Donald, D. Cracking the codes: How doctors and hospitals have collected billions in questionable Medicare fees. *Center for Public Integrity*, May 19, 2014.
30. Livingston, S. Insurers profit from Medicare Advantage's incentive to add coding that boosts reimbursement. *Modern Healthcare*, September 4, 2018.
31. Geruso, M, Layton T. Up-coding inflates Medicare costs in excess of $2 billion annually. *UT News*, University of Texas at Austin, June 18, 2015.
32. Schulte, R. As seniors get sicker, they're more likely to drop Medicare Advantage. *Kaiser Health News*, July 6, 2017.
33. Silvers, JB. This is the most realistic path to Medicare for All. *New York Times*, October 2019.
34. Abelson, RD. With mergers, concerns grow about private Medicare. *New York Times*, August 25, 2015.
35. Tomlinson, C. Biden moves forward with Trump Medicare Advantage plan. *Houston Chronicle*, November 8, 2021.
36. Hilzic, M. Trump plans a Trojan horse. Los Angeles Times, October 5, 2019.
37. Abelson, R, Sanger-Katz, M. Private Medicare plans misled customers into signing up, Senate report says. *New York Times*, November 3, 2022.

38. McCanne, D. CMS smothers us with inconsequential regulations for Medicare Advantage. *Health Justice Monitor*, December 22, 2022.
39. Conley, J. Jayapal laments Biden's cave to insurer industry on Medicare Advantage. *Common Dreams*, April 6, 2023.zz
40. Geruso, M, Layton, TL, Wallace, J. Are all managed care plans created equal? Evidence from random plan assignment in Medicaid. NBER Working Paper No. 27762, National Bureau of Economic Research, August 2020.
41. Potter,W. Elevance Health is denying care for Medicaid patients at high rates, according to Department of Health and Human Services Report. wendellpotter@substack, August 1, 2023.
42. Herman, B. Medicaid's unmanaged managed care. *Modern Healthcare*, April 30, 2016.
43. Cohen, D, Mikaelian, A. *The Privatization of Everything: How the Plunder of Public Goods Transformed America and How We Can Fight Back*. New York. *The New Press*, 2021, pp. 172-173.
44. Hall, D, Nguyen, TA. Economic Benefits of Public Services. *Real-World Economics Review* no. 84, 2018.
45. The Advisory Board. How Much of Americans' Paychecks Go to Health Care, *Charted*, May 2, 2019.
46. Tribble, SJ. Rural hospitals feel the pinch as Medicare Advantage plans grow. *The Progressive Populist*, Dec. 1, 2023. p.1.
47. Reich, RB. *The System: Who Rigged It, How We Fix It*. New York. *Alfred A. Knopf*, 2020, p. 69.
48. Zibel, A. Oil & gas company executives pocketed millions in payouts. *Public Citizen News*, August 12, 2021.
49. Dayen, D. Tom Scully is as responsible as anyone for the way health care in America works today. *The American Prospect*, August 1, 2023.
50. Abelson, R, Sanger-Katz, M. 'The cash machine was insatiable': How insurers exploited Medicare for billions. *New York Times*, October 8, 2022.
51. Hartmann, T. *The Hidden History of Monopolies: How Big Business Destroyed the American Dream*. Oakland, CA. *Berrett-Koehler Publishers*, Inc. 2020, pp. 7, 2.
52. Business Roundtable redefines the purpose of a corporation to promote 'an economy that serves all Americans.' https://opportunity.businessroundtable.org/ourcommitment/.
53. Evans, M, Rust, M, McGinty, T. Hospitals shun poorer areas. *Wall Street Journal*, December 27, 2022: A 1.
54. Nader, R. Center for the Study of Responsive Law, December 2, 2021.
55. Diamantis, M, As quoted by *Corporate Crime Reporter*. 37 (15), April 10, 2023, pp 1, 12-13.

Chapter 4

WALL STREET AND PLUNDER BY PRIVATE EQUITY

Private equity is among the worst sources of financial abuse. Private equity firms enjoy a blanket exemption from disclosures to the SEC, epitomizing the failure to regulate finance and the systemic abuses that result. They borrow money that is tax-deductible to buy up companies in retail, health care, media, and other sectors. The debt must be served by the cash flow of the company. They often bleed these companies dry, in order to pay themselves special dividends, cutting wages, laying off workers, and stinting on investments that the company needs to survive. If the company goes broke, the private-equity owner can declare bankruptcy, having already made back its actual investment many times over. More than 11 million Americans now work for companies owned by private equity.[1]

—Robert Kuttner, cofounder and coeditor of *The American Prospect* and author of the 2019 book, *The Stakes: 2020 and the Survival of American Democracy*

Many of us had not heard of private equity in past years, but it has become a major predator infiltrating the economy with a vengeance from its Wall Street base, as reflected by the above quote. The goals of this chapter are (1) to briefly discuss its history in this country; (2) to discuss its common approaches, examples, and adverse impacts; and (3) to consider whether and how it might be reined in.

I. Where Did Private Equity Come From?

Well into the 1960s, U. S. corporations were generally viewed as owing something to the community that provided their economic support and legal protections, with a goal of service outweighing financial gain.[2] Much of that changed during the 1970s after this edict from Milton Friedman, Nobel Laureate in economics at the University of Chicago and author of *Capitalism and Freedom*:

> *Few trends could so thoroughly undermine the very foundations of our free society as the acceptance by corporate officials of a social responsibility other than to make as much money for their shareholders as possible.*[3]

Thus began what became known as the "shareholder revolution," with the overall corporate goal shifting to maximizing profits for investors of its stock over a service ethic. Financial gain became the overriding goal as many corporations became targets to be bought and sold in a new way—through leveraged buyouts (LBOs). That led to the beginning of "private equity," whereby institutional investors on Wall Street made high-risk, high-return investments outside of public markets.[4]

The 1980s saw rapid growth of private equity (PE). By 1989, such firms as Blackstone and Carlyle had carried out more than 2,000 LBOs valued at more than $250 billion. Discussing this new phenomenon, Matt Stoller, whom we met in Chapter 2, observed:

> *By the end of the 1980s, Wall Street had permanently changed corporate America. A new type of business model existed. The leveraged buyout industry, stung with bad publicity, rebranded as "private equity." While some PE firms made productive investments, they were largely tools of floating capital that sought to use the corporation for the purpose of financier. . . Strategically, the only businesses that were sustainable in the new legal environment were those that could withstand the pressures of financial raiders.*[5]

Further growth of private equity was fostered in 1999, when private equity firms successfully lobbied Congress to repeal the Glass-Steagall Act, which had put brakes on risky investments by commercial banks during the Great Depression of the 1930s. Figure 4.1 shows continuing growth of private equity from 2000 to 2020, with one-half of private equity deals through LBOs, and with most of these transactions "walled off" from public markets. (Figure 4.2)

Figure 4.1

Assets Managed by Private Capital, 2000-2020

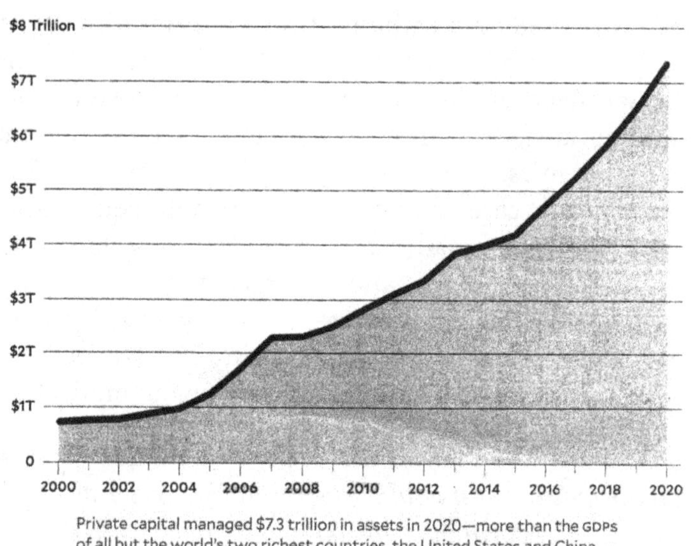

Source: Center for Economic and Policy Research

Figure 4.2

PRIVATE EQUITY DEALS THROUGH LBOs, 2020

In 2020, 50.6% of private equity deals were leveraged buyouts.

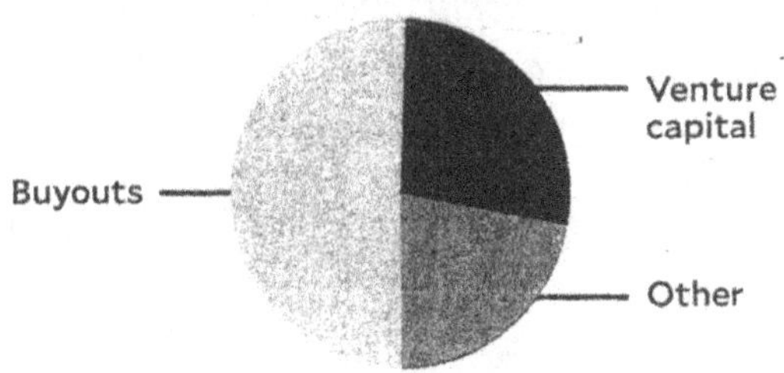

Source: Center for Economic and Policy Research

II. Common Approaches and Adverse Impacts of Private Equity

Today, the private equity industry manages more than $7 trillion in global assets, typically financing its deals with debt while generating profits for its clients and fees for its managers. Its investments range across a wide area, from firefighting services to health care and insurance companies.

Taking health care as one example, private equity firms have been active across a broad range, including hospitals, outpatient facilities, physician staffing and emergency room services, and medical debt collecting. In their in-depth Working Paper from the Center for Economic and Policy Research in 2020, Eileen Appelbaum and Rosemary Batt described the leveraged buyout model this way:

> *PE firms have been at the forefront of the M & A [mergers and acquisitions] mania in the healthcare sector as they take advantage of opportunities to consolidate markets, reduce competition, and increase market power . . . This model is low risk, as third-party government and private insurers guarantee payments. These payments provide a steady cash flow to service the debt . . .*
>
> *Over the last decade, PE firms have exited their healthcare investments on average in less than five years—their preferred window . . . They began buying out hospitals and nursing homes in the 2000s before moving into more lucrative niches post-2010—ambulatory surgery, radiology, anesthesiology, emergency room management, neo-natal units, burn clinics, and trauma units, IT health and bill collecting. More recently, they have moved into non-hospital-based physician specialties—dermatology, dental practice management, case management, ophthalmology, and orthopedics—as well as behavioral health.*[6]

These are other examples of private equity looting that is commonplace:

Hospitals

Private equity firms investing in hospitals take this general approach:

> *They begin by acquiring a small hospital system, referred to as a platform company, in a leveraged buyout. Then they add smaller hospitals in geographically dispersed regions, creating a national, multi-state hospital chain. The purchases are all financed with borrowed money, and the private equity firms transfer the debt load onto the hospitals . . . The private equity owners plan to exit investments they acquire in three to five years . . . These acquisitions usually fall below the size that triggers review by antitrust regulators, allowing them to go unchallenged.*[7]

Nursing homes

Again, a common PE strategy is to buy up nursing homes at discounted prices, add them to a chain, cut their budgets, lay off staff, and extract as much profit as possible before selling them.[8] Along the way, the National Bureau of Economic Research has recently found that PE ownership was responsible for an appalling and estimated 20,000 premature deaths over a 12-year period.[9]

Air ambulance services

After buying up ambulance services, PE owners raise their prices and charge four to nine times higher than Medicare would pay for these services.[10] These became another source of high surprise medical bills, a boon to investors, but not to patients who had no other choice of air ambulance provider.

Reproductive care

Private equity backed firms have found increased profits in this area as well. Examples of profiteering include labeling normal births as emergencies and recommending more expensive fertility procedures than are recommended by non-private equity facilities.[11]

Oncology clinics

A recent study found that oncology clinics in the U. S. have become another highly profitable target for PE investors, with PE-affiliated clinics now established in 45 states dealing especially with radiation and chemotherapy.[12]

Home care

PE investors have found another lucrative market in the home care industry by cutting costs, again extracting higher profits at the expense of employees and patients, then later selling at a big profit. Caregivers lose through lower compensation, while patients lose through fewer visits and higher rates of hospitalization.[13]

Hospice care

PE investors extract higher profits from purchasing for-profit hospices, selecting less sick patients that will survive longer at home, reducing visits and even neglecting patients dying at home.[14]

Prison Care

P.E. firms have almost monopolized the market in prison health care, food services, and prison telecommunications, making exorbinate profits in all three.[15]

Adverse impacts of private equity

Continuing with health care as an example, PE investments invariably lead to consolidation, less competition, and increasing profiteering. As a result, these are the adverse impacts on patients, families and taxpayers:

- prices to what the traffic will bear;
- uncontained prices and costs;
- decreased choice and access to care;
- variable, often poor quality of care;
- erosion of what safety net we have left; and
- rampant profiteering and fraud.[16]

Private equity ownership of hospitals typically brings staff reductions and worse quality of care as part of the way to increase profits, predictably associated with increased numbers of hospital errors, such as central line infections (up by more than falls by patients) in a recent national study.[17]

Elevance Health gives us an example of diversified involvement in health care with high returns. It sells health insurance to individuals and employers, manages Medicaid and Medicare Advantage plans, and owns a pharmacy benefit management company. Its stock price has soared from $53.18 per share in 2010, when the Patient Protection and Affordable Care Act was passed, to $495.70 per share in 2022.[18]

A closer look at private equity's takeover of staffing of emergency rooms in U. S. hospitals sheds a bright light on what has become the corporate practice of medicine. PE-backed staffing companies manage one quarter of the country's emergency rooms; the two largest are Tennessee-based Envision Healthcare, owned by investment giant KKR & Co., and TeamHealth, owned by Blackstone. Seeking maximal profits without expertise in emergency care, these kinds of companies have largely replaced physicians' clinical autonomy at the expense of patients' care. They have evaded rules against the corporate practice of medicine in 33 states plus the District of Columbia. Court filings are in process in a number of states, including what could be a landmark case in a California federal court starting in January 2024.[19]

Jim Hightower, author of *The Hightower Lowdown* whom we met in Chapter 2, sums up the typical strategy of private equity investments this way:

> *With some notable exceptions, the business of hedge funds and private equity outfits is corporate plunder: They amass a pile of money from big investors and banks and use it to buy foundering businesses on the cheap; slash workforces; degrade quality; jack up prices; strip productive assets and sell them at a premium; and extract outlandish managerial fees for all the above, eventually selling off the hollowed-out carcasses as scrap or just shutting them down.*[20]

All of these nefarious activities on Wall Street, largely under the public radar, are firmly in place today, as Matt Stoller notes:

> *In previous eras in American history, the wreckage caused by such widespread looting would have led to substantial legal reforms. And there were some. But the key innovation, that the corporate structure exists as a mechanism for the extraction of cash from insiders from either the company itself or from the market that company monopolized, was here to stay.*[21]

III. Can the Abuses of Private Equity be Reined In?

Despite their harms to the public interest, the exploitive practices of the private equity industry continue on in relative safety from regulation or reform through the protection of powerful corporate stakeholders. The Internal Revenue Service almost never audits PE firms, even when whistle-blowers have alerted it to illegal tax avoidance. With almost 200 lobbyists, the industry has sent almost $600 million in campaign contributions to Congress over the last ten years. One day before the January 6 insurrection attack on the Capitol, outgoing President Trump assured PE executives that they would not have to pay income taxes.[22]

PE firms are generally insulated from the consequences of their actions as they enjoy disproportionate benefits from hard-fought tax battles that allow them to pay minimal taxes, especially through the so-called carried interest loophole. Reform attempts have been blocked by lobbyists since 2006.[23] Attempts to rein in private equity can also be blocked by machinations of Wall Street markets, as illustrated by their responses to the attempts of the Federal Trade Commission to block the proposed mergers of Microsoft's acquisition of videogame maker Activision Blizzard and Amgen's merger with Horizon Therapeutics. In both instances, the share values of both corporations soared to new highs as investors spooked, then resulting in big profits for hedge funds as the FTC's antitrust efforts went nowhere.[24]

The prospects for regulation of private equity are poor in the near term with control of the House having shifted to the Republicans. Had the Democrats retained control of the House, prospects would have been much improved. If Democrats gain control of both chambers in Congress after the 2024 elections, the Stop Wall Street Looting Act that was introduced in the 117th Congress on October 20, 2021 could be re-introduced by Senators Warren, Baldwin and Brown and Representatives Jayapal and Pocan. If that bill can be passed, these kinds of provisions would take effect:

- increase financial and legal liability in the event of certain violations of law;
- give employee compensation higher priorities in bankruptcies;
- prohibit the payment of dividends for two years from an acquired asset firm to a PE fund; and
- modify the tax treatment of carried interest and treat the capital income with respect to a PE fund as ordinary income.[25]

Conclusion:

Given the corporate power backing ongoing profiteering by private equity forces on Wall Street, these kinds of necessary reforms will be difficult to accomplish. Laura Olson, Distinguished Professor of Political Science at Lehigh University and author of the 2022 book, *Ethically Challenged: Private Equity Storms U. S. Health Care,* describes the challenge for effective reform this way:

> *Only a radical transformation of the U. S. tax laws, financial system, and regulatory bodies will truly stop PE from gaming the system and looting everything of value.*[26]

That observation sets the stage for the next chapters in Part II, where we will see just how unaccountable U. S. corporations have become within an oligarchy resistant to change.

References:

1. Kuttner, R. *The Stakes: 2020 and the Survival of American Democracy.* New York. *W. W. & Norton & Company*, 2019, p. 137.
2. Pearlstein, S. When shareholder capitalism comes to town. *The American Prospect*, March/April 2014, pp. 40-48.
3. Friedman, M. The Social Responsibility of Business is to Increase Profits. *The New York Times Magazine*, September 13, 1970.
4. Levintova, H. Grab economy: Private equity billionaires are looting the country, leaving everyday Americans to clean up the mess—and fight for the scraps. *Mother Jones*, May/June 2022, pp. 14-19.

5. Stoller, M. *Goliath: The 100-Year War Between Monopoly Power and Democracy*. New York. *Simon & Schuster*, 2019, p. 405.
6. Appelbaum, E, Batt, R. Private equity buyouts in healthcare: Who wins, who loses? Working paper no. 118, *Center for Economic and Policy Research*, March 15, 2020, pp. 1-2.
7. Applebaum, E. How private equity makes you sicker. *The American Prospect*, Fall 2019, pp. 62-66.
8. Laise, E. As the pandemic struct, a private equity firm went on a nursing home buying spree. *Barrons' Online*, August 6, 2020.
9. Ballou, B. Private equity is gutting America—and getting away with it. Guest essay. *New York Times*, April 28, 2023.
10. Bai, G, Chanmugam, A, Valerie, Y et al. Air ambulances with sky-high charges. Johns Hopkins University, June 10, 2019.
11. Kemp, E. Private equity's path of destruction in health care continues to spread. *Public Citizen News*, 43 (2) March/April 2023, pp. 8-10.
12. Tyan, K, Lam, MB, Milligan, M. Private equity acquisition of oncology clinics in the U. S. from 2003 to 2022. JAMA Internal Medicine on line, May 1, 2023.
13. Johnson, J. Report rings alarm over private equity's grip on home health, hospice industries. *Common Dreams*, March 18, 2022.
14. Waldman, P. Preparing Americans for death lets hospices neglect end of life. *Bloomberg*, July 22, 2011.
15. Fenne, M. Privatized prison healthcare seeks profit at patients' expense. Private Equity Stakeholder Project, October 17, 2023.
16. Geyman, JP. Private equity looting of U. S. health care: An under-recognized and uncontrolled scourge. *Intl J Health Services, on line, November 3, 2022.*
17. Abelson, R, Sanger-Katz, M. Private equity ownership linked to hospital errors. *New York Times*, December 27, 2023, B:5.
18. Potter, W. Elevance Health's 2022 earnings are in, outperforms Wall Street expectations. *Wendell Potter NOW*, January 25, 2023.
19. Wolfson, BJ. ER doctors call private equity staffing practices illegal and seek to ban them. *Kaiser Health News*, December 22, 2022.
20. Hightower, J. The priority is profit. *Hightower Lowdown*, January, 2020, p. 2.
21. Ibid #5, p. 406.
22. Drucker, J, Hakim, D. Private equity: How a powerful industry conquered the tax system. *New York Times*, June 12, 2021.
23. Ibid # 9.
24. McCabe, C, Dummett, B. Hedge funds make big profits betting against FTC and Khan. *Wall Street Journal*, September 25, 2023, A:7.
25. S. 3022—Stop Wall Street Looting Act, introduced by Sen. Elizabeth Warren into the 2021-2022 117th Congress on 10-20-21.
26. Olsen LK. *Ethically Challenged: Private Equity Storms U. S. Health Care*. Baltimore, MD, *John Hopkins University Press*, 2022, p. 295.

PART II

HOW THE OLIGARCHS DEFEND THEIR POWER

The Republican Party has literally become the party of fear—of domestic terrorism, of hatred, of deceit, of division, and of ending the American experiment of democracy.

Our democracy has been softened up for this final assault for decades, by the substitution of money for broad participation, by assaults on the fundamental right to vote that began with repression of the Black franchise and then in the last decade became general. Our democracy has been weakened by the extreme use of gerrymanders, by the filibuster, by social media as a vehicle for systemic lies, and by ultra-partisan discipline on the part of the Republicans. All of this became more explicit and more extreme after 2016.

—Robert Kuttner, author of *Going Big: FDR's Legacy, Biden's New Deal,* and the *Struggle to Save Democracy*

CHAPTER 5

LIES AND DISINFORMATION

Facts don't cease to exist because they are ignored.

—Aldous Huxley, well known English writer, philosopher, and leading intellectual of his time (1894-1963)

America grew even more polarized in the Trump years. It was already a divided country when he took over; the schisms of society did not start with him. But he profited from the divisions and widened them. After four years of Trump's war on truth—and on the independent media that challenged him—three quarters of Americans said that Republican and Democratic voters could no longer agree on even basic facts, much less plans and policies.[1]

—Peter Baker and Susan Glasser, co-authors of the 2022 book *The Divider: Trump in the White House*, 2017-2021.

The above two quotes call attention to the crucial importance of distinguishing truth from untruth. The war on truth and the comfort with untruths, though a trademark of Trump's presidency, are hardly new in American politics. In his 2020 book, *Evil Geniuses: The Unmaking of America: A Recent History*, Kurt Anderson pulled together these main messages of the GOP playbook over the last several decades:

Government is bad
Believe in our perfect mythical yesteryear
Establishment experts are wrong, science is suspect
Entitled to our own facts
Short-term profits are everything
Liberty equals selfishness
Inequality's not so bad
Universal health care is tyranny.[2]

The goals of this chapter are three-fold: (1) to give examples of increasing lies and disinformation in today's politics that endanger our country at this pivotal time in its history; (2) to discuss their adverse impacts on the body politics during the 2022 midterms and 2024 election cycle; and (3) to briefly consider what is being done to safeguard our democracy against the attacks on facts and truth by the purveyors of lies and untruths.

I. Lies and Alternative Facts during the Trump Years

Historians are already finding the Trump years consistently more saturated with deception and abandonment of facts than in previous times. As Dana Milbank reports in his 2022 book, *The Destructionists: The Twenty-Five-Year Crack-Up of the Republican Party*:

> *Before launching his presidential run in 2015, he conveniently selected the precise basket of issues Republican voters wanted to hear about: Repealing Obamacare. Anti-abortion. Anti-tax. Anti-China. Against Common Core education standards. Virulent in challenging President Obama's legitimacy. The thrice-married Trump claimed he was for traditional marriage. The developer who relied on (often undocumented) immigrant labor came out against immigrants. A hotelier whose properties offered copies of the Koran talked of banning Muslims from entering the United States.*[3]

Presidential candidate Trump reached huge audiences on social media, tweeting disinformation to 100 million people at a time on Twitter, and attacking national news media as "fake news,"[4] A BuzzFeed analysis found that Trump's own fake news stories about the 2016 election generated more engagement on Facebook than the top election stories from 19 major news outlets combined.[5]

Throughout 2016, Facebook was allowing posts on its site that included far right extremist talk as "free speech." These included some 3,000 disinformation ads posted by Russian hackers, posing as Americans and paid for by Russia, trying to manipulate the 2016 election campaign against Hillary Clinton, while Trump was cheering the hackers on.[6] In September, two months before the election, Trump had almost 87,000 Facebook interactions on his page, more than CNN, ABC, NBC, *the New York Times*, *the Washington Post*, and *Buzzfeed* combined.[7]

Early on after Trump won the 2016 election, Ben Rhodes, author of the 2021 book, *After the Fall: Being American in the World We've Made*, described the role of Facebook in these terms:

> *In the weeks since the U. S. election, it had become clear just how symbiotic Facebook's model was to Trump's victory. Cannibalizing traditional media that dealt in facts by posting unverified stories for free (and selling ads). Elevating conspiracy theories and partisan vitriol that travelled faster and farther through its algorithm (and selling ads). Serving as an open vessel for Russian disinformation that tore down Clinton and elevated Trump (and selling ads). Collecting massive amounts of users' data, which was in turn used to build a more efficient grievance-based campaign shaped around the likes and dislikes of users (and helping to elect Trump).*[8]

By the end of his presidency, according to fact-checking by the *Washington Post*, Trump had accumulated 30,573 false and misleading claims (more than 21 a day in office).[9] The truth suffered badly in that process. A 2018 study of some 126,000 tweets in all categories by the Massachusetts Institute of Technology found that the time taken by falsehoods to reach 1,500 people on Twitter was six times quicker than for the truth.[10] According to internal Facebook documents, it allowed foreign and domestic groups to post divisive content and peddle false information on its site as it pursued a larger audience.[11]

Unfortunately, Facebook has continued to play a divisive role that fuels further polarization and violence. It has been shown that members of the Oath Keepers and Proud Boys messaged each other on Facebook about plans for the January 6th insurrection attack on the Capitol, including bringing weapons for the expected confrontation. One Facebook page, posted on January 5 as "Red-State Secession," said: "If you are not prepared to use force to defend civilization, then be prepared to accept barbarism."[12]

David Dayen, executive editor of *The American Prospect* and author of the 2020 book, *Monopolized: Life in the Age of Corporate Power*, had this to say about what happened the next day:

> *The well-documented events of January 6th have enabled us to learn a lot about the rioters quickly. There were the led and misled, their anger stoked by social media and encouraged by a mountain of lies, from election fraud to a secret society of elite pedophiles . . . There were off-duty policemen and Air Force veterans, personifying the links between cops and military figures and the far right . . . There were very clearly organized and determined nationalists and racists, extremist leaders and militia members, sporting zip ties and weapons, explicitly seeking to do much more than scare the political class . . . Puffed up with decades of hate, these disparate figures lashed out with violence against the state, justifying it as the only way to save America.*[13]

Here are examples of lies and disinformation during the runup to the 2022 midterms:

> *Think how bad they are. Think how evil they are . . . These are bad people. They're trying to destroy our country. And we can't let it go on any longer . . . The radical Democrats are engaging in a desperate attempt to keep me from returning to the White House.*[14]
>
> —Trump campaigning for Republicans at a rally two months before the mid-terms in Pennsylvania

These are factual responses to three lies spread widely by the GOP in an effort to fool voters in the mid-terms:

1. *Democrats are soft on crime and want to defund the police.* Democratic policies support background checks, the rule of law, and strong law enforcement. GOP policies, on the other hand, have made it easier for people to get and carry guns, with gun sales at record numbers and as many guns out there as our entire population.[15]

2. The Democrats are responsible for high prices and inflation. Corporate greed is responsible for much of the inflation we have seen, even during the pandemic; the Economic Policy Institute and the Roosevelt Institute have just confirmed that corporate profits in the U. S. have jumped up to 53.9% since the 2020 pandemic compared to 11.4% increases from 1979 to 2019.[16] The Federal Reserve Board, as well as many in the mainstream media, have been slow to acknowledge the role of monopolistic corporate control of supply chains and price gouging as a driver of inflation.[17]

3. Democrats have hired 87,000 IRS agents to go after the middle class.

These IRS agents, phased in over time, are needed to restore the IRS to previous staffing levels before GOP cuts; their target will be the richest 1% who hide a fifth of their income from the federal government, not the middle class.[18]

II. Adverse Impacts of Lies and Disinformation

The continuous run of lies and disinformation in the U. S. in recent years has been harmful in several ways:

1. Distrust of national news organizations.

Between 2016 and 2021, Americans' trust in national news organizations dropped sharply, and also along party lines—Republicans' drop of 35% vs. Democrats of 5%.[19] (Figure 5.1) Today, according to the Pew Research Center, less than 6 in 10 Americans trust information coming from national news organizations, with confidence in newspapers and television news at all-time low.[20]

Figure 5.1

PORTION OF AMERICANS WHO TRUST INFORMATION FROM NATIONAL NEWS ORGANIZATIONS, 2016-2021

% of U.S. adults who say they have a lot or some trust in the information that comes from ...

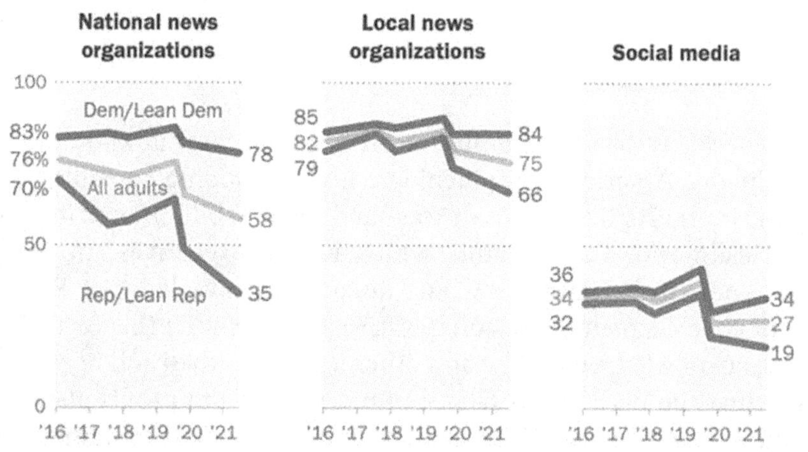

Note: In 2016, trust of information from social media was only asked of and based on internet-using U.S. adults.

Source: Survey of U.S. adults conducted June 14-27, 2021. For dates of other surveys, see the topline.

2. *Increased polarization—beyond that already with us.*

More than 7 in 10 Americans believe social media sites censor political views; 9 in 1 Republicans suspect political censorship (6 in 10 Democrats do). (Figure 5.2)[21]

Figure 5.2

PORTION OF AMERICANS WHO THINK SOCIAL MEDIA SITES CENSOR POLITICAL VIEWS

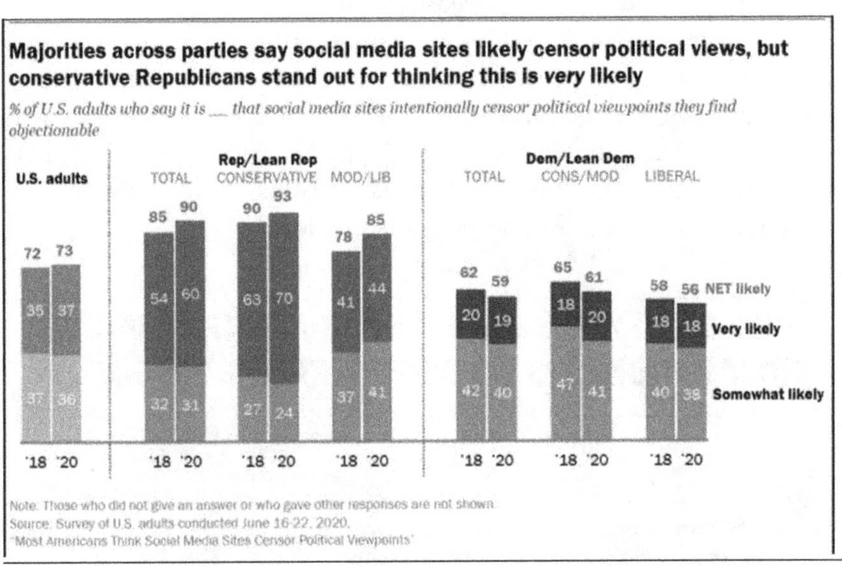

Source: Pew Research Center

Fox News has been guilty of propagating false news for years that divides America along ideologic lines, including spreading the Big Lie in the 2020 elections. It was sued for $1.6 billion over its false fraud claims for that election, which its top executives and news hosts knew to be untrue.[22] Court documents revealed that Rupert Murdoch, chairman of the conservative media empire that owns Fox News, acknowledged that he and other lead executives and hosts also knew that the Big Lie was false, but put ratings and profits ahead of broadcasting the truth.[23] Those lies harken back to Mark Twain's days. (Figure 5.3)

Figure 5.3

LIES BY FOX NEWS

Source: Reprinted with permission from Nick Anderson

Before the case went to trial, Fox News and Dominion Voting Systems agreed to a settlement of $787.5 million. Fox News was spared the further loss of any credibility by avoiding testifying under oath in trial. Compared to its estimated value of about $17 billion, the settlement was more like pocket change and the cost of doing business for Fox, which never offered any kind of apology for promulgating Trump's Big Lie.[24] Figure 5.4 displays what happened.

Figure 5.4

THE SETTLEMENT

Source: Reprinted with permission from Nick Anderson

Soon after its settlement with Dominion Voting Systems, Fox News fired Tucker Carlson, its latest lead host and purveyor of offensive, racist and white supremacy rhetoric. He promulgated a revisionist account of the January 6 insurrection attack on the U. S. Capitol. After Dominion, Fox faced a defamation suit by the software company Smartmatic. Meanwhile, the *New York Times,* the Associated Press, and National Public Radio challenged the redactions of Carlson's earlier remarks that had escaped legal filings.[25]

As Paul Krugman observed in the *New York Times*:

> *Fox has become a prisoner of the audience it created. It found itself endorsing claims about a stolen election, even though its own people knew they were false, because it feared losing market share among viewers who wanted to believe the Big Lie . . . Rupert Murdoch's organization, then, has effectively been taken hostage by the very forces he helped conjure up . . . This isn't a simple story of plutocratic rule. It is, instead, a story in which the attempts of the superrich to get what they wanted have unleashed forces that may destroy America as we know it. And that's terrifying.*[26]

After building a media empire over seven decades, Rupert Murdoch stepped down as chair of Fox and News Corp in November 2023, passing the torch to his elder son, Lachlan, who had served as co-chair of News Corp. Rupert continues as a major shareholder of the two companies, and it remains to be seen how his retirement affects policies of the two companies.[27]

3. Some lies have lethal results.

As one example, QAnon believers spread a false theory on Facebook in 2020 that liberal elites and celebrities ran a global child trafficking ring. That lie led to a conspiracy theory that Hillary Clinton and other prominent Democrats were abusing children in the basement of a Washington D.C. restaurant (which was later proven false with that restaurant not even having a basement!).[28]

Although Zuckerberg had agreed to take down some of QAnon's content from Facebook for fear that it could lead to violence, it was not done. Soon thereafter, an administrator of a Facebook page named

"Kenosha Guard" spread the word across Ohio and neighboring states "to take up arms and defend our City tonight from the evil thugs." An event called "Armed Citizens to Protect Our Lives and Property" was posted. More than 300 Facebook users marked that they would attend, inciting a 17-year-old shooter to cross state lines that night to Kenosha, Wisconsin, where he killed two and wounded one with an AR 15 assault rifle.[29]

Over the next month, Facebook pages were created for the Kenosha shooter as right-wing groups began to rally around him, even celebrating him as a patriot. More than 6,500 Facebook pages and groups dedicated to militias were added over the next month. Facebook removed these as it became clear how its pages made it possible for fringe movements, including militias and conspirators, to organize and recruit followers on its site.[30] NBC News later found that QAnon members and followers exceed 3 million users on Facebook.[31]

Early in the pandemic, Trump issued all kinds of advice to people to take various treatments despite their risk and lack of any scientific merit. One was the malaria drug, hydroxychloroquine, which led to the death of an Arizona man after he swallowed fish tank cleaner containing chloroquine.[32]

Later in the pandemic, Facebook and Instagram spread disinformation pushing back on COVID-19 vaccine mandates under the guise of freedom, thereby contributing to the anti-vaccination movement being promulgated by Republicans.[33] According to research by the Commonwealth Fund, the anti-vaccination movement accounted for 18.5 million additional hospitalizations and proved fatal for 3.2 million Americans whose deaths would have been averted by vaccination.[34]

4. Loss of trust in government

In the aftermath of the World War II years during the 1950s, Americans were together in support and trust in their government. Figure 5.5, however, shows a steep decline in that trust since the 1960s, with a drop from almost 80% to just 17% today, according to the Pew Research Center.[35,36] Gallup polls in 2021 also showed sharp declines in public confidence in the Presidency, Congress and television news.[37]

Figure 5.5

PUBLIC TRUST IN GOVERNMENT, 1958-2020

% who say they trust the government to do what is right just about always/most of the time

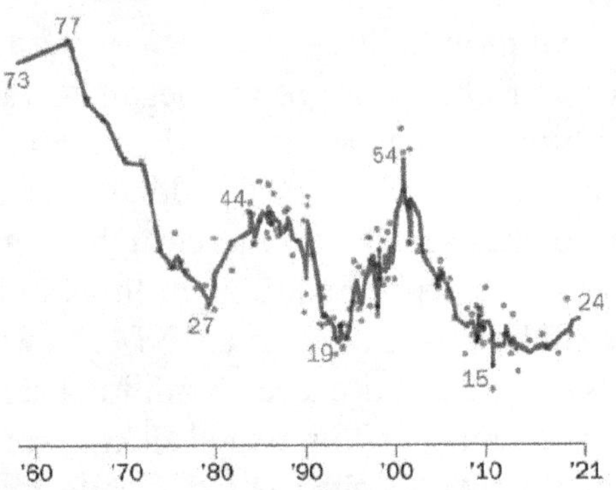

Note: From 1976-2020 the trend line represents a three-survey moving average.
Source: Survey of U.S. adults conducted April 5-11, 2021.
Trend sources: Pew Research Center's American Trends Panel (2020-2021), Pew Research Center phone surveys (2019 and earlier), National Election Studies, Gallup, ABC/Washington Post, CBS/New York Times and CNN polls.

Source: Pew Research Center

5. *Threat to democracy*

Today's Republican party has no vestiges of its strengths in past years. It still can't get away from the Trump cult and advances no policies of its own. A May 2021 Reuters/Ipsos poll found that 61 percent of respondents believe Trump's Big Lie that the 2020 election was stolen from him.[38] Election denial is growing, enabled by Facebook and posing a threat to our democracy, with more than 20 million people believing that violence is justified to restore Trump to the presidency.[39] Less than two months before the midterm elections, Five Thirty Eight reported that 60 percent of Americans will have an election denier on the ballot this Fall.[40] Representative Jamie Raskin (D-MD), Professor of Law at American University and member of the House Select Committee investigating the January 6 insurrection, recently observed:

> *It's shocking that one of America's major political parties, the one founded by Abraham Lincoln, has now wrapped itself around lies, propaganda, conspiracy theory, and disinformation. They attack our constitutional system. They attack the outcome of our election . . . They no longer act like a political party.*[41]

At this writing, with just months away from the 2024 elections, Trump's reelection campaign is putting out disinformation about voter fraud in an effort to resuscitate the Big Lie of 2020 by claiming that any results not favorable to him will be fraudulent. Senior advisors to his campaign have recently posted a statement on social media calling on the Republican National Committee to refocus its manpower and money on preventing Democrats from stealing that election.[42]

The purchase of Twitter by Elon Musk, the wealthiest person in the world, poses a continuing and escalating threat to democracy. He let Trump back onto Twitter despite his previous abuse of the platform. Asserting that he is a "free speech absolutist," he promptly fired much of the staff, many having been involved in countering harassment and disinformation. Since then, the daily numbers of hate speech posts grew sharply.[43] During his suspension from Facebook, Trump fanned the flames of conflict on his own social media site, Truth Social, with about 5 million followers, which increased by 18 times when he joined Twitter.[44]

A little-known shadowy network of dozens of pro-Trump Facebook pages, now known as Facebook "Maga mills" run by a small group of for-profit corporations, has emerged over the last five years. With an audience of at least 38 million readers, they are making large profits by spreading highly inflammatory, racially charged posts full of disinformation and conspiracy theories.[45]

6. The hazards of artificial intelligence (A.I.)

Various kinds of A.I. are spreading like wildfire as Microsoft, Google, Snap and other companies have incorporated A.I. into their products. As one example, the recently launched ChatGPT, developed by OpenAI, is a large language module that is touted to "take us to a form of artificial general intelligence," delivering efficiency in operations, ideas, discoveries and insights in many languages "that have never been attainable before across every domain." Developed rapidly by private for-profit companies in a global economy, these kinds of possible advances bring new unrecognizable hazards that raise these kinds of warnings about their impacts on future workplaces through automation, amplified income equality, and yet unknown impacts on professions, labor unions, and societies.46 One new hazard involves deepfake technology whereby hackers can impersonate voices of bank customers, and hack personal bank data. According to the Federal Trade Commission, that scam involved more than 300 million people between 2020 and 2022, with more than $8.8 billion in losses.[47]

These recent warnings should grab our attention:

> *A.I. systems with the power of GPT 4 and beyond should not be entangled with the lives of billions of people at a pace faster than cultures can safely absorb them. A race to dominate the market should not set the speed of deploying humanity's most consequential technology. We should move at whatever speed enables us to get this right. . . The time to reckon with A.I. is before our politics, our economy and our daily life become dependent on it. Democracy is a conversation, conversation relies on language, and when language itself is hacked, the conversation breaks down, and democracy becomes untenable. If we wait for the chaos to ensue, it will be too late to remedy it.*[48]
>
> —Yuval N. Harari, historian —Tristan Harris and Aza Raskin, co-founders and a founder of Sapienship, of the Center for Humane Technology a social impact company

Ms. Timmit Gebru, founder and executive director of the Distributed Artificial Intelligence Institute, a non-profit she launched in 2021 and inside Silicon Valley skeptic, brings us this insight:

> *We talk about algorithms, but we don't talk about who's constructing the data set or who's in the data set. If the input is biased, then the output can amplify such biases.*[49]

More recently, a group of A.I. experts including Elon Musk called for a six-month pause on systems more powerful than GPT-4, in order to have time to institute "shared safety protocols;" and that if such a moratorium cannot be enacted quickly, governments should step in and institute a moratorium.[50] Even more recently, this open letter was signed by more than 350 executives, researchers, and engineers working with A.I.

> *Mitigating the risk of extinction from A.I. should be a global priority alongside other society-scale risks, such as pandemics and nuclear war.*[51]

Although some A.I. companies have attempted to add guardrails to some of the leading chatbots to prevent harmful information and hate rhetoric from being widely distributed, researchers at Carnegie Mellon and the Center for A.I. Safety have shown that these guardrails can be easily circumvented.[52] A recent two-page article in the *New York Times* exposed the wide extent to which Musk's X platform is full of misinformation after his reversal of guardrails, including reversing its prior policy against COVID-19 misinformation.[53]

III. What's Being Done to Counter Lies and Disinformation?

As the harms of unregulated social media accumulate in our society and country, Dr. Nicholas Carr, visiting professor of sociology at Williams College and author of *How to Fix Social Media in The New Atlantis*, describes the challenge before us:

> *The problems unleashed by social media, and the country's inability to address them, point to something deeper: Americans' loss of a sense of the common good. Lacking any shared standard of assessing social media content, we've ceded control over that content to social media companies.*[54]

In his important 2022 book, *The Chaos Machine: The Inside Story of How Social Media Rewired Our Minds and Our World*, Max Fisher, international reporter for the *New York Times*, describes the accelerating adoption of artificial intelligence (A.I.) on various platforms, including Meta, Open A.I., Snap, Twitter, and My A.I. Basic questions are still being asked about the validity of algorithms, who develops them, and their safety. Fisher brings us this warning about the future of social media:

> *Whatever the counsel, for a great many serious researchers, analysts, or human rights advocates, it comes down to some version of turning it off . . . Some combination of ideology, greed and the technological opacity of complex machine-learning blinds executives from seeing their creations in their entirety. The machines are, in the ways that matter, essentially ungoverned.*[55]

As one example of their many problems, Snap recently acknowledged this problem with its OpenAI technology customized for Snapchat:

> *My A.I. is prone to hallucination and can be tricked into saying just about anything. Please be aware of its many deficiencies and sorry in advance. Please do not share any secrets with My A.I. and do not rely on it for advice.*[56]

Unfortunately, the U. S. Supreme Court has completely missed the boat in protecting the public from these kinds of lies and disinformation. It recently handed down twin victories to two Big Tech giants. In Googles' case, it ruled that a section of the Communications Decency Act does not apply that would limit its liability for user content. In a separate case involving Twitter, it ruled unanimously that another law allowing lawsuits for aiding terrorism did not apply to the ordinary activities of social media companies.[57]

These are some of the efforts being taken to bring social media under some kind of social responsibility:

- In late 2020, the Democrat-controlled House antitrust subcommittee released a 449-page report recommending sweeping regulations against Facebook, Google, Amazon and Apple that in some cases, could break them up. Their concerns were about monopolistic behavior, but also about the companies' threat to our economy and democracy.[58]
- The Justice Department filed suit against Google in October, 2020 for abuses in line with the House report; soon thereafter, the Federal Trade Commission filed a similar suit against Facebook, suggesting that it might seek to break the company up.[59]

- Near the end of 2021, a non-profit Integrity Institute was established to discuss solutions to platform design problems at social media companies, while a bipartisan group of senators began drafting legislation to compel Facebook and other social media companies to provide data to outside researchers.[60]
- The Southern Poverty Law Center has launched new initiatives to fight online extremism, including investigation and exposure of ways that far-right extremists exploit mainstream digital technology, and the efforts to inoculate young people against online radical extremism.[61]
- Privacy regulators in the European Union, representing a 27-nation bloc and home of about 450 million people, have hit Facebook owner Meta with a $1.3 billion fine for sending user information to the U. S., a record privacy penalty for the bloc.[62]
- The Department of Justice has filed a lawsuit against Google claiming that it has engaged in anti-competitive practices in digital ad-brokering, and is seeking a breakup of Google's "illegal monopoly."[63]
- President Biden has urged action in the 118th session of Congress for federal protections for Americans' privacy and fundamental reform of the Communications Decency Act;[64] he has also recently issued an Executive Order invoking emergency powers to increase federal oversite of A.I.[65]
- NPR is quitting Twitter after it designated itself "U. S. state-affiliated media."[66]
- As ChatGPT reaches 100 million users, the U. S. Commerce Department put out a formal public request for comment on accountability measures.[67]
- *The New York Times* filed suit against Microsoft and Ope-nAI over alleged copyright infringement, seeking damages that the Tech companies are using its content to destroy data sets that include the *Times*' work.[68]

As the battle between truth and disinformation/misinformation rolls on, the *New York Times* brings us this essential description of truth this way:[69]

The truth is hard.
The truth is hidden.
The truth must be pursued.
The truth is hard to hear.
The truth is rarely simple.
The truth isn't so obvious.
The truth is necessary.
The truth can't be glossed over.
The truth has no agenda.
The truth can't be manufactured.
The truth doesn't take sides.
The truth isn't red or blue.
The truth is hard to accept.
The truth pulls no punches.
The truth is powerful.
The truth is under attack.
The truth is worth defending.
The truth requires taking a stand.
The truth is more important now than ever.

Conclusion:

The results of the 2022 midterms cut both ways. Although Democratic control of the Senate is a positive outcome, loss of the House to Republicans, without policies except to conduct vengeful investigations, is negative. We can expect a do-nothing Congress, with little if any bipartisanship, as the country's problems simmer and worsen leading up to the 2024 election cycle. Disunity is the rule as democracy is once again on the ballot for 2024. We have to realize that, much as we have touted our democracy, we still have not achieved a multi-cultural democracy, even after more than 240 years.

In the next chapter, we will see how the GOP has been working diligently for the last several decades to stack the U. S. Supreme Court in its favor and against the equality of all of our citizens.

References:

1. Baker, P, Glasser, S. *The Divider: Trump in the White House*, 2017-2021. New York. *Doubleday*, 2022, p. 647.
2. Anderson, K. *Evil Geniuses: The Unmaking of America: A Recent History*. New York. *Random House*, 2020, pp. 368-370.
3. Milbank, D. *The Destructionists: The Twenty-Five-Year Crack-Up of the Republican Party.* New York. *Penguin Random House*, 2022, pp. 218-219.
4. Ibid #4.
5. Silverman, C. This analysis shows how viral fake election news stories outperformed real news on Facebook. *BuzzFeed News*, November 16, 2016.
6. Frenkel, Kang, C. *An Ugly Truth: Inside Facebook's Battle for Domination.* New York. *HarperCollins Publishers*, 2021, pp. 116-137.
7. Ibid # 6, p. 283.
8. Rhodes, B. *After the Fall: Being American in the World We've Made*. New York. *Penguin Random House*, 2021, pp. 299-300.
9. Ibid # 1, p. 644.
10. Dizikes, P. Study: On Twitter, false news travels faster than true stories. Massachusetts Institute of Technology, March 8, 2018.
11. Hagey, K, Horwitz, J. Facebook rife with stolen content. *Wall Street Journal,* November 10, 2021: A:1.
12. Ibid # 6, p. 288.
13. Dayen, D. Quelling our national riot. *The American Prospect*, January/February 2021, p. 4.
14. Schiff, A. Election denial is now Republican dogma. Adam Standing Strong campaign email, September 12, 2022.
15. Wernau, J, Elinson, Z. New buyers rush to acquire guns. *Wall Street Journal,* July 15, 2020: A 20.
16. Jones, S. Factcheckers agree with Katie Porter and her whiteboard that corporate profits drive inflation price increases. *Politicus* USA, October 22, 2022.
17. Kuttner, R. The Fed keeps throttling the economy. Kuttner on TAP. *The American Prospect*, December 14, 2022.
18. Reich, R. These blatant lies could swing the midterms. Inequality Media Civic Action, October 22, 2022.
19. Gottfried, J, Liedke, J. Partisan divides in media trust widen, driven by a decline among Republicans. *Pew Research Center*, August 30, 2021.
20. Brenan, M. Americans' confidence in major U. S. institutions dips. *Gallup,* July 14, 2021.
21. Anderson, M, Perrin, A, Vogels, EA. Most Americans think social media sites censor political viewpoints. *Pew Research Center*, August 19, 2020.
22. Lee, E. 'Shockingly reckless': Fox News hosts privately shot down Trump's 'big lie' over election fraud. *USA Today*, February 17, 2023.
23. Peters, JW, Robertson, K. Murdoch acknowledges Fox News hosts endorsed election fraud falsehoods. *New York Times*, February 27, 2023.
24. Reich, R. The settlement: "Accountability" is just another cost of doing business. Substack, April 19, 2023.

25. Rutenberg, J, Peters, JW, Schmidt, MS. Carlson's texts ignited crisis for Fox chiefs. *New York Times*, April 27, 2023: A: 1.
26. Krugman, P. Plutocratic power and its perils. *New York Times*, April 18, 2023: A: 18.
27. Flint, J, Sharma, A. Rupert Murdock to step down, elder son to take over empire. *Wall Street Journal*, September 22, 2023, A:1.
28. Ibid # 6, p. 278.
29. Ibid # 6, p. 278-280.
30. Ibid # 6, p. 281.
31. Sen, A, Zadrozny, B. QAnon groups have millions of members on Facebook. *NBC News*, August 10, 2020.
32. Ibid # 3, p. 222.
33. Oshinsky, D. The long history of vaccine mandates in America. *Wall Street Journal*, September 18-19, 2021: C 1-2.
34. Fitzpatrick, MC, Moghadas, SM, Pandey, A. Two years of U. S. COVID-19 vaccines prevented millions of hospitalizations and deaths. To the Point (blog), *Commonwealth Fund*, December 13, 2022.
35. Hartmann, T. Why conservatives want government to fail everywhere. *The Progressive Populist*, September 15, 2021, p. 13.
36. Drum, K. Mad as Hell: What's fueling America's political rage? *Mother Jones*, September/October 2021, p. 21.
37. Reich, R. *The Common Good*. New York. *Alfred A. Knopf*, 2018, pp. 95-97.
38. Smoking Gun. What Americans believe. *The Progressive*, August 24, 2021, p. 17.
39. McManus, D. Letter from Washington. Election denial means January 6 was just the beginning. *Los Angeles Times*, October 3, 2021.
40. FiveThirtyEight staff. 60 percent of Americans will have an election denier on the ballot this Fall. *ABC News*, October 23, 2022.
41. Raskin, J, as quoted by Easley, J. Rep. Jamie Raskin warns that the GOP is acting like a religious cult. *Politicus USA*, January 17, 2022.
42. Ludwig, M. Trump's election disinformation machine is already kicking into gear for 2024. *Truthout*, October 4, 2023.
43. Frenkel, S, Conger, K. Hate speech's rise on twitter is unprecedented, researchers find. *New York Times*, December 2, 2022.
44. The proliferation of Trump's lies leads to violence. *Indivisible Team*, January 30, 2023.
45. Reich, R. Have you heard about Facebook's "MAGA mills"? *Inequality Media Civic Action*, March 23, 2023.
46. DePillis, L, Lohr, S. For workers, promise of AI is a threat, too. *New York Times*, March 29, 2023: A 1.
47. Flitter, E, Cowley, S. A.I. copies your voice, then calls up your bank. *New York Times*, September 1, 2023, B:1.
48. Harari, Y, Harris,, T, Raskin, A. If we don't master A.I., it will master us. *New York Times*, March 27, 2023: A: 18.

49. Timmit Gebru. An A:I ethicist wants to draw attention to the technology's pitfalls. *Wall Street Journal*, February 25-26, 2023: C:6.
50. Metz, C. What makes A.I. chatbots go wrong? *New York Times*, April 8, 2023: B 6.
51. Roose, K. A.I. poses risk of 'extinction,' industry leaders warn. *New York Times,* May 30, 2023.
52. Metz C. It's easy to thwart A.I. safety. *New York Times,* July 28, 2023, B1.
53. Myers, SL, Thompson, SA, HSUC, T. Swirl of vitreol and false posts, *New York Times*, October 28, 2023, B:1.
54. Carr, N. Social media should be treated like broadcasting. *Wall Street Journal*, October 30-31, 2021: C 2.
55. Fisher, M. *The Chaos Machine: The Inside Story of How Social Media Rewired Our Minds and Our World.* New York. *Little, Brown and Company*, 2022, 339-340.
56. Bobrowsky, M. Meta, Snap embrace artificial-intelligence chatbox. *Wall Street Journal* February 28, 2023, B: 4.
57. Liptak, A. Supreme Court delivers 2 wins to tech giants. *New York Times*, May 19, 2023, A:1.
58. Ibid #55, p. 332.
59. Ibid #55, p.
60. Hagey, K, Wells, G, Glazer, E. et al. Facebook's pushback: political spin, no apologies. *Wall Street Journal*, November 26, 2021: A 4.
61. SPLC Report. SPC launches new initiatives to fight online extremism. 51 (4) Winter 2021.
62. Schechner, S. Meta's targeted ads face scrutiny in Europe. *Wall Street Journal*, December 7, 2022: A 1.
63. Kruppa, M. Google prepares for battles on multiple fronts. *Wall Street Journal*, January 27, 2023: B 1.
64. Biden, J. Unite against Big Tech abuses. *Wall Street Journal*, January 12, 2023, A: 15.
65. McKinnon, JD, Siddiqui, S, Volz, D. Biden emergency powers to assist oversite of A.I. systems, *Wall Street Journal*, October 31, 2023, A:3.
66. Kelly, L, Robertson, K. NPR is quitting Twitter over 'government funded' label. *New York Times*, April 13, 2023.
67. Tracy, R. U. S. weighs regulating A.I. tools. *Wall Street Journal*, April 12, 2023: A: 1
68. Bruell, A. N.Y. Times accuses AI firms of copyright violations. *New York Times*, December 28, 2023, A:1.
69. *New York Times*, September 19, 2023, A:14.

CHAPTER 6

THE STACKED AND CAPTURED U. S. SUPREME COURT

There are more instances of the abridgement of the freedom of the people by gradual and silent encroachments of those in power than by the violent and sudden usurpations.

—James Madison

Why should there not be a patient confidence in the ultimate justice of the people? Is there any better or equal hope in the world?

—Abraham Lincoln, First Inaugural Address

As we have seen in earlier chapters, the GOP is no longer the party of Lincoln. Michael Beschloss, the well-known historian of the American presidency, notes that today's Republican Party has become one of power and Big Money, which has fostered the largest income and wealth inequality in our country's history. As he further observes, this has become a moral issue, one of national conscience.[1]

The U. S. Supreme Court has come under widespread criticism and disapproval in recent years, to the point that it has become a threat to the future of this country. This chapter has three goals: (1) to bring historical perspective to how this has come to be; (2) to discuss the rulings of today's Supreme Court that are at odds with the public interest; and (3) to consider how today's politicized Supreme Court, captured by Big Money corporate interests, puts our democracy at risk. [1]

I. Historical Perspective

The 50-year GOP scheme to control the Supreme Court:

The Republican Party has patiently and persistently held to its goal to control the Supreme Court over much of the last 50 years.

In an extensive policy essay in the *Harvard Journal on Legislation* in 2020, Senator Sheldon Whitehouse (D-RI), dates the start of that effort to a secret memo from Lewis Powell, then a prominent corporate lawyer, to an official at the U. S. Chamber of Commerce warning that "the American economic system (ie., corporate America) "is under broad attack from academics, the media, leftist politicians, and other progressives," further arguing for an "unprecedented influence campaign on behalf of corporate America against progressive gains."[2]

Leonard Leo has been a kingpin in charting this course for the Supreme Court for many years. Described by some as "the most influential person no one has ever heard of," he was an executive at the Federalist Society for almost 30 years until 1991. Since then, he has led an under-the-radar network of dark money donations for two major goals—to pull the U. S. judiciary to the right in order to "roll back dominance of many important sectors in American life", and also to "punish some of the country's biggest corporations for pushing environmental, social and governance causes that generally align with a Democratic agenda."[3] Leo was largely responsible for packing the Supreme Court with three very conservative Justices as well as blocking the nomination of Merrick Garland to the High Court. As a result, the numbers of 5-4 conservative Supreme Court rulings have increased markedly—80 from the 2004 to 2018 terms benefiting big corporate and Republican donor interests.[4] Moreover, the conservative Supreme Court helped Trump to nominate and confirm more than 200 nominees to the federal bench, thereby shifting the balance of power throughout the judiciary from federal district and appellate courts to state supreme courts.

An investigation by POLITICO based on dozens of financial, property and public records from 2000 to 2021 found that Leo's lifestyle took a lavish turn starting in 2016, when Leo was tapped as an unpaid advisor to incoming President Trump on Supreme Court Justices. As an executive for the Federalist Society for many years, he received somewhere between $125,000 and $435,000 per year, according to its IRS filings.[5]

In his excellent 2022 book, *The Scheme: How the Right Wing Used Dark Money to Capture the Supreme Court*, Senator Sheldon Whitehouse saw this end game unfolding:

> *As I watched Senate rules and norms bent and broken in the rush to appoint Trump judges—and especially to rig the Supreme Court—I realized that the Supreme Court wasn't just a target of the Scheme; it was enabling the Scheme. There was a feedback loop between the Scheme and the Court. And my heart sank to realize that if the right-wing oligarchs succeeded in capturing the Court, the results would forever damage our American republic, its integrity, and its principle of majority rule. They weren't just in it to win cases; they were out to change America.*[6]

Retiring two years ago from his position with the Federalist Society in order to devote full-time to raising dark money, Leo received *$1.6 billion* (not a misprint!) from Barre Seid, a 90-year-old manufacturing magnate through a tax-free transaction for his new "non-profit" venture, the Marble Freedom Trust. The largest donation in political history ever, it gives Leo new full rein to pursue its stated mission "*to maintain and expand human freedom consistent with the values and ideals set forth in the Declaration of Independence and the Constitution of the United States.*"[7]

These are Supreme Court rulings that encouraged corporate greed and have led to an increasingly unequal society:

1. ***1976: Buckley decision.*** This ruling re-defined politicians taking money from billionaires away from being "political corruption" and "bribery" to "exercise of free speech."
2. ***1978: Boston v. Bellotti.*** This ruling gave giant corporations the same "free speech" right.
3. ***2010: Citizens United.*** This ruling gave corporations the political equivalence of personhood and allowed unmonitored campaign contributions from billionaires and corporations for whatever purpose they desired.[98]

   This ruling has been especially damaging to our democracy by opening the flood gates to very large campaign donations that undermine popular sovereignty, majority rule, and representative government. Between 2010 and 2020, groups that don't disclose their donors spent almost $1 billion in elections, almost 8 times their donations over the previous decade.[9] As Senator Whitehouse observes:

> *Today, corporations wield commanding power in our democracy. They do so directly, and through a network of trade associations, think tanks, front groups, and political organizations. That power too often is directed by corporate forces to dodge accountability for harms to the public; to subvert the free market to their advantage; and to protect their own political power by undermining democratic institutions.*[10]

And further:

> *Citizens United and other Supreme Court decsions empowering all this anonymous influence represent one side of a vicious cycle, the side in which the Court cossets and protects dark money. The other side of the cycle is how dark money has helped the Scheme to stack the Court, just as industry stacks a captured regulator agency. To perpetuate this is no small deed. It has required an arsenal of tactics, including a doctrine factory where useful legal theories are created, an auditioning process by which judges compete for advancement, a Senate rubber stamp for confirming them, and an armada of amici to signal the donors' wishes to the Court. And the Scheme has it all.*[11]

4. ***2021: Americans for Prosperity Foundation v. Bonta.*** This ruling was a big win for Charles Koch. It will likely make dark money even darker by establishing a precedent that could be used to hide donor identities from state governments, potentially undermining accountability for bribery, fraud and corruption in politics and policy making.[12]

II. Rulings by Today's Supreme Court Against the Public Interest

With Leonard Leo actively involved in the appointments of five conservative Justices in recent years, the Supreme Court is now a dependable ally for corporate and Republican partisan interests, so much so that it has damaged our democracy. Bill Blum, a Los Angeles attorney and former State of California administrative law judge, issued this warning in 2021:

> *The U. S. Supreme Court is not a democratic institution. It consists of nine unelected elite lawyers armed with the tools and techniques of judicial review. They, not "The People," often get the last word on vital questions of social, economic, and even political policy.*[13]

By the end of its 2021 term, the Supreme Court, with its 6-3 conservative majority, had issued these three extremist rulings:

1. *Reproductive rights.*

The 1973 Roe v. Wade ruling by the Supreme Court recognized, as a core democratic value, the right of women to terminate an unwanted pregnancy at any point up to viability, about 24 weeks. That was overturned in June, 2022 through the Dobbs v. Jackson Women's Health Organization. The decision ignited widespread anger and protests across the country as 26 states restricted access to abortion pills or banned abortion altogether. (Figure 6.1).[14] Maternal mortality has increased almost twice as fast in those states with such restrictions.[15] Of further concern in terms of inadequate access to women's reproductive health care, a recent survey of more than 2,000 current and future physicians found that 76% of them would no longer consider practicing or training in abortion-restricted states.[16]

Figure 6.1

WHERE ABORTION IS LEGAL AND WHERE IT LOSES PROTECTIONS WITHOUT ROE V. WADE

Abortion access across the U.S. now depends on state laws after Supreme Court overturned 1973 decision that established constitutional right to an abortion

Source: Guttmacher Institute

The issue heated up further when GOP state attorneys general sent letters to pharmacies opposing the use of medication abortion, which involves the sequential use of mifepristone and misoprostol. Then a federal judge in Texas took on the FDA as not qualified to approve mifepristone as a safe and effective drug, as took place in 2000.[17] In a rapid turn-around, Washington State filed a lawsuit arguing that the drug was in fact safe and effective, as has been demonstrated by its use over the past 23 years.[18] As the situation became even more confused, the Supreme Court in late April 2023 deferred to rule on removal from the market of mifepristone and return the issue to the Fifth Circuit Court of Appeals in New Orleans.[19] It remained likely that the matter would be appealed back to the Supreme Court, likely during the 2024 election campaigns.

As the legal status of reproductive rights remained unresolved, an updated NPR/PBS News Hour/Marist poll found that two-thirds of Americans oppose laws banning medication abortion. (Figure 6.2) It also found that 62% of respondents have not very much or little confidence in the Supreme Court, the lowest level of confidence in the Supreme Court since Marist has been asking that question.[20]

Figure 6.2

NEARLY TWO-THIRDS OF AMERICANS OPPOSE LAWS BANNING MEDICATION ABORTION

Respondents were asked: "A medication abortion is the use of a prescription pill or a series of pills taken to end a pregnancy. Do you support or oppose a law that bans access to a medication abortion?"

Source: NPR/PBS NewsHour/Marist poll of 1,291 U.S. adults conducted April 17-19. The margin of error for the overall sample is 3.4 percentage points. Some results may not add up to 100% due to rounding.
Credit: Alyson Hurt/NPR

2. *Gun rights.*

On another 6-3 vote, the Supreme Court cast aside longstanding strict limits in New York State on granting permits for carrying concealed hand guns outside the home and in public places. Predictably, that has led to judges in lower courts across the country striking down other gun regulations. As one example, a federal judge in Texas ruled that the Constitution protects the right of 18- to 20-year-olds to carry hand guns for self- defense outside the home.[21] Figure 6.3 illustrates the incredible hypocrisy and uncaring of Texas Governor Greg Abbott in the aftermath of a shooting that claimed the lives of five people, including a 9-year-old girl.

Figure 6.3

ABBOTT TORCHED FOR CALLING MASS SHOOTING VICTIMS 'ILLEGAL'

Source: Reprinted with permission from Nick Anderson

Since then, those kinds of rulings have had an increasingly dangerous impact across the country to the point that the numbers of mass shootings keep increasing and that 25% of guns sold today are AR 15s, weapons of war. Jack Rakove, Professor of History and

American Studies Emeritus at Stanford University, challenges the faulty originalist "history" used by the Court in its rulings on gun rights this way:

> *It is a tragic irony that the miniscule evidence ostensibly supporting the Supreme Court's recent decisions on gun regulation are the real outliers in the historical record. This is a tradition that the Supreme Court has largely invented, not one it has discovered, and it is sadly consistent with the evolution of the U. S. into a nation uniquely vulnerable to gun deaths of every kind, from suicides to mass shootings.*[22]

3. *Environmental protection.*

In a case about whether the Environmental Protection Agency (EPA) can regulate coal fired power plants, the Supreme Court ruled that neither the Environment Protection Agency nor any other agency can adopt rules that are "transformational to the economy" unless Congress has specifically authorized it to do so. That ruling throws a big wrench into what this country can do to control carbon emissions and combat climate change.[23]

Growing concerns about these Supreme Court rulings.

Eric Holder, 82nd Attorney General of the United States, issued this statement after the Roe and EPA rulings:

> *This week, the Supreme Court cemented the fact that it is wildly out of touch with the American people and heretofore guiding legal principles . . . Today, the Supreme Court is at its worst. The Court's majority has caustically reversed long-held precedent to give us a country where our daughters and granddaughters will have fewer rights than their mothers and grandmothers and where our gun violence problem is unnecessarily worsened . . . The Supreme Court must be reformed in order to ensure that the Court serves the interests of the people instead of the interests of an extreme, minority faction.*[24]

Michael Waldman, president and CEO of the Brennan Center for Justice at NYU School of Law and author of the excellent 2023 book, *The Supermajority: How the Supreme Court Divided America*, adds this:

> *Over three days in June 2022, the Supreme Court changed America. It overturned Roe v. Wade, repealing the protection for abortion rights in place for American women for a half century, and putting at risk all other privacy rights. It radically loosened curbs on guns, amid an epidemic of mass shootings. And it hobbled the ability of government agencies to protect public health and safety and stop climate change when the topic is a "major question." The Court crammed decades of social change into three days.*[25]

In the aftermath of these rulings, the Supreme Court has once again raised increased public concern that its decisions are politicized in favor of conservative political interests. Its nine justices have been the only U. S. judges—state or federal—not governed by a code of ethical conduct. For too long it has rejected the need for such a code, even after criticism over the last two decades of most of its members having engaged in behaviors forbidden to other federal court judges. According to the Brennan Center for Justice, these behaviors include "participating in partisan convenings or fundraisers, accepting expensive gifts or travel, making partisan comments at public events or in the media, or failing to recuse themselves from cases involving apparent conflicts of interest, either financial or personal." Its 2019 white paper called for the Supreme Court to "adopt its own Code of Conduct, establish a regular practice of explaining its own recusal decisions, and strengthening its rules governing gifts and financial disclosures."[26]

President Joe Biden's Commission on the Supreme Court of the United States, in its 2021 final report, noted that "most public and private entities have adopted Codes of Conduct for their organizations and employees, and that it is not obvious why the Court is best served by an exemption from what so many consider best practice." The Commission's 34 members also expressed bipartisan support for non-renewable terms of 18 years, and saw an advisory ethics code for the High Court as "a positive step." [27]

One behind-the-scenes organization, the Supreme Court Historical Society, gives large, often corporate donors special access to High Court Justices when the donors have a significant stake in the way future cases are decided. As a non-profit, it is not required to disclose its donors. An investigation by the *New York Times* found that the Society has raised more than $23 million over the last 20 years.[28]

Of particular concern today is the refusal of Justice Clarence Thomas to recuse himself in a case that related to the January 6th insurrection after his wife, Ginny Thomas, had sent text messages to the former White House chief of staff concerning plans for that criminal conspiracy. Transcripts released by the House Committee investigating the January 6 insurrection, as reported by *MSNBC Nightly News*, revealed that texts to her husband made her feel better about the fight ahead in the coup attempt.[29]

Of further concern is a recent investigative report by ProPublica revealing that right-wing Justice Clarence Thomas has been taking luxury trips funded by Republican billionaire Harlan Crow for more than two decades. It is a long list of gifts received from Crow, never disclosed by Thomas, that include a gift of a house where the Thomas family has been living. There is precedent for ousting a Supreme Court justice—the removal of Justice Abe Fortas, a Democratic appointee, in 1969 when he was involved in such a scandal. At that time Congress dealt with the problem in a bipartisan way.[30]

Legislation requiring the Supreme Court to develop its own ethical code of conduct was drafted by the House Judiciary Committee in the last Congress, May, 2022—the Supreme Court Ethics, Recusal and Transparency Act (SCERTA), which passed 22-16 along party lines.[31] In June, 2022, some 190,000 Move On members called for Clarence Thomas to be impeached.[32] In February 2023, the *Washington Post* reported that the Supreme Court justices discussed, but did not agree on an ethical code of conduct.[33]

Another serious ethical transgression by Justices of the Supreme Court has recently come to light that once again shows that the highest court in the land has the lowest ethical standards. Justice Neil Gorsuch did not disclose his sale of a $2 million vacation home to the CEO of a major corporate law firm that has argued hundreds of cases before Court.[34] Chief Justice Roberts has been asked to testify before the Senate Judiciary Committee, but has chosen to decline. As this book goes to press in 2024, SCERTA has still not been taken up in Congress. While the Supreme Court did adopt its own new ethics code in November, 2023, there seem to be no real ways to enforce what has been called a public relations pablum.[35]

All of this has led Randall Eliason, former chief of the fraud and public corruption section of the U. S. Attorney's Office for the District of Columbia, to conclude that the Supreme Court has a corruption problem. As he says:

> *Over more than two decades, the Supreme Court has gutted laws aimed at fighting corruption and at limiting the ability of the powerful to enrich public officials in a position to advance their interests. As a result, today wealthy individuals and corporations may buy political access and influence with little fear of legal consequences, either for them or for the beneficiaries of their largess.*[36]

III. How the Supreme Court Puts Our Democracy at Risk

The extent to which the Supreme Court has been politicized and captured by powerful corporate interests puts our democracy at risk in several ways. Katrina vanden Heuvel, editorial director and publisher of *The Nation*, brings us this insight:

> *The Supreme Court is the country's least democratic branch of government. Its appointed, unelected justices serve lifetime terms. They select the cases they hear. And now, after a 40-year campaign by conservatives, the court has a six-person, transparently partisan majority. This session, they will continue to forward the right's agenda—undermining civil rights, elevating religious doctrine, rolling back the power to regulate.*[37]

The Supreme Court is no longer in step with the mainstream of American society. Figure 6.4 shows a marked drop in trust over the last 10 years, with sharp differences by political party. A recent national poll by NPR, PBS Newshour, and the Marist Institute for Public Opinion found that 62% of Americans have either no confidence at all or not very much confidence in the Supreme Court. Moreover, 68% think that Supreme Court justices should have term limits instead of lifetime appointments.[38]

Figure 6.4

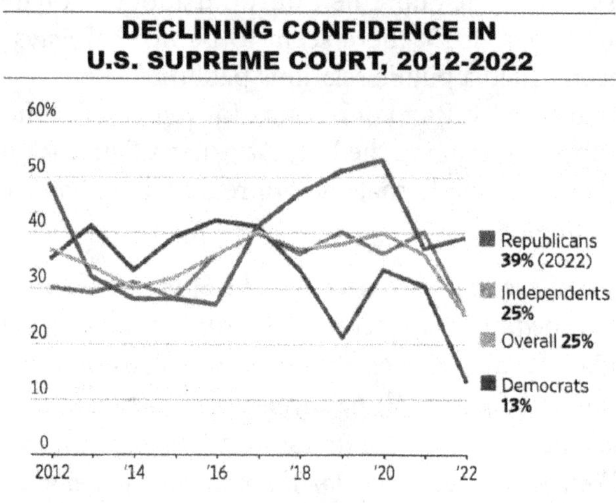

Source: Gallup polls since 2022

These are some of the extremely damaging rulings by the Supreme Court handed down during the last days of its 2023 term:

• *Affirmative action:*

It held that race-conscious admissions programs at Harvard and the University of North Carolina violate the Constitution's guarantee of equal protection, rolling back decades of precedent. In its 6-3 vote by the conservative majority, it cast aside precedent in the same way that the Dobb's decision of 2022 had done for reproductive rights of women. In this latest ruling, dissenting Justice Sonia Sotomayor wrote this blistering dissent:

> *The Court subverts the constitutional guarantee of equal protection by further entrenching racial inequality in education, the very foundation of our democratic government and pluralistic society."*[39]

Three months later, Justice Ketanji Brown Jackson, the first Black female Supreme Court Justice, issued this forceful rebuke to the affirmative action ruling on the occasion of the 60th anniversary of the Ku Klux bombing at the Sixteenth Street Baptist Church in Birmingham, Alabama that killed four young girls:

> *With let-them-eat-cake obliviousness, today, the majority pulls the rip cord and announces 'colorblindness for all' by legal fiat. But deeming race irrelevant in law does not make it so in life.*[40]

- *Free speech:*

In a ruling involving a Colorado man who sent disturbing messages to a singer-songwriter on the internet, the Supreme Court ruled that the First Amendment imposes limits on laws that make it a crime to issue threats on the internet. It held that prosecutors must prove that an offender was acting recklessly in making such threats.[41] In another case, the High Court held that a Colorado web designer can refuse to serve a same sex couple's wedding plans based on protections from the 1964 Civil Rights Act, which have been shown to be constitutional on many past occasions. This gave Justice Sotomayor another occasion to dissent in this way:

> *The concept of a public accommodation thus embodies a simple, but powerful social contract: A business that chooses to sell to the public assumes a duty to serve the public without unjust discrimination.*[42]

- *Cancellation of student debt:*

In another 6-3 party line vote, the Supreme Court rejected President Biden's authority to cancel some $1.6 trillion in student debt held by more than 45 million college students in the absence of clear congressional authorization.[43]The majority claimed that his student loan policy exceeded his authority under the HEROES Act, while he had directed his Secretary of Education to provide debt relief under the Higher Education Act of 1965.[44]

As one exception to these kinds of flagrant rulings by the Supreme Court, one very recent ruling by the U. S. Supreme Court was positive for the country. North Carolina had asked the High Court to rule that the U. S. Constitution empowers its state legislature alone to determine how elections are run—the "independent state legislature theory." In 2021, the Republican-dominated state legislature in North Carolina had passed, on a party-line vote, an extreme partisan gerrymander that locked in a supermajority of the State's 14 congressional seats. The Supreme Court has rejected that theory for more than 100 years, including as recently as 2015 and 2019. Fortunately, it did so once again in a 6-3 ruling on June 27, 2023, thereby averting unchecked power of state legislatures to set rules for federal elections warped by partisan gerrymandering.[45]

Elie Mystal, attorney and justice correspondent for *The Nation*, describes what we now have is a juristocracy, with the 6 conservative Justices on the Supreme Court "continuing to do all the things that Republicans cannot persuade voters to do." [46] The Voting Rights Act is the next target of the High Court, which already made a worrisome ruling 10 years ago with its 2013 ruling, *Shelby County v. Holder*, which gutted a requirement of prior federal approval for voting changes in states with a record of partisan gerrymandering. [47] Writing for the Court at that time, Chief Justice John Roberts ignored history and the record to render his own finding that racial discrimination was no longer a problem in the United States.[47]

In light of these kinds of conservative rulings, the 2023-2024 Supreme Court term may continue to render worrisome rulings, as it has agreed to review cases involving voting rights, workers' rights, regulation of health and safety, taxing the wealthy, and the environment.[48] The Koch network of billionaire business money will be trying to bring cases to the Court that can reduce government regulations by the "administrative state."[49] On December 5, 2023, the Supreme Court did hear oral arguments in *Moore v. United States*, a case that threatens the ability of Congress to fairly tax corporations and the ultra-wealthy, both now and in the future, with any ruling pending. Four Justices of the Court have major conflicts of interest, such as having received lavish gifts and vacations from wealthy donors, and it remains to be seen whether or not they will recuse themselves.[50]

As Robert Reich warns:

> *No Supreme Court case in recent history has had the extreme potential economic impact that Moore v. United States does, limiting opportunities for social change for generations to come . . . The integrity of the Court demands they must recuse themselves now.* [51]

Based on the research for his important 2022 book, *The Scheme: How the Right Wing Used Dark Money to Capture the Supreme Court*, and as a participant in President Biden's Commission on the Supreme

Court of the United States that published its report in 2021, Senator Whitehouse comes away with this takeaway:

> *As we battle for the soul of the Court, no reform will be meaningful if we do not disrupt the flow of undisclosed dark money into all stages of the pipeline: the pseudo-academic hothouses that make it worth someone's while to manufacture reverse-engineered theories; the organizations that indoctrinate, groom and audition judicial candidates; a Senate that has abandoned its own institutional processes and prerogatives to install reliable policy agents on the courts; and a Supreme Court whose "ethics" program has neither binding rules nor referees. Nor will it be meaningful if we do not grapple with the damage already done, procured through unprincipled decisions that rewarded unprincipled special interests. The worst of the damage is the damage done to American democracy.*[52]

Conclusion:

In view of the evolution of *The Scheme* with its capture of the Supreme Court and the rise of corporate power in governance, it is an open question whether our democracy of 245 years can survive against today's emerging oligarchy. As polarization within American society reaches new highs of polarization, toxic debate and increasing violence, our Republic is at a political and moral tipping point.

Louis Brandeis came of age in the Progressive Era that followed the Gilded Age of the 1890s. As Associate Justice on the Supreme Court from 1916 to 1939, he fought for small business and supported President Woodrow Wilson's campaign to "Bust the Trusts." He warned that we can't have democracy when so much of our wealth is concentrated in the hands of the few, as it is today. He also warned of "the insidious menace inherent in large aggregations of capital, particularly held by corporations."[53]

We can learn from Abraham Lincoln's experience in leading our Republic during the height of its upheaval during the Civil War years. Jon Meacham, Pulitzer Prize-winning biographer of U. S. presidents and author of the 2022 book, *And There Was Light: Abraham Lincoln and the American Struggle,* describes Lincoln's motives in this way:

> *In life, Lincoln's motives were moral as well as political—a reminder that our finest presidents are those committed to bringing a flawed nation closer to the light, a mission that requires an understanding that politics divorced from conscience is fatal to the American experiment in liberty under law. In years of peril he pointed the country toward a future that was superior to the past and to the present; in years of strife he held steady. Lincoln's life shows us that progress can be made by fallible and fallen presidents and peoples—which, in a fallible and fallen world, should give us hope.*[54]

In the next chapter, we will consider another way whereby oligarchs defend their power—weak anti-trust regulations.

References:

1. Beschloss, M. As quoted on Alex Wagner Show, MSNBC, October 23, 2022.
2. Whitehouse, S. *Dark money and U. S. Courts: The Problems and Solutions. Harvard Journal on Legislation* 57: 281, 2020.
3. Vogel, KP. Leonard Leo pushed the Courts right. Now he's aiming at American society. *New York Times*, October 12, 2022.
4. Ibid # 2, 289-290.
5. Przybyla, H. Dark money and special deals: How Leonard Leo and his friends benefited from his judicial activism. *ProPublica*, March 1, 2023.
6. Whitehouse, S. *The Scheme: How the Right Wing Used Dark Money to Capture the Supreme Court*. New York. *The New Press*, 2022, p. 6.
7. Ibid # 6.
8. Mystal, E. Objection! Dark money windfall. *The Nation*, September 19-26, 2022.
9. Hartmann, T. When will America break free from the clutches of the grifters? *The Progressive Populist*, November 1, 2021, p. 12.
10. Ever-Hillstrom, K et al. *More Money, Less Transparency: A Decade Under Citizens United*. Center for Responsive Politics: Open Secrets News, January 14, 2020.
11. Ibid #2, p. 273.
12. Gibson, C. Charles Koch's campaign to make dark money even darker. *The Center for Media and Democracy*, December 19, 2022.

13. Blum, B. Taking back the Supreme Court. Major changes are warranted to save a broken institution. *The Progressive.* August/September 2021, pp. 46-49.
14. Dapena, K, Calfas, J. Where abortion is legal and where it loses protections without Roe v. Wade, *Wall Street Journal,* June 28, 2022.
15. Declercq, E, Barnard-Mayers, R, Zephyrin, L et al. The U. S. maternal health divide: The limited maternal health services and worse outcomes of states proposing new abortion restrictions. *The Commonwealth Fund,* December 2022.
16. Rovner, J. 76 percent of surveyed doctors don't want to work in abortion-restricted states. *Kaiser Health News,* May 24, 2023.
17. Kusisto,, L., Whyte, LE. Abortion-pill approval suspended by U. S. judge, *New York Times,* April 7, 2023.
18. Vansickle, A. Justice, for now, safeguard access to abortion pills. *New York Times,* April 22, 2023: A: 1.
19. Calfas, J. Abortion pill fight engulfs Walgreens. *Wall Street Journal,* March 9, 2023, p. A:6.
20. Montanaro, D. Poll: Two-thirds oppose banning medication abortion. *00.5 WESA, Pittburgh's NPR News Station,* April 24, 2023.
21. Gershman, J. Judges across U.S. expand gun rights. *Wall Street Journal,* October 11, 2022: A 4.
22. Rakove, J. The Justices are bad gun historians. *Wall Street Journal,* November 4-5, 2023, C:6.
23. Totenberg, N. Supreme Court restricts the EPA's authority to mandate carbon emissions reductions. *NPR,* June 30, 2022.
24. Holder, E. It's time to reform the Supreme Court. National Democratic Redistricting Committee, June 24, 2022.
25. Waldman, M. *The Supermajority: How the Supreme Court Divided America.* New York. *Simon & Schuster,* 2023, p. 1.
26. Kalb, J, Bannon, A. Supreme Court ethics reform. *Brennan Center for Justice,* September 24, 2019.
27. Erskine, E. Presidential court commission approves final report, identifying disagreement on expansion. *SCOTUS NEWS,* December 8, 2021.
28. Becker, J, Tate, J. A charity tied to the Supreme Court offers donors access to the Justices. *New York Times,* December 30, 2022.
29. Johnson, J. Calls for Clarence Thomas impeachment vote after report exposes billionaire-funded trips. *Common Dreams,* April 6, 2023.
30. Cohen, A. There's a precedent for ousting a justice. *New York Times,* April 13, 2023.
31. Crawley, J. Supreme Court ethics code advances in House. *Bloomberg Law,* May 11, 2022.
32. Omar, J. Petition to MoveOn members to impeach Clarence Thomas, June 8, 2022.
33. Barnes, R, Marimow, AE. Supreme Court justices discussed, but did not agree on, code of conduct. *The Washington Post,* February 9, 2023.

34. Reich, R. Supreme Court Neil Gorsuch caught red-handed. *Inequality Media*, April 27, 2023.
35. VanSickle, A, Liptak, A. Supreme Court announces ethics code for Justices. *New York Times*, November 13, 2023.
36. Eliason, RD. The Supreme Court has a corruption problem. *New* York Times, May 19, 2023, A:23.
37. vanden Heuvel, K. The Supreme Court's majority reconvenes its assault on democracy. *The Progressive Populist*, November 1, 2022, p. 12.
38. Otten, T. Poll: Two-thirds of Americans don't have confidence in Supreme Court. *The New Republic*, April 24, 2023.
39. Sotomajor, S, as quoted by Wilkins, B, "With let-them-eat-cake oblivious-ness", Supreme Court ends affirmative action for colleges. *Common Dreams*, June 29, 2023.
40. Green, EL, Vansicle, A. A call in Birmingham for a nation to recall ugly truths about the past. *New York Times*, September 16, 2023, A:18.
41. Liptak, A. Supreme Court puts first amendment limits on bans to online threats. *New York Times*, June 28, : A:15.
42. Kuttner, R. The Roberts Court's cynical use of free speech to allow discrimination. Today on Tap, *The American Prospect*, June 30, 2023.
43. Liptak, A. Justices say no to student loan relief. *New York Times*, July 1, 2023, A: 1.
44. Shear MD. Court's decision unravels a signature plan of Biden's. *New York Times*, July 1, 2023, A:12.
45. Liptak, A. Supreme Court rejects theory that would have transformed American elections. *New York Times*, June 27, 2023.
46. Mystal, E. Welcome to the juristocracy. *The Nation*, October 17-24, 2022, p. 17.
47. Bravin, J. Conservative shift marks historic term. *Wall Street Journal*, July 1, 2022, A:7.
48. Pilkington, E, Surgey, N. 'Get the right cases to the supreme court': inside Charles' Koch's network. the guardian.org, October 26, 2023.
49. Cohn, M, Right-dominated Supreme Court is poised to do grave harm in upcoming term. *Truthout*, September 28, 2023.
50. Tulley, E. Compromised Supreme Court Justices cannot rule on this case. *Daily Kos*, October 30, 2023.
51. Reich, R. Four Justices must recuse due to massive financial interests in Moore v. U. S. robert@imcivicaction.org.
52. Ibid # 6, pp. 225-226.
53. Louis Brandeis, as quoted by Whitehouse, S., Ibid # 6, p. 26.
54. Meacham, J. *And There Was Light: Abraham Lincoln and the American Struggle*. New York. *Penguin Random House*, 2022, pp. 419-420.

CHAPTER 7

CORPORATE POWER VS. ANTITRUST REGULATION: CAPITALISM OUT OF CONTROL

Our economy has changed a great deal since our antitrust laws were first introduced . . . Competition law has been excessively narrowed, and excessively influenced by presumptions concerning a competitive marketplace. Today, our competition laws and antitrust practices need to be reformed, to incorporate the realities of the twenty-first century and the insights of modern economics . . . We also need to curb the power corporate leaders have to advance their own interests at the expense of the other stakeholders in the corporation, including shareholders, workers, and the communities in which the firm operates.[1]

—Joseph Stiglitz, Ph.D., Nobel Laureate in Economics and author of the 2012 book, *The Price of Inequality: How Today's Divided Society Endangers Our Future* and the 2019 book, *People, Power and Profits: Progressive Capitalism for an Age of Discontent.*

Despite the many books on corporate crooks, there have been no corporate crime law reforms, no additional prosecutions of these CDOs, not even comprehensive congressional or state legislative hearings. The corporate crooks at the top of giant companies still get away with profiting from their corporate crime wave.[2]

—Ralph Nader, author of *Wrecking America: How Trump's Lawbreaking and Lies Betray Us All,* and founder of the Center for the Study of Responsive Law

We have seen in the last two chapters how lies and disinformation from the Republican Party, despite the extent of their untruth, have gained broad support from an uninformed electorate, while the Supreme Court is surprisingly detached from dealing fairly with important issues facing our democracy. Now we address another way in which the developing oligarchy protects itself from government regulation. This chapter has three goals: (1) to touch on the highlights of how antitrust policies have been developed and applied since the early 1900s; (2) to describe some of the ways that mega corporations have evaded antitrust enforcement to the detriment of everyday Americans; and (3) to discuss what is being done today under the Biden administration to develop and enforce new antitrust initiatives.

I. Historical Background

Although *The Sherman Antitrust Act of 1890* prohibited "monopolization" by such industry-dominating companies as U. S. Steel, Standard Oil and some railroads, it was more a statement of principles without effective results.[3] Administrative neglect and judicial hostility carried the day through the 1890s, during which Louis Brandeis, a brilliant corporate attorney out of Harvard Law School, earned the title of "the people's lawyer" for his exposure of the corruption of the New Haven Railroad, a mismanaged consolidated company controlled by J. P. Morgan.[4]

Highlights of four previous cycles of antitrust policy and enforcement since 1900:[5]

1. 1900-1920:

Theodore Roosevelt served two terms as President from 1901-1909 and, though a Republican, issued this warning in 2010 that "corporate funds used for political purposes were one of the principal sources of corruption that tended to create a small class of enormously wealthy and economically powerful men whose chief object is to hold and increase their power, which could destroy American democracy."[6]

Two important pieces of legislation were enacted in the years to follow during the administration of President Woodrow Wilson:

- ***The Clayton Act of 1914*:**

It prohibited, among other things, mergers or acquisitions when the effect may be "substantially to lessen competition, or to tend to create a monopoly." The Clayton Act was amended in 1976 by the

Hart-Scott-Rodino Antitrust Improvements Act, which required that antitrust agencies be notified of certain mergers depending on the size of the parties and the size of the transaction. The Clayton Act also set rules to protect workers and stop predatory pricing by trusts.

- ***The Federal Trade Commission Act of 1914:***

This law created the Federal Trade Commission (FTC), which was empowered to prevent unfair methods of competition and unfair and deceptive acts or practices in or affecting commerce, conducting investigations, provide reports to Congress, and enforce, with the Department of Justice, the antitrust laws.

2. 1920s-1930s:

Antitrust enforcement was unusual during this period as FDR planned and put in place his New Deal programs based on industry-government cooperation. In 1936, however, FDR called for the need to "redeem democracy from the despotism of concentrated economic power."[7]

3. 1940s-late 1970s:

Robust anti-trust policy was seen in those years as a central condition for effective competition. In 1958, the Supreme Court had recognized the Sherman Act of 1890 as"a comprehensive charter of economic liberty aimed at preserving free and unfettered competition as the rule of trade. It rests upon the premise that the unrestrained interaction of competitive forces will yield the best allocation of our economic resources, the lowest prices, the highest quality and the greatest material progress, while at the same time providing an environment conducive to the preservation of our democratic political and social institutions.[8]

4. Late-1970s-mid-2010s:

That was not to last with the arrival of laissez-faire thinking spread by the Chicago's School of Economics. The earlier moral case for antitrust was thrown aside and mergers were rarely challenged. There was no need for antitrust enforcement since market forces could be relied upon to correct problems of the market better than government intervention.[9] With the arrival of the Reagan presidency in the 1980s, antitrust enforcement was very much loosened as consolidation and mergers became common through the Bush administration.[10]

5. *Rise of a 5th Cycle, a progressive, anti-monopoly, New Brandeis School*

We have seen a renewed interest in, and priority for strong antitrust policy as the unimpeded market power has become monopolistic in many parts of the economy to the gain of Wall Street stakeholders and shareholders at the expense of consumers. Joseph Stiglitz, former chief economist at the World Bank, brings us this observation about this major new change:

> *The "greed-is-good" ethic of twenty-first century American capitalism works against creating the right norms . . . One of the most invidious ways that influence is exerted is the "revolving door," in which politicians get payoffs, not today but in the future, in the form of good jobs in the private sector when they leave office. The revolving door is pervasive and corrosive. That those in the U. S. Treasury and elsewhere in government quickly go from serving their country to working on Wall Street leads to questions about whether they have been serving Wall Street all along.*[11]

II. Corporate Abuses with Weak Antitrust Laws

Antitrust enforcement collapsed under both parties in recent years as rigging of the rules of patents, trademarks and copyrights by mega corporations intensified under administrations of both parties.[12] We do not have to look far to find many examples of corporate profiteering today that serve mega-corporations, Wall Street, and Big Money at the expense of everyday Americans and their families. Here are just several of many:

- After decades of unchecked mergers, giant medical systems now monopolize health care from top to bottom in many cities, states and even regions of the country; 75% of markets are now highly consolidated, resulting in higher prices, less patient choice, and worse quality of care.[13]
- While Exxon posted net profits of $19.66 *billion* in the third quarter of 2022, it increased dividends and paid $15 billion to shareholders in that year.[14]

- Prices charged by U. S.-based manufacturers of COVID vaccines exceed production costs by 10-fold or more.[15] Pfizer has recently announced a huge price increase for its publicly funded COVID-19 shot to between $110 and $130 per dose in the U. S., up from about $30 per shot.[16]
- The typical employee at 50 publicly traded corporations would have to work for at least 1,000 years to earn what their CEOs make in just one year.[17]
- The U. S. now has the highest economic inequality of any major developed nation in the world, with the wealthiest 1% now owning one-third of the country's wealth. [18]

Challenging the basis for one of the above examples of corporate greed—the rationale by PhRMA for its high prices of COVID-19 vaccines—is both instructive and a potential avenue for reform. Drug companies have long argued that the costs of research and development are so immense that innovation and bringing out new drugs would be stifled without large amounts of government support and long-term patent protection. In earlier years, insulin and the polio vaccine were developed and brought to market at very reasonable prices without such government support.

Dean Baker, co-director of the Center for Economic and Policy Research and author of *Rigged: How Globalization and the Rules of the Modern Economy Were Structured to Make the Rich Richer*, brings us another example in today's economy—Corbevax, another vaccine for COVID-19—that has also done so. It was developed by Drs. Peter Hotez and Maria Elena Botazzi at the Center for Vaccine Development at Texas Children's Hospital, is open sourced, highly effective, and priced at less than $2 per shot. They were nominated for the Nobel Peace Prize for that breakthrough, which was soon made available overseas in large numbers.[19]

Such a contrast with the COVID vaccines developed by Pfizer and Moderna with large amounts of R & D money and patent protection, yet selling for at least $20 per shot. Baker makes an effective argument for replacing patent monopolies for drugs with long-term government contracts for research and development, similar to those used by the Defense Department for development of weapon systems.[20]

It has now become standard practice to buy up rivals more than any time in history, as exemplified by Google, Amazon and Facebook, as Matt Stoller, author of *Goliath: The 100-Year-War Between Monopoly Power and Democracy*, points out:

> *Today, with Google, Amazon, Facebook, we find ourselves in America, and globally, with perhaps the most radical centralization of the power of global communications that has ever existed in history. One company controls roughly 90 percent of what we search for. And they also know what we think, because we tell them, through our searches. Another company controls our book market, and a third controls how we interact with our social worlds. Meanwhile, the free press is dying.*[21]

Robert Reich adds this observation about how American wealth and income have changed over the last 40 years, during which anti-trust and securities laws have been relaxed and bankruptcy laws loosened:

> *These changes stem from a dramatic increase in the political power of large corporations and Wall Street to change the rules of the market in ways that have enhanced their profits, while reducing the share of economic gains going to the majority of Americans. Higher corporate profits have meant higher returns for and, directly and indirectly, to the executives and bankers themselves.*[22]

Figure 2.3 (page 30) shows the marked impact of these changes on CEO-Worker Compensation.

III. What Is Being Done to Strengthen Anti-Trust Regulation

There are many areas where Congress and the administration can start to improve anti-trust regulation. They could close the loophole that permits hedge fund and private equity abuses, and increase reserve requirements for very large banks. They could also take on these anti-competitive practices that need to be controlled:

- Use and sale of massive amounts of information on the buying habits of users of Amazon, Apple, Google, Facebook and Microsoft;
- "tying arrangement", when Apple makes it very difficult to use non-Apple products by charging exorbitant prices for must-have accessories;
- when Amazon uses privileged information against competitors that rely on its platform to reach customers;
- or when Facebook, Google and Amazon traffic in users' personal data.[23]

Fortunately, the advent of the Biden administration after the 2020 election cycle has brought renewed interest and energy to antitrust policies and enforcement. Early on, he issued an Executive Order, *Promoting Competition in the American Economy*, while declaring that "capitalism without competition isn't capitalism, it's exploitation."[24] His appointment of Lina Khan, a former law professor, as chair of the Federal Trade Commission represented a major departure from what had become conventional antitrust policy. Her 2017 groundbreaking article in the *Yale Law Journal* showed how existing antitrust law could be applied to big platform companies like Google, Facebook and Amazon that buy up or destroy potential rivals, or use their access to customer data to undercut competitors who used their platforms in their marketing.[25]

With a goal to prevent companies from building up too much power and stifling competition, Ms. Khan and the FTC have issued 42 letters of investigation over mergers or similar transactions, the highest number in more than 10 years. In one instance, the FTC is suing to break up Meta, alleging that it has created a social-media monopoly by buying up nascent competitors such as Instagram.[26] States' attorney generals are also taking an active antitrust role, as shown by the State of California alleging that Amazon's online retailers' contracts with third-party sellers and wholesalers inflate prices, stifle competition and violate the State's antitrust and unfair competition laws.[27] Still another case showing new antitrust enforcement is the blocking by the Department of Justice of the proposed merger of Penguin Random House, the world's largest consumer-book publisher, with rival publisher Simon & Schuster, because of its reduction of competition in the market.[28]

Currently, the DOJ and 38 states are suing Google for using its deep pockets and dominant position to cut out rivals and entrench its search engine. To that end, they have charged that Google has paid $10 billion a year to Apple and others to be the default provider on smartphones.[29]

According to a recent report by Public Citizen, Big Tech has pulled out all the stops fighting against the American Innovation and Choice Online Act (AICOA). It would prohibit large platform owners, such as Google, Meta, Microsoft and TikTok, from using their dominant market power to unfairly advance their economic interests over their competitors. According to Forbes, Amazon, Apple, Google and Facebook have a combined market value of $6.2 trillion, and they spent $106 million lobbying over the last two years as monopoly power translates to political power.[30]

In what may well become a landmark case, a federal lawsuit by three attorneys general, from Washington, D.C, California and Illinois, was recently filed against the supermarket chains Kroger and Albertsons. The announced purchase of Albertsons by Kroger Co. would combine two chains with more than 5,000 stores across the country under well-known banners like Ralph's, Safeway and Vons, with a total combined revenue of more than $209 billion. The federal suit argues that the deal would be in violation of that long-standing pillar of antitrust law, the Sherman Act.[31]

Meanwhile, the House of Representatives passed a package of these three bills that will help to update America's antitrust laws for the first time in decades:

1. *The Merger Filing Fee Modernization Act*, which gives the Department of Justice more funding to pursue cases by increasing merger filing fees on large companies and reducing them for small and medium-sized companies;
2. *The State Antitrust Enforcement Venue Act*, which would end the practice of state antitrust suits getting merged with private suits and put into a Multidistrict Litigation process, which has enabled monopoly deals by getting around state-level antitrust enforcement; and
3. *The Foreign Merger Subsidy Disclosure Act*, which would force any merging entities to disclose subsidies received from the Chinese government.

Those three bills, merged into a package, passed the House with a vote of 242-184, and were passed on to the Senate in a lame duck session in December 2022.[32] The first two of the above bills were passed in the Senate by a bipartisan vote, whereby merger filing fees were increased for the first time since 2001 and state-based antitrust enforcement was empowered.[33] In July 2023, the Federal Trade Commission and Department of Justice released updated merger guidelines aimed to limit mergers and acquisitions as a main driver of corporate consolidation.[34]

Conclusion:

While the above progress is significant, we can expect that the mighty corporate industrial complex will fight tooth and nail against further antitrust enforcement, with all the forces that it can assemble. In the next chapter, we will consider another big way that U. S. oligarchs defend their power—through tax evasion and evasion of corporate accountability.

References:

1. Stiglitz, J. *People, Power and Profits: Progressive Capitalism for an Age of Discontent*. New York. *W. W. Norton. & Company*, 2019, pp. 77-78.
2. Nader, R. Center for the Study of Responsive Law, Washington, D.C., December 2, 2021.
3. Letwin, WL. Congress and the Sherman Antitrust Law: 1887-1890. *The University of Chicago Law Review* 23 (2): 221-258, 1956.
4. Berk, G. *Louis D. Brandeis and the Making of Regulated Competition*, 1900-1932, pp. 41-43.
5. Stucke, ME, Ezrachi, A. The rise, fall and rebirth of the U. S. Antitrust Movement. *Harvard Business Review*, December 15, 2017.
6. Anderson, K. *Evil Geniuses: The Unmaking of America: A recent History*. New York. *Random House*, 2020, p. 17.
7. Reich, R. The three myths used by the ultra-wealthy to justify the ultra-wealthy. *The Progressive Populist*, November 1, 2022, p. 13.
8. Ibid # 5.
9. Ibid # 5.
10. Leonard, C. *Kochland: The Secret History of Koch Industries and Corporate Power in America*. New York. *Simon & Schuster*, 2019, p. 473.
11. Stiglitz, JE. *People, Power and Profits: Progressive Capitalism for an Age of Discontent*. New York. *W. W. Norton & Company*, 2019, p. 173.
12. Kuttner, R. *The Stakes: 2020 and the Survival of American Democracy*. New York. *W. W. Norton & Company, Inc*. 2019, p. 154.
13. Rosenthal, E. Your exorbitant medical bill, brought to you by the latest hospital merger. *New York Times*, July 25, 2023.
14. Jones, S. Exxon swims in unprecedented windfall profits while Americans suffer at the pump. *PoliticusUSA*, October 28, 2022.

15. Light, DW, Lexchin, J. The costs of coronavirus vaccines and their pricing. *J Royal Society of Medicine*, November, 2021.
16. Johnson, J. 'Daylight robbery': Pfizer condemned for hiking U. S. COVID vaccine price by 10,000% above cost. *Common Dreams*, October 21, 2022.
17. Anderson, S, Pizzigati, S. Executive excess 2019: Making corporations pay for big pay gaps. Institute for Policy Studies. 26th Annual Report, September 2019.
18. Wilkins, B. 'Obscene,' says Sanders after CBO reports richest 1% now owns over1/3 of U. S. wealth. *Common Dreams*, September 28, 2022.
19. Brooks-Harper, K. From obscurity to a Nobel Peace Prize nomination, Houston scientists acclaimed for their patent-free COVID-19 vaccine. *The Texas Tribune*, February 10, 2022.
20. Baker, D. We don't need government-granted monopolies to finance drug development. *CounterPunch*, December 16, 2022.
21. Stoller, M. *Goliath: The 100-Year-War Between Monopoly Power and Democracy*, New York. *Simon & Schuster*, 2019, p. 449.
22. Reich, R. The great power shift (Part I), substack.com, October 28, 2022.
23. Biden, President J. As quoted by Kuttner, R. Going Big: FDR's Legacy, Biden's New Deal, and the Struggle to Save Democracy. New York. *The New Press*, 2022, p. 179.
24. Khan, L. Amazon's antitrust paradox. *Yale Law Journal* 126 (3), 2017.
25. Ibid # 12, pp. 218-219.
26. Michaels, D, Tracy, R. FTC's antitrust posture spurs companies to rethink mergers. *Wall Street Journal*, August 16, 2022, A: 1.
27. Mai-Duc, C, Mattioli, D. Amazon hit with California antitrust suit. *Wall Street Journal*, September 15, 2022: A 1.
28. Trachtenberg, JA, Wolfe, J. Penguin Random House blocked from acquiring rival publisher Simon & Schuster. October 31, 2022.
29. McCabe, D, Kang, C. Government casts Google as a bully of rivals. *New York Times*, September 13, 2023, B:1.
30. Tanglis, M. Big Tech's big money inside game. *Public Citizen News*, 43 (1), January/February 2023, p.1.
31. Hirsch, L. Attorneys general sue to stop dividend tied to Kroger-Albertsons deal. *New York Times*, November 2, 2022.
32. Dayen, D. Dayen on TAP. Antitrust action moves forward. *The American Prospect*, September 30, 2022.
33. Klobuchar, A. Klobuchar bipartisan legislation to restructure merger fees, strengthen antitrust enforcement passes Congress, News release. Washington, D. C., December 23, 2022.
34. New merger enforcement guidelines. *Corporate Crime Reporter*, July 24, 2023.

CHAPTER 8

TAX EVASION, TAX SHELTERING AND CORPORATE UNACCOUNTABILITY

As we have seen seen in the last chapters, the elite corporate class has gained and held power and advantage over the rest of American society for the last 40 or more years. It has gained a large treasure trove after stacking the Supreme Court and profiting from Citizens United with overwhelming funds to lobby their political candidates, and warding off antitrust regulators. Tax evasion and sheltering have been another weapon in their arsenal to gain further economic power, as we will see here.

The goals of this chapter are three-fold: (1) to review the history of how tax evasion and sheltering by corporations and wealthy individuals have enabled them to become unaccountable; (2) to describe adverse impacts of these practices on the rest of the country; and (3) to consider approaches to more progressive tax policies and corporate accountability.

I. Historical Perspective on Corporate Taxation and Accountability

Corporations have paid income taxes in the U. S. since the start of the 20th century. Corporate tax rates of 20% in 1910 increased to 50-60% from the Great Depression years to the post- World War II years in the 1950s and 1960s. While many wealthy people complain about taxes today, they are nothing compared to the 1950s during the Eisenhower administration. Figure 8.1 shows the average tax rate of 55% for the wealthy during those years, as well as a comparison of the top 0.1% vs. the lowest 90% of income earners.[1]

FIGURE 8.1

AVERAGE TAX RATE OF 55% FOR THE RICH UNDER EISENHOWER

(Average tax rates: top 0.1% versus bottom 90% income earners)

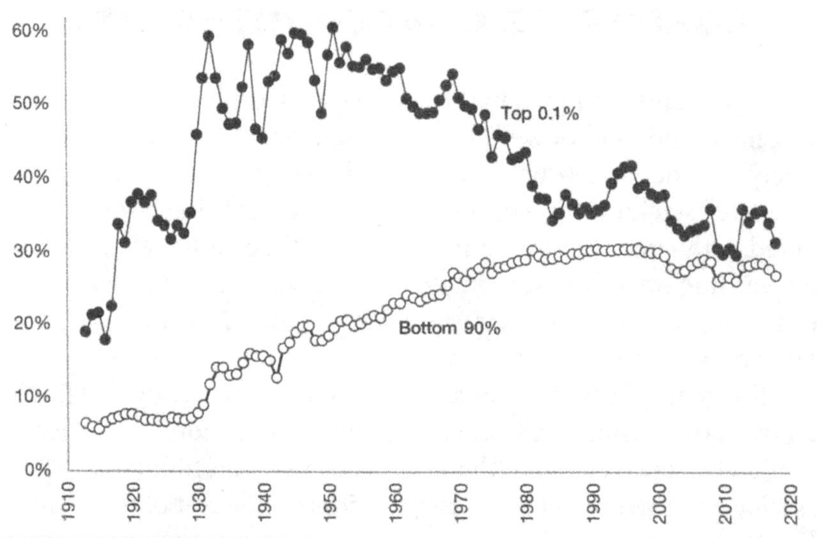

Source: www.taxjusticenow.org

Although corporate tax avoidance became common from the 1970s on, that practice had been promoted many years earlier by J. P. Morgan, that early titan of wealth, who paid *no* income tax for 1931 and 1932 during the Great Depression. He made a distinction between tax *evasion* and tax *avoidance*, arguing that tax avoidance wasn't illegal and that it was just smart business to use loopholes in a tax code to maximize one's income.[2]

Tax avoidance became common for large companies in the 1970s, when corporate executives began to address their goal as maximizing shareholder value. By paying less tax, they could have more profits to distribute in dividends to shareholders. A corporate tax-dodging industry took root, with tax avoidance legal firms, sham partnerships to generate tax-deductible paper losses, moving accounts offshore, and other strategies to avoid paying U. S. taxes. Figure 8.2 shows how effective corporate tax avoidance efforts have been since the 1960s, with corporate income tax revenue dropping far below revenue from individual taxes.[3]

Figure 8.2

CORPORATE VS. INDIVIDUAL INCOME TAX REVENUE, 1910-2020

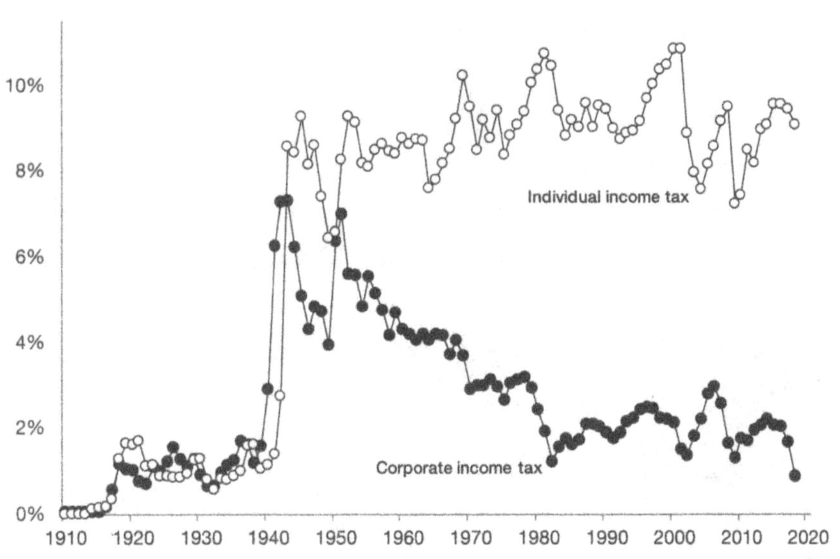

Source: www.taxjusticenow.org

In the 1980s, the Reagan years brought a new ideology under a libertarian creed that taxation was "theft" and that it was patriotic to avoid paying taxes. Previous administrations had fought the tax-avoidance industry, but in 1981 that industry took off as it became government-approved.[4] Since then, tax evasion has itself become big business for most corporations and the wealthy.

Large multinational U. S. corporations have the resources to exploit our complex tax code as they move profits to shell companies offshore to countries with zero or low tax rates. In so doing, they can avoid paying much or all of their taxes and increase shareholder value. As examples, Facebook shifted its profits to the Cayman Islands while Google transferred its intellectual property to zero-tax Bermuda.[5] Figure 8.3 shows the extent to which U. S. multinationals have moved their profits and capital to tax havens since the 1970s.[6]

FIGURE 8.3

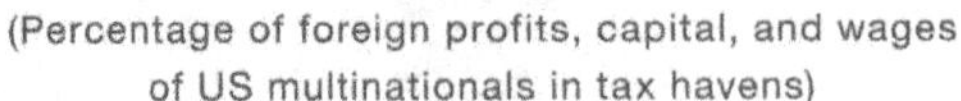

PAPER PROFITS AND CAPITAL OF U.S. MULTI-NATIONALS MOVING TO OFFSHORE TAX HAVENS

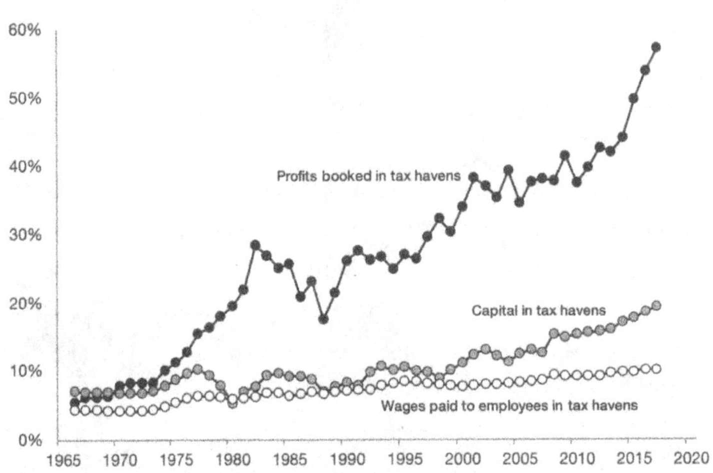

Source: www.taxjusticenow.org

By 2000, more than one-quarter of the profits of large U. S. corporations were registered in tax havens abroad. In 2010, in an attempt to rein in this practice, Congress passed the Foreign Account Tax Compliance Act (FATCA), signed into law by President Obama. It imposed an automatic exchange of data between foreign banks and the IRS, but it wasn't long before it was found to be ineffective. In 2016, more than one half of U. S. corporate profits were registered in tax havens,[7] and 210,000 shell companies had been incorporated out of the country, mostly in the British Virgin Islands and Panama.[8]

During the Trump administration, the Tax Cut and Jobs Act was pushed through Congress by Republicans, reducing the corporate income tax rate from 35% to 21%. But again, that was on paper and nowhere close to what happened. Companies continued to pay tens of billions each year to attorneys and accountants to minimize their taxes, so that the effective tax rate was just 13.3% in 2019.[9] Figure 8.4 shows a 40% drop in corporate tax receipts as the federal deficit rose by an estimated $1.45 trillion. A 2020 study by the Congressional Budget Office found that the richest 1% of Americans is responsible for 70% of unpaid taxes, averaging $381 billion a year.[10]

FIGURE 8.4

CORPORATE TAX RECEIPTS BEFORE AND AFTER 2017 TAX CUT

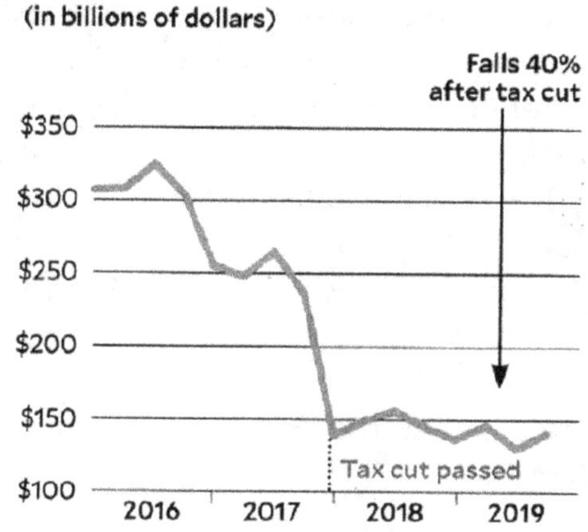

Source: Americans for Tax Fairness, and the Institute for Policy Studies Inequality Program

Source: Americans for Tax Fairness, and the Institute for Policy Studies and Inequality Program

We can expect tax avoidance by wealthy baby boomers to continue well into the future. A 2022 report from Americans for Tax Fairness, *Dynasty Trusts: Giant Tax Loopholes, the Supercharge Wealth Accumulation*, estimates that $21 trillion of that wealth will pass internally within America's already dynastically wealthy families between now and 2045. Closer in, it is estimated that these wealthy families will avoid as much as $8.4 trillion in estate and generation-skipping taxes between now and 2024 through the use of dynasty trusts and other currently legal loopholes.[11]

II. Adverse Impacts of Corporate Tax Evasion and Sheltering

The extreme gains of corporate executives and the ultra-wealthy has come at the expense of labor and most of the rest of the U. S. population. These are the major results of corporate tax evasion and sheltering:

1. *Increased inequality by income and wealth*

As shown by Figure 8.2 (p.113), the top 0.1% of Americans paid little more than the bottom 90% over the last 50 years. As a result, billionaire wealth has soared while labor has not shared in the low corporate income tax rates available to their corporate bosses. According to a recent report from Americans for Tax Fairness (ATF) and the Institute for Policy Studies Program (IPS), most of the surge of billionaire income is from growth of wealth income, largely untaxed due to a loophole in the tax code, as opposed to wage-income.[12]

These markers illustrate the depth of inequality that has taken place in recent decades:

- America's billionaires and ultra millionaires held more than $8.5 trillion in untaxed wealth gains in 2022.[13]
- The ultra-wealthy's $8.5 trillion of untaxed income.
- The $4 trillion in total wealth of all U. S. billionaires is almost double the $2.1 trillion in total wealth held by the bottom half of the population—165 million Americans.
- One half of the companies studied by the U. S. Department of Labor paid their CEOs at least 186 times what a median worker earned, even in a tight labor market.[14]
- Another study found that bonuses on Wall Street have soared by 1,743% since 1985, which would have corresponded to growth in the federal minimal wage to $61.75 an hour instead of $ 7.25.[15]
- A recent GAO study found that 34% of large corporations pay no federal taxes at all.[16] These big companies paid *no* federal income taxes in 2020: Nike, FedEx, HP, Salesforce, Dish Network, Charter Communications.[17]

- In the five years since the GOP passed the Trump tax cuts in 2017, U. S. corporations have spent $4.2 trillion of their new-found wealth on stock buybacks, which could have been used to raise workers' wages, lower consumer costs, and invest in workplace protections and public safety.[18] That tax cut also added $1.9 trillion to the national debt.[19]
- Almost two-thirds of new wealth amassed since the start of the COVID pandemic has gone to the richest 1% as the rise in extreme wealth has been accompanied by an increase of extreme poverty.[20]
- Because of the loophole-ridden U. S. tax system, individuals can pass almost $13 million in assets to heirs without paying the federal estate tax, which applies to just two of every 1,000 American estates.[21]

Figure 8.5 shows how the annual income of the heads of America's largest 350 companies by revenue went up by 21 times in 1965 compared to an astronomical 351 times in 2020, leaving the annual income of their workers far behind.[22] Bernie Sanders brings these sea changes home in this overview:

> *In the United States today, at a time of unprecedented income and wealth inequality, weekly wages for the average American worker are actually lower than they were 50 years ago after adjusting for inflation. In other words, despite a massive increase in worker productivity, despite CEOs now making nearly 400 times more than what their employees earn, despite record-breaking corporate profits, dividends and stock buyouts, average American workers are worse off than they were 50 years ago.*[23]

2. Inequities between corporate and individual tax rates

As we can see from Figure 8.1 (p.112) the average tax rates of 55% for the top 0.1% in the 1950s during the Eisenhower administration are virtually the same as the bottom 90% of us today—hardly fair from any standpoint.

Figure 8.5

CEO-Worker Compensation Ratio, 1965 and 2020

Top 350 American companies by review

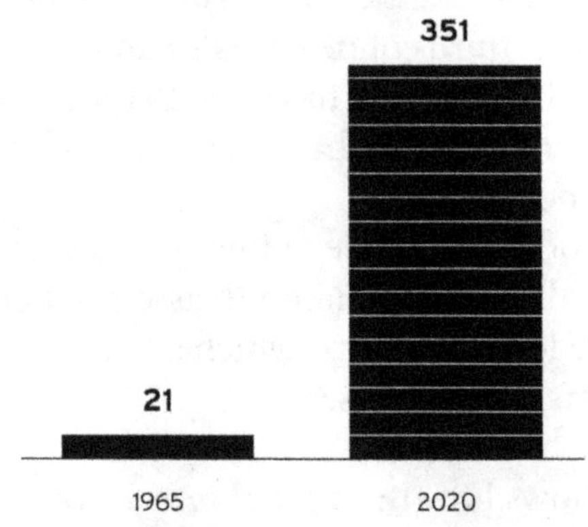

Source: Economic Policy Institute

3. Deleterious impacts on education, health care, and other parts of the safety net

The present injustices of tax policy that allow the extreme widened gap in income available to the ultra-wealthy compared to the rest of Americans leaves little money left to fund essential public needs. Emmanuel Saez and Gabriel Zucman, Professors of Economics at the University of California Berkeley and co-authors of the 2019 book *The Triumph of Injustice: How the Rich Dodge Taxes and How to Make Them Pay*, remind us that:

> *Similar levels of tax progressivity were reached in the 1950s, before the collapse in taxes at the top, the explosion of health care costs, and the rise of payroll taxes transformed the U. S. tax system into an engine of injustice. It's through collective spending on education, health, and other public goods that rich countries have become wealthy, not through the deification of a tiny minority of the ultra-rich. If history is any guide, the prosperous nations of the future will continue to be those that invest in the success of all.*[24]

There are all kinds of areas where a marked increase in public funding is urgently needed to keep up with urgent needs for the future, ranging from road and bridge repair and dealing with climate change to meeting currently underfunded parts of our safety net. These are markers of the extent of damage to our safety net:

- Rising inequality within the U. S. population has led to a growing gulf between the haves and have nots, with 43 million Americans living in poverty.[25]
- More than 31 million children in the U. S. live at or near the federal poverty level, often leading to stunted cognitive development, impaired immune function, and psychiatric disorders.[26]
- 41 million Americans are food insecure, a growing problem, defined as not knowing where the next meal is coming from.[27]
- Public health has been underfunded and neglected at county, state and federal levels for many years, leaving us open to being short on readiness for the next pandemic, as we were with COVID-19.[28]
- There are now about 30 million Americans without health insurance, with an additional 87 million underinsured, leading one-third of Americans to skip essential health care due to unaffordable costs.[29]

4. Adverse impacts on the electorate and democratic elections

Billionaires spent millions through super PACs to elect right wing candidates in the midterms who will maintain our rigged anti-democratic tax system. They want to continue taking big tax handouts while they cut back Social Security for the rest of us. As one example, hedge fund billionaire Ken Griffin has been a long-time Republican mega-donor, having contributed more than $146 million to federal candidates and PACs over the last ten years.[30] As another example, Facebook billionaire Peter Thiel spent $15 million in each of two states bankrolling election-denier candidates for the U. S. Senate—J. D. Vance in Ohio and Blake Masters in Arizona. [31]

5. Adverse impacts on the federal debt.

As Robert Reich has recently clarified, the half-century switch from times when the the wealthy paid higher taxes to their tax avoidance today negatively impacts the federal debt. The decline in tax revenue from the wealthy adds to the federal budget deficit, which is further accentuated by the federal government paying the wealthy interest on their savings in treasury bonds, personal trusts, estates, and other ways that they park their savings. As a result, a growing amount of most Americans' taxes are going to the wealthy through interest payments rather than to the needs for essential government services.[32]

Those impacts have been extreme—by the end of 2023, the original George W. Bush tax cuts and their extensions will have added $8.4 trillion to the federal debt, while the 2017 Trump tax cuts will have added another $1.7 trillion to the debt.[33]

The Freedom Caucus in the House of the 118th Congress would take our tax policies back to the Dark Ages. It introduced supposed "Fair Tax" legislation that would repeal the federal income tax, replace it with a 30 percent national sales tax, and abolish the IRS! Predictably, it would benefit the rich far more than lower-income taxpayers—a tax cut in the first year of $175,710 for those in the top 0.1% vs. for those making less than $75,000 a year, an average tax cut of just $329 a year. (Figure 8.6) Although a political dead letter, its blatantly unfair policy would have the poorest fifth of Americans pay 70% of their income in taxes, the second poorest fifth 38%, and the richest fifth just 17%.[34]

In late April 2023, as the national debt limit loomed requiring action by Congress by the end of June to avert a potentially catastrophic default on the debt, House Republicans barely passed a debt ceiling bill (217-215) that would raise the debt ceiling into 2024 in exchange for freezing spending at last year's level for a decade. Its across the board spending cuts would include cuts to federal agencies, including repeal of IRS funding needed to crack down on wealthy and corporate tax cheats, and sharp reductions in funding of President Biden's domestic agenda. Fortunately, as discussed in Chapter 12, a bipartisan deal was struck at the last moment in Congress to avert defaulting on the debt, but controversies over spending priorities will continue on.

Figure 8.6

AVERAGE TRUMP TAX CUTS FOR WEALTHY DWARF THOSE FOR WORKING FAMILIES

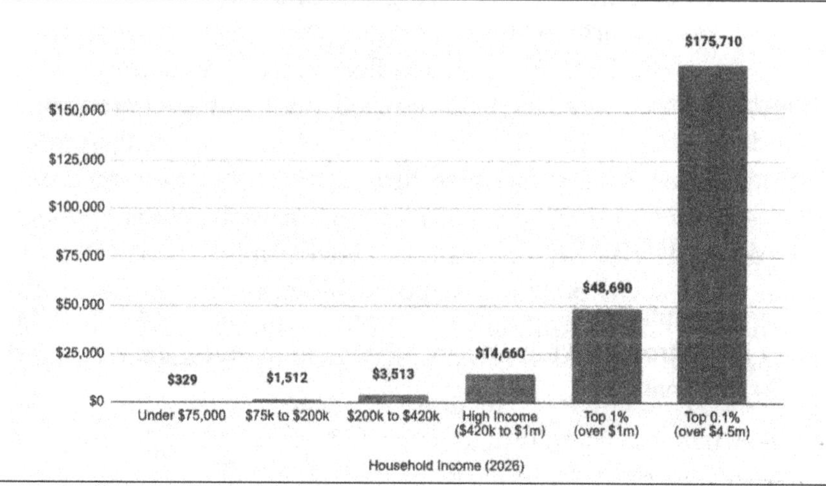

Source: Tax Policy Center TCJA extensions distributional analysis

III. Toward More Progressive Tax Policy and Corporate Accountability

In their new book, *The Corporate Sabotage of America's Future and What We Can Do About It*, Robert Weissman and Joan Claybrook describe many ways whereby corporate power works against the public interest in their drive for increased profits and control. They also describe the degree to which Americans are united around the need to confront corporate power, including:

- Roughly 90% of Americans want Medicare to negotiate drug prices.
- More than 80% of Americans want to end Dark Money—secret spending—in elections.
- There is virtual unanimity among the public about the need to transform the campaign funding system.
- Over two-thirds of Americans favor increased taxes on corporations and the wealthy.
- Almost all Americans believe there should be increased enforcement of laws and regulations in the U. S. against corporations.[35]

The Biden administration can claim important progress toward bringing increased disclosure and accountability to corporate business practices. In September 2022, the Treasury Department issued a new anti-money laundering rule that will require disclosure of primary owners of both foreign and domestic companies registered in the U. S. It will take effect in 2024. Enactment of the Inflation Reduction Act (IRA) reduced the top corporate tax rate from 37% to 20%. The IRA will also raise more than $500 billion in taxes from wealthy interests through a 15% minimum tax on billion-dollar corporations, a 1% tax on corporate stock buybacks, and beefing up IRS enforcement. Moreover, in his 2023 State of the Union address to Congress, President Biden called on Congress to pass the Billionaire Minimum Income Tax requiring that households with net worth more than $100 million will pay an effective tax rate of at least 20% on their full income each year, including the increased value of their stock and other assets whether they sell them or not.[36]

Other signs of progress:

1. On December 6, 2022, the criminal conviction of Trump's enterprises on 17 counts for tax fraud. On January 13, 2023, the maximal $1.6 million fine for felony tax fraud.[37]
2. Release of Trump's tax returns by the House Ways and Means Committee in December 2022. Despite a legal requirement that the IRS audit his tax returns during his presidency, that never happened. When his tax returns were finally released in December 2022, they revealed bogus deductions over many years, his reporting of $60 million in losses during his presidency, that he paid no federal income tax at all in 2020, and that he never donated his presidential salary to charity despite having claimed to do so.[38]
3. Nine more Truth to Power candidates were seated in Congress, increasing the number in Congress to 72 who reject corporate PAC money. That organization was started by Katie Porter (D-CA) in 2020, when 56 members joined the initial group. [39]

4. In response to continued corporate stock buybacks amounting to some $3.5 billion in the first half of 2023, the Biden administration is calling for an increase in the stock buybacks tax from 1% to 4% through the Stock Buyback Accountability Act of 2023.[40]

In order to get back to the kind of progressive tax policies in the 1950s, Saez and Zucman recommend three components for effective reform of U. S. tax policy:

1. *a progressive income tax that ensures that high earners pay more;*
2. *a corporate tax, that ensures that all profits are taxed, whether or not distributed; and*
3. *a progressive wealth tax, a critical component for effective reform, at a rate of 2% above $50 million in wealth and 3.5% above $1 billion in wealth.*[41]

In response to the concentrated wealth that has been suffocating our democracy and undermined social cohesion for many years, Representatives Barbara Lee (D-CA) and Summer Lee (PA-12) have recently introduced the Oppose Limitless Inequality Growth and Reverse Community Harms (Oligarch Act). When enacted, it would establish a wealth tax with four brackets:

- 2% for all wealth between 1,000 and 10,000 times median household wealth.
- 4% for all wealth between 10,000 and 100,000 times median household wealth.
- 6% for all wealth between 100,000 and 1,000,000 times median household wealth.
- 8% for all wealth over 1,000,000 times median household wealth.

Since the richest households are the largest tax evaders, the bill would impose at least a 30% audit rate on households covered by this tax, together with penalties for substantial valuation understatements.[42]

More recently, Senator Bernie Sanders (I-VT) introduced the For the 99.5% Act, an estate tax bill that would require families of the billionaire class, who inherit more than $3.5 million in wealth each year, to start paying their fair share of taxes. If and when enacted, families of 657 billionaires in America would pay up to $2.7 trillion in estate taxes each year, which would go a long way toward reversing the increasing social inequities of most Americans. Predictably, Republicans oppose such a bill unless they could pay for it by making massive cuts in Social Security, Medicare, Medicaid, and other critical programs.[43]

Interestingly, a group of 205 millionaires and billionaires at Davos for the World Economic Forum called on world leaders and business executives to support wealth taxes at a high priority.[44] Nobel prize winner economist Joseph Stiglitz even called for wealth taxes as high as 70% to address widening inequality.[45]

Conclusion:

Reform of U. S. tax policy in the near term is very unlikely at best given the Republican-controlled House of the 118th Congress. Although U. S. corporations are enjoying the highest profit margins in more than 70 years, we can expect that Republicans will try to renew these three major tax breaks for big corporations: allowing them to write off research expenses all at once; expanding their net interest deduction tax break; and extending a 100% bonus deduction.[46] With the GOP at war within itself and lacking in policies of its own, it may well be that the 2024 elections will return policy direction to the Democrats, when ongoing progress toward justice in tax policy can be established.

References:

1. Saez, E, Zucman, G, *The Triumph of Injustice: How the Rich Dodge Taxes and How to Make Them Pay*. New York. S. W. *Norton & Co., Inc.* 2019, pp. 41-43
2. Galloway, S. *Adrift: America in 100 charts*. New York. *Penguin Random House*, 2022, p. 12.
3. Ibid # 1, p. 70.
4. Ibid # 1, p. 51.
5. Ibid # 1, pp. 80-82,
6. Ibid # 2, p. 32.

7. Ibid # 7.
8. Ibid # 1, p. 64.
9. Baker, D. How to decimate the corporate tax-avoidance industry. *The Progressive Populist*, October 1, 2022, p. 11.
10. Under cover of Kavanaugh, Republicans passed huge tax cuts for the wealthy. *The Progressive Populist*, November 1, 2018.
11. Collins, S. The dynastic wealth of U. S. oligarchs is a threat to democracy. *Common Dreams*, February 7, 2022.
12. Updates: Billionaire wealth, U. S. job losses and pandemic profiteers based on report from Americans for Tax Fairness and the Institute for Policy Studies Program on Inequality, August 21, 2021. \
13. Kass, D., *Americans for Tax Fairness*
14. Francis, T. CEO pay increases, heads for a new record. *Wall Street Journal*, April 4, 2022: A 1.
15. Johnson, J. 'An absolute outrage': Sanders rips wealthy tax cheats. CBO estimates $381 billion in annual unpaid taxes. *Common Dreams*, July 9, 2020.
16. Easley, J, Jones, S. Let's talk about fairness as 34% of large profitable corporations pay 0 in federal taxes. *PoliticusUSA*, January 14, 2023.
17. Queally, J. On greed and tax avoidance, says Bernie Sanders, 'Trump is not alone'. *Common Dreams*, December 31, 2022.
18. Souza, M. These companies are taking advantage of inflation to enrich shareholders. *Daily Kos*, February 20, 2023.
19. Clemente, F. New Republican plan: $200 grocery bill would cost $320. *Americans for Tax Fairness*, February 3, 2023.
20. Neate, R. Joseph Stiglitz: tax high earners at 70% to tackle widening inequality. *The Guardian*, January 22, 2023.
21. Johnson, J. 'We are not taxing the very wealthy enough': Runaway inequality about to get worse. *Common Dreams*, May 15, 2023.
22. Ibid # 2, pp. 92-93.
23. Sanders, B. Morally grotesque and growing inequality. *The Guardian*, September 12, 2023.
24. Ibid # 1, p. 194.
25. Powers, N. Fear of a black planet: Under the Republican push for welfare cuts, racism boils. *Truthout*, January 21, 2018.
26. Healy, M. Doctors group calls on pediatricians to address child poverty. *Los Angeles Times*, March 9, 2016.
27. Ungar, L, Lieberman, T. Starving seniors: How America fails to feed its aging. *Kaiser Health News*, September 3, 2019.
28. Press release. Six takeaways of the KHN-AP investigation into the erosion of public health. *Kaiser Health News/Associated Press*, July 1, 2020.
29. Picchi, A. Surge in Americans skipping medical care due to cost, Gallup says. *CBS News*, December 14, 2021.
30. Billionaires buying elections. *Americans for Tax Fairness*, July 2022.
31. Schroeder, R. Trump-backed Blake Masters looks set to win Arizona's Republican Senate primary with $15 million in help from Peter Thiel. *Market Watch*, August 2, 2022.

32. Reich, R. The biggest story you've never heard about today's federal debt. (robertreich@substack.com), January 31, 2023.
33. Clemente, F. Renewing the Trump Tax Cuts benefits the rich & threatens Social Security, Medicare, Medicaid & more. *Americans for Tax Fairness*, March 3, 2023.
34. Cooper, R. The Freedom Caucus has a harebrained plan to jack up taxes on the poor. *The American Prospect*, January 26, 2023.
35. Weissman, R, Claybrook, J. The pervasive problem of corporate power. *Public Citizen News* 43:6, Nov/Dec 2023, p. 1.
36. Talley, I. New rule mandates corporate ownership disclosure. *Wall Street Journal*, September 30, 2022.
37. Bromwich, JE, Protess, B, Rashbaum, WK. Trump's company gets maximal punishment for evading taxes. *New York Times*, January 13, 2023.
38. Kuttner, R. The tax evader in chief. Today on Tap, *The American Prospect*, December 21, 2022.
39. Porter, K. From 56 to73. info@katieporter.com, January 2, 2023.
40. Kass, D. Fight back against corporate greed. *Americans for Tax Fairness*, September 7, 2023.
41. Ibid # 1, pp. 146-149.
42. Tell your representative: Co-sponsor and pass the Oligarch Act. *Patriotic Millionaires*, August 19, 2023.
43. Sanders, B, How would Republicans pay for this $1.75 trillion tax break for billionaires? *Americans for Tax Fairness*, December 28, 2023.
44. Gomelsky, V. Rolex now has a resale program. The watch world quakes. *New York Times*, January 18, 2023.
45. Ibid # 19.
46. Clemente, F. A major victory for tax fairness. *Americans for Tax Fairness*, December 22, 2022.

PART III

HOW THE OLIGARCHY THREATENS FAIR ELECTIONS

Our country faces unprecedented challenges today. They cannot be resolved with half-steps or compromises. There is not a middle ground between the insatiable greed of uber-capitalism and a fair deal for the working class. There is not a middle ground as to whether or not we save the planet. There is not a middle ground as to whether or not we preserve our democracy and remain a society based on equal protection for all.

Democrats face the most fundamental of all choices. They must choose whether to be on the side of the working-class men and women who create the wealth of this country, or to be on the side of the billionaire class, the corporate elites, and the wealthy campaign donors who hoard wealth for their own self-interest.

By making an unequivocal decision as to which side they are on in the class war, Democrats can finally enact policies to overcome uber-capitalism and the greed, inequality, and bigotry that have denied the promise of "liberty and justice for all."[1]

—Senator Bernie Sanders (I-VT), author of the 2023 book, *It's OK to be Angry about Capitalism*.

As the United States approaches majority-minority status (the white population, 76 percent of the country in 1990, is now 58 percent and will drop below 50 percent around 2045) Republicans have chosen to become the voice of white people, particularly those without college degrees, who fear the loss of their way of life in a multicultural America. White grievance and white fear drive Republican identity more than any other factor—and drive the tribalism and dysfunction in the U. S. political system.[2]

—Dana Milbank, political columnist for *The Washington Post* and author of *The Destructionists: The Twenty-Five-Year Crack-Up of the Republican Party*[2]

References:

1. Milbank, D. *The Destructionists: The Twenty-Five-Year Crack-Up of the Republican Party.* New York. *Doubleday*, 2022, p. 7.
2. Sanders, B. *It's OK to be Angry about Capitalism*. New York. *Penguin Random House LLC*, 2023, p. 292.

CHAPTER 9

CITIZENS UNITED AND CORRUPT ELECTION SPENDING

With all due deference to separation of powers, last week the Supreme Court reversed a century of law that I believe will open the floodgates for special interests—including foreign corporations—to spend without limit in our elections. I don't think American elections should be bankrolled by America's most powerful interests, or worse, by foreign entities. They should be decided by the American people.[1]

—President Barack Obama, in his annual State of the Union address to both houses of Congress six days after the U. S. Supreme Court's Citizens United ruling in 2010

As Democrats rose to applaud President Obama's above statement, Supreme Court Justice Samuel Alito, who was sitting just in front of him, was seen to grimace and silently utter "not true" as the rest of the Justices sat stony faced looking straight ahead.[2] But the searing truth of the President's prediction has been proven far beyond true over the next 12 years, as so graphically represented by David Cay Johnston's initial prediction that "Citizens United is to the expansion of corporate power what the big bang was to the beginning of the universe."[3] (See page 12).

This chapter has three goals: (1) to bring brief historical perspective to how the Citizens United law came to be; (2) to discuss its anti-democratic impacts on national elections; and (3) to describe some of the approaches that have and are being taken to redress its flaws.

I. Brief Historical Perspective

The Citizens United case didn't come out of nowhere, since the U. S. Supreme Court had acted 34 years earlier in the *Buckley v. Valeo* case that, while the *number* of campaign contributions could be limited, *expenditures* of campaign contributions could not be limited because that would violate the donors' First Amendment freedom of speech. That set up a system of campaign contributions favoring the ultra-wealthy that has come down to the present, since they can easily bundle multiple donations.[4]

As a conservative nonprofit organization, Citizens United in 2008 wanted to use corporate funds for cable and satellite transmissions of a video-on-demand film critical of then presidential candidate Hillary Clinton. It also wanted to air commercials for the film shortly before the 2008 Democratic primaries. But since that would have violated existing campaign finance law that prohibited such communications close to an election, it brought a case that ended up at the U. S. Supreme Court. Two years later, its monumental ruling *Citizens United v. Federal Election Commission* was handed down, by a 5-4 decision, overturning more than 50 years of campaign finance regulation. Under the First Amendment, corporations could then spend unlimited amounts of money to influence elections. In the next presidential election in 2012, the difference was marked—outside spending reached $1.03 billion, three times more than four years earlier.[5]

Two subsequent Supreme Court decisions soon followed that opened the flood gates still wider:

- In *SpeechNow.org v. FEC* (2010), a federal appellate court held that outside groups can accept unlimited contributions from corporations or individuals. "Independent expenditure" committees had previously been limited to $5,000 per year.
- *McCutcheon v. FEC* (2014) struck down limits on the aggregate amounts that individuals can contribute to all federal candidates and political parties combined, exceeding the previous aggregate limit of $123,200 per election cycle.

With those restrictions removed, just 25 ultra-wealthy donors accounted for almost one-half (47%) of all individual contributions to super PACs from 2010 to 2020.[6]

These two subsequent statements by former President Jimmy Carter reflect the negative gravity of the 2010 Supreme Court ruling Citizens United v. Federal Election Commission:

> *Citizens United has turned America into an "oligarchy with unlimited political bribery."*
>
> *Citizens United has led to "a complete subversion of our political system as a payoff to major contributors."*[7]

II. How Citizens United Has Undermined Fair Elections and Democracy

Examples of "corrupted political system where billionaires can buy elections", as Bernie Sanders charges:

- A right-wing dark money group controlled by Leonard Leo, the Marble Freedom Trust, receives $1.6 billion from Tripp Lite CEO and longtime Republican benefactor Barre Said, "perhaps the largest single contribution ever made to a politically focused nonprofit."[8]
- A pair of super PACs charged with securing Republican majorities in the House and Senate—the Congressional Leadership Fund and the Senate Leadership Fund—raised a combined $188 million through the first 16 months of the 2022 campaign cycle, 86% of which came from just 17 billionaires. The Democratic counterparts of these two super-PACs—the House Majority PAC and the Senate Majority PAC—raised $154 million over the same time period, with 17% coming from 19 billionaires. According to Americans for Tax Fairness, billionaires pumped $1.2 billion into the 2020 elections, almost 40 times more than the $31 million they donated in 2010 when Citizens United was enacted.[9]
- In the first 8 months of 2022, Fortune 500 companies and trade groups donated about $25 million to election deniers, according to the watchdog Accountable U.S.[10]

- The Senate Leadership Fund, aligned with Senate Majority Leader Mitch McConnell, spent more than $32 million and $56 million on the 2022 Republican Senate races in Ohio and Pennsylvania, respectively.[11]
- U. S. billionaires spending almost $900 million on this federal election cycle.[12]
- Congressional Republicans and their two super PACs spending $148 million, mainly regarding tax cuts for billionaires and corporations.[13]

Figure 9.1 shows the striking increase in federal campaign contributions from billionaires after the passage of Citizens United in 2010.

FIGURE 9.1

FEDERAL CAMPAIGN CONTRIBUTIONS FROM BILLIONAIRES, 2000-2020

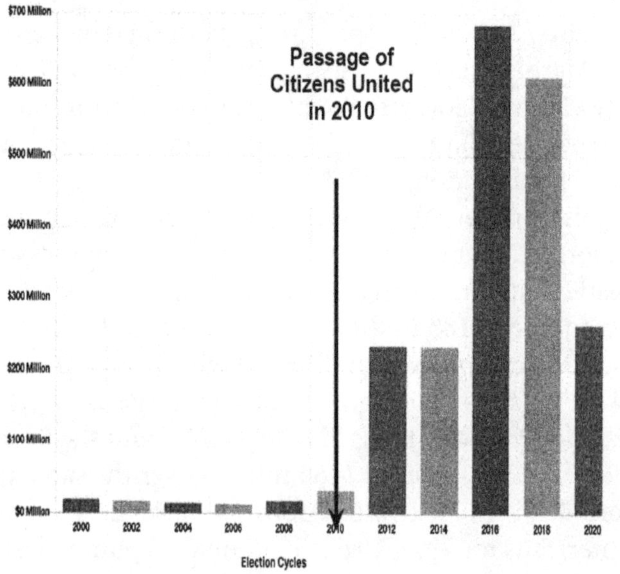

Source: Americans for Tax Fairness and the Institute for Policy Studies Inequality Program

Another major threat to democracy, mostly under the radar of public awareness, is the work of ALEC (the American Legislative Exchange Council), backed by big corporations and the Heritage Foundation, which bankroll an ongoing effort to distrust American elections.[14]

Shortly after the 13th anniversary of the Supreme Court's Citizens United ruling, *Daily Kos* pulled together these results:

- "Election spending has exploded; an estimated $16.8 billion was spent on the 2022 midterm elections.
- The ultra-wealthy hold enormously outsized power, transforming our democracy into more and more of an oligarchy each day.
- Super PACs have brazenly ignored campaign finance laws, and corporations are hiding their political spending—and even bribing politicians—in secretive entities.
- Foreign powers have exploited the loopholes *Citizens United* created to influence our elections from abroad."[15]

This current example illustrates how the brazen use of Big Money can negatively impact the public interest:

> *Kelcy Warren, a Texas billionaire who made his fortune from gas and propane pipelines and has an estimated net worth of $5 billion, made a $1 million donation to Texas Governor Greg Abbott's campaign against former Democratic gubernatorial candidate Beto O'Rourke in 2021. Soon thereafter, O'Rourke criticized Abbott for failing to hold Texas oil and gas companies responsible to their role in the February 2021 ice storm that left more than 4.5 million state residents without power, caused hundreds of deaths, and produced a $2.4 billion profit for Warren's company, Energy Transfer Partners. Warren delivered his cash donation to Abbott's campaign two weeks after Abbott had signed legislation that included a loophole allowing natural gas companies like Energy Transfer Partners to opt out of energy infrastructure winterization mandates. Because O'Rourke publicly criticized that donation, Warren is suing him for defamation.*[16]

Ben Horton, a Harvard Law School Public Service Venture Fund Fellow at Free Speech for People, called out the motivations of U. S. corporations in this way:

> *Corporations have no structural interest in a functioning democracy; they're interested in a government that responds primarily to their needs, and their need is to amass as much wealth as possible . . . The January 6 insurrection and the craven response [by corporations not to assign responsibility] reminds us that we must reclaim the promise of a true democracy in our country, responsive not to corporate slush funds but to the people of the U. S.*[17]

Figure 9.2 illustrates the power of corporate money on election spending. These donations "... enabled corporations to spend unlimited amounts of money from their own treasuries to influence elections." [18]

Figure 9.2

THE GREEN WAVE OF DARK MONEY

Source: *Matson Roll Call*. Reprinted with permission

III. Can Anything Be Done to Re-Establish Fair and Democratic Elections?

Some things have been attempted, but haven't seen the light of day due to Republican opposition:

- Public Citizen started a wave of activism to overturn *Citizens United* soon after its approval, so that 20 states and more than 800 localities had called for a constitutional amendment for its overturn by 2020; in 2014, 54 U. S. senators voted in favor of that amendment, just 12 shy of the needed two-thirds majority, while more than 200 House members co-sponsored it in the 2020 Congress.[19]
- In March 2019, the House passed *H. R. 1*, the *For the People Act*, the most sweeping pro-democracy legislation in the last 50 years, but it was blocked by the GOP Senate without a hearing. It also called for a constitutional amendment, to be passed separately, together with small-donor and public financing of elections and tightening of rules on super PACs and end dark money spending.[20]

As corporations were enjoying record profits from inflated prices while paying historically low tax rates, some members of Congress were pushing for more tax breaks in year-end legislation. As we saw in the last chapter, their goal was to expand these three major tax loopholes:

- Increase write offs for research expenses
- Expand the net interest deduction tax break
- Extend the 100% bonus depreciation

The two-year cost of these tax breaks would have been about $100 billion and up to $600 billion over 10 years.[21]

What finally happened with tax legislation in 2022 was corporate friendly through the Inflation Reduction Act, which set a minimal tax rate of 15% for corporations making more than $1 billion a year, together with an excise tax of 1% on stock buybacks. These were not expected to make much change in corporate behaviour.[22] The

Americans for Tax Fairness Action Fund was calling for President Biden to issue an executive order requiring contractors receiving more than $1 million in federal dollars to disclose their political spending in federal elections.[23]

Meanwhile, quiet but effective lobbying by Big Money interests has continued to prevent any groundswell to reject the Citizens United decision. Audit rates for millionaires and large corporations are still considerably lower than for low-income families.[24] One third of big corporations avoid paying *any* tax,[25] while the 15% federal tax bite is but a tiny part of the 55% in the Eisenhower years of the 1950s.

Conclusion:

With that background on the deleterious impacts of uncontrolled campaign contributions of the very wealthy, we move to the next chapter to examine other ways that voting rights are suppressed, again in favor of big corporate money.

References:

1. Obama, B. As quoted by Bernstein, A. *American Oligarchs: The Kushners, the Trumps, and the Marriage of Money and Power.* New York. *W. W. Norton & Company*, 2020, pp. 221-222.
2. Bernstein, *A., as quoted in American Oligarchs: The Kushners, the Trumps, and the Marriage of Money and Power*, pp. 220-221.
3. Johnston, DC. *The Fine Print: How Big Companies Use "Plain English" to Rob You Blind.* New York. *Penguin Group*, 2013, p. 26.
4. Ibid # 2, p. 128.
5. Bradberry, A. Ten years after Citizens United. *Public Citizen News*, March/April 2020, pp. 1, 6.
6. Ibid # 5.
7. Carter, J. Jimmy Carter calls it "unlimited political bribery." As quoted by *Public Citizen*, February 23, 2023.
8. Johnson, J. Right-wing dark money group gets $16 billion donation from tax-dodging business mogul. *Common Dreams*, August 22, 2022.
9. Stancil, K. Just 27 billionaires have spent $90 million to buy GOP Congress: Report. *Common Dreams*, July 18, 2022.

10. Johnson, J. Koch network showers fascist election deniers with campaign cash ahead of midterms. *Common Dreams*, September 23, 2022.
11. Opinion. Trump's $89 million debt to McConnell, *Wall Street Journal*, November 9, 2022, A 20.
12. Johnson, J. 'That's oligarchy': Sanders rips billionaires for trying to buy midterm victories. *Common Dreams*, November 7, 2022.
13. Clemente, F. Voters didn't buy Republican lies. *Americans for Tax Fairness.* November 10, 2022.
14. Harrison, V. UPS and other major companies bankrolling far-right legislation. *Common Cause*, December 19, 2022.
15. Easley, J. Wake up Democrats: Powerful right-wing groups are funding attack to rig every election. *PoliticusUSA*, August 3, 2021.
16. Roth, AL, Macek, S. Billionaire's lawsuit against O'Rourke may stifle criticism of money in politics. *Truthout*, January 28, 2023.
17. Horton, B. January 6 shows why corporate political spending is bad for democracy *Truthout*, December 5, 2021.
18. Cass, D., Kass, D., January 6 Shows Why Corporate Political Spending Is Bad for Democracy, *Truthout* Americans for Tax Fairness
19. Ibid #5.
20. Clemente, F. Corporations want billions in tax breaks before the end-of-year. We're fighting back! *Americans for Tax Fairness Action Fund.* November 11, 2022.
21. Cox, C. Biden's corporate tax hike in the Inflation Reduction Act won't hurt most U. S. companies, Wall Street analysts say. *CNBC*, August 16, 2022.
22. Clemente, F. President Biden must issue an executive order to get dark money out of our elections. *Americans for Tax Fairness*, December 1, 2022.
23. Congress needs to take two steps to fund the IRS for the short and long term. Center on Budget and Policy Priorities, February 1, 2022.
24. Payne, E. Tell Congress we need a billionaire minimum income tax now. *Patriotic Millionaires.* May 22,2023.
25. Easley, J, Jones, S. Let's talk about fairness as 34% of large profitable corporations pay $0 in federal taxes. *PoliticusUSA*, January 14, 2023.

CHAPTER 10

ANTI-DEMOCRATIC SUPPRESSION OF VOTING RIGHTS

With the country's high level of inequality, the Supreme Court seemed to approve of a system which ensured that there would be 'government of the 1 percent, for the 1 percent, and by the 1 percent.'[1]

—Joseph Stiglitz, Nobel Laureate in Economics and author of *People, Power, and Profits: Progressive Capitalism for an Age of Discontent,* commenting on the U. S. Supreme Court's Buckley v. Valeo ruling in 1976

Following up on the last chapter's coverage of what the U. S. Supreme Court has done to distort and cancel so much of what the right to vote should mean, this observation by David Rubenstein brings us this helpful insight about how long this has been a problem:

The United States has clearly struggled with the right to vote throughout its history— (for African Americans) not allowing them to vote (by law before the Fifteenth Amendment and by practice through the ensuing Jim Crow period) . . . Even today, efforts are regularly made in some jurisdictions to suppress minority voter turnout by making voting a complicated, time-consuming, and somewhat arduous and painful process, thereby discouraging some citizens from voting. Those efforts accelerated in many states following the 2020 election, initially most visibly in Georgia and Florida.[2]

This chapter has just 2 goals: (1) to examine various ways by which our claimed democracy has been falling far short of the U. S. Constitution's guarantees of voting rights; and (2) to ask whether reform is possible within today's polarized political climate, and if so, how?

I. Obstacles to Democratic Voting Rights and Representative Government

1. Big Money funding of election campaigns.

The role of Big Money from mega corporations is not obvious, but nevertheless a dominating factor that undermines majority rule and representative government. These are some of the factors that fly below the radar of public awareness:

- Billionaires control election spending.[3]
- Quiet but effective lobbying by Big Money interests has prevented any groundswell to reject the Citizens United decision.
- Lack of criminal justice for corporations.[4]
- Many big corporations pledged to stop donations to the 147 Republican members of Congress who voted against certification of the 2020 election results. However, Fortune 500 and corporate trade groups later proceeded to donate more than $32 million to the campaigns of those members.[5]
- Another report found that just one ultra-wealthy right-wing couple, owners of Uline packing supplies, gave $63 million to election deniers running for federal, gubernatorial and secretary of state candidates, who vowed, if elected, to undermine future elections.[6]
- The American Legislative Exchange Council (ALEC) is an extremist group of lobbyists funded by the Kochs and big corporations that has worked for many years to put out disinformation to fuel voter suppression laws and force far-right legislation through state legislatures; it planned on how to be so involved in 2023 states' legislative sessions.[7]

2. Gerrymandering

Partisan gerrymandering is still allowed and common in some states whereby redistricting commissions that are controlled by one party (usually the GOP) redraw districts' maps. The goal in each case is to give that party a decisive advantage during elections through "cracking", when mapmakers break up a cluster of certain types of voters (such as some minorities) or "packing", where maps are redrawn to cram particular groups of voters of the opposing party into one or as few districts as possible.[8] As one example of the effectiveness of gerrymandering, the GOP has controlled the House of Representatives in 10 of the last 15 elections despite losing the popular vote in 7 of them.[9] Going into the 2022 midterms, the GOP had control of redrawing the boundaries of some 181 congressional districts in 18 states.[10]

Gerrymandering can be used to prevent fair and democratic elections by erecting racist barriers against minority voters. Texas gives us an example of how undemocratic this can be. Latinos have accounted for almost one half of the state's population growth over the last ten years, so that Whites are now a minority with 39.8 percent of the population. In defense of the future White vote, Greg Abbott, its Republican Governor, approved new congressional and legislative districts in 2021 whereby 23 districts have White majorities and the number of Latino-majority districts is reduced from eight to seven.[11]

Other extremes in gerrymandering

What's been happening in Wisconsin has in effect thrown out democracy itself. It started in 2011 when Republicans controlled all branches of state government and drew what political scientists have called among the biggest partisan gerrymanders in modern U. S. history. After that, even when Democratic candidates have performed well statewide, Republicans have maintained large majorities in the Legislature, to the point that in the November 2022 election, when Democrats received 51% of the vote statewide, they got *just 30% of the seats* in the state legislature![12]

The back story of this fiasco involves the Wisconsin State Supreme Court as well as the U. S. Supreme Court. In April 2022, the State Supreme Court ruled to accept, by a 4-3 decision, a legislative map for the 2022 elections drawn by Democratic Governor Tony Evers. When that ruling was sent up to the U. S. Supreme Court, however, it was struck down and sent back to the State Court saying that there was not enough evidence to show why race should be a factor in drawing Assembly districts in Milwaukee.[13,14] Fortunately, progressives gained sway on Wisconsin's State Supreme Court with the election of Justice Janet Protasiewicz in April, 2023, as future issues likely to be heard include voting rights and the State's 1849 abortion ban.[15]

Another extreme example of unfair gerrymandering is the ongoing battle between the U. S. Supreme Court and the Republican-controlled state legislature in Alabama. The legislature drawn map in 2022 had packed one-third of Alabama's Black population into just one district, thereby preserving White political power in remaining districts. A special court found that to be illegal and ordered the legislature to redraw the map with a second majority Black district.[16] Alabama then appealed its case to the U. S. Supreme Court, resulting in a surprise 5-4 decision written by Chief Justice John Roberts finding this to be racial discrimination and a violation of the Voting Rights Act of 1965.[17] That defiance was similar to Alabama state leaders ignoring the Supreme Court's Brown v. Board of Education 1954 ruling calling for stopping segregating Black and White children in Alabama's public schools.[18]

3. Voter suppression

These are examples, among many, of various forms of voter suppression that have become widespread in recent election cycles:

- The Voting Rights Act of 1965 has been under sustained legal and political assault since it was signed by President Lyndon B. Johnson; the most recent examples include the Shelby County v. Holder case, with a ruling by the U. S. Supreme Court in 2013 that states with a history of racial discrimination could change their election laws without advance federal approval. Predictably, that led to a wave of voting restrictions since then in Republican-led state legislatures.[19]
- According to a report by States United Action, Republican lawmakers introduced more than 240 bills in 33 states during 2022 that would obstruct the fair administration of elections by usurping control over results, seizing power over election responsibilities, requiring partisan or unprofessional election "audits", or even imposing draconian criminal or other penalties.[20]
- Many Republican-led states are now implementing a strategy they're calling "radical incrementalism" to pass, piece by piece, such restrictions on voting rights as limiting voting by mail, banning ballot drop boxes, and placing new restrictions on voter registration groups.[21]
- Many large corporations sponsored voting suppression bills in 12 states, as shown in Table 10.1, which never received much public attention.[22]

- Intimidation of local election workers, even death threats, with more than 100 such incidents in Arizona leading up to the midterms.[23]

TABLE 10.1

Corporate Sponsors of Voter Suppression Bills in 2020 Election Cycle

FORTUNE 100 RANK	COMPANY	2020 ELECTION CYCLE CONTRIBUTIONS	TOTAL CONTRIBUTIONS 2015 - 2020
1	Walmart	$146,000	$376,617
3	Exxon Mobil	$49,700	$131,250
5	CVS Health	$81,100	$174,050
7	UnitedHealth Group	$201,600	$411,200
9	AT&T	$312,780	$810,915
13	Cigna	$66,325	$109,225
15	Chevron	$51,700	$116,200
18	General Motors	$86,200	$185,100
20	Verizon Communications	$111,575	$246,075
22	Marathon Petroleum	$85,965	$205,365
28	Comcast	$167,400	$439,700
29	Anthem	$73,650	$138,150
30	Wells Fargo	$58,900	$113,709
36	State Farm	$121,500	$315,370
39	Raytheon / Raytheon Technologies	$68,500	$154,050
43	UPS	$56,250	$165,900
62	Caterpillar	$63,000	$157,250
64	Pfizer	$133,925	$308,085
69	Merck	$90,900	$180,200

Sources: Public Citizen's analysis of data from The National Institute on Money in Politics (FollowTheMoney.org) and *Fortune*.

- Election deniers installing loyalists in states' secretaries of state positions with the goal to change election results in those states and overturn close elections nationally.[24]
- Republicans in Detroit, Michigan, tried to prevent tens of thousands of the city's absentee ballots from being counted in 2022 until they were blocked by a judge.[25]

The Electronic Registration Information Center (ERIC), was established more than 10 years ago as a bipartisan, non-profit organization in order to maintain accurate voting rolls. With 30 member states today, it has been especially helpful in identifying voters who have died or may no longer live in the state. For more than a year, however, it has been besieged by false claims by Trump allies claiming that it is a voter registration vehicle for Democrats.[28] Despite its importance to keeping election rolls accurate and up to date, however, eight Republican-led states (with more likely to follow) have resigned their membership in ERIC.[27] That has led Danielle Lang, senior director to the voting rights program at the Campaign Legal Center, to observe:

> *It seems like their goal is to create chaos—to lead to bloated rolls so they can point at them and say, 'Look at the problem we have,' even though its a problem entirely of their own making.*[29]

4. The Hastert Rule in the Senate

This was introduced by Dennis Hastert, Republican Speaker of the House (1999-2007), whereby a majority vote by Senate Republicans was required before a full hearing would be held in the Senate. We have seen how Senate Majority Leader McConnell has disallowed so many bills from a hearing in the Senate in recent years, even including the Voting Rights Act, when 41 GOP Senators blocked the bill. That bill would have required states with a history of voter discrimination to obtain federal approval for their redrawn political maps.

5. Excessive influence of small states in elections for the U. S. Senate

The Senate is undemocratic and unrepresentative of the country. More than one-half of the U. S. population lives in 9 states, represented by only 18 senators, while a voter in Wyoming has 68 times the voting power as one in California. According to census projections by the University of Virginia, that imbalance will be even more marked by 2040, when 8 states will have one-half of the U. S. population and 30 percent of the population will control 68 percent of Senate seats.[29]

6. Deepfake technology to mislead or confuse voters.

The rapid, and at times reckless development of A.I. for the purpose of misleading voters, has become a problem. Online watchdogs are warning that it could be used for such nefarious purposes as spreading false information about polling hours and locations and how voters can cast their ballots. [30] Public Citizen has concluded that:

> *Artificial intelligence poses a significant threat to truth and democracy as we know it.* [31]

In view of that threat, Public Citizen has formally called on the Democratic Party and the Republican Party not to use artificial intelligence or deepfake technology to mislead or defraud the electorate. Public Citizen has also petitioned the Federal Election Commission (FEC) to use its existing authority to make political deepfakes illegal.[32]

II. Is Reform Possible?

One important step to reform the election process has already been taken—the Electoral Count Reform Act (ECRA), passed with bipartisan support as part of the annual omnibus spending package in late December 2022. It eliminated the so-called "failed choice exception" that previously had allowed states to claim without evidence that voter fraud had occurred and/or to submit their own set of electors if voters "failed" for one reason or another to make their choice on Election Day. In effect, it will Trump-proof future presidential elections from attempts to steal the results.[33]

Wisconsin shows how dangerous SCOTUS decisions can be for democracy. The absence of the "red wave" in the 2022 midterms led Steve Kornacki, critical examiner of election returns, to say "The only seats where the Republicans are making gains right now is when the seats were drawn to give them an advantage."[34]

Amending the Constitution has been a bridge too far for many years. When the Supreme Court considered ending partisan gerrymandering in 2019, Chief Justice Roberts suggested in the *Rucho v. Common Cause* case that the Guarantee Clause does not provide the basis for a justifiable claim against objections to a legislative map in North Carolina. In a turnabout reversal on this issue, however, he recently wrote the 5-4 majority opinion in the Allen v. Milligan case that Alabama's gerrymandered congressional map likely violates the Voting Right's Act's prohibition against discriminatory voting practices.[35]

Perhaps the ultimate reform needed to assure voting rights for every American will be to pass legislation for universal voting, as has been recommended by two experts:

> *There is a powerful democracy movement in the United States that has spearheaded reforms to reduce barriers to voting. . . Our polling has found that 61% of Americans agreed with the premise underlying the proposal that voting is both a right and a duty. Support for this idea was as strong among Republicans as among Democrats.*[36]
>
> —E. J. Dionne, Jr., Professor of Public Policy at Georgetown University, senior fellow at the Brookings Institution, and co-author of the 2022 book, *100% Democracy: The Case for Universal Voting*
>
> —Miles Rapoport, Executive Director of 100% Democracy: An Initiative for Universal Voting, and co-author of *100% Democracy: The Case for Universal Voting*

These are other important approaches to modernizing and reforming the election process in this country:

1. *Automatic voter registration*—registering every eligible voter automatically on his or her 18th birthday, as proposed by Reverend Jesse Jackson.[37]
2. *Establish a National Popular Vote Interstate Compact,* which would avoid controversies of electoral college results and guarantee the presidency to the candidate receiving the most popular votes nationwide.[38]
3. *Increase the membership of the House of Representatives*—today, with 435 House members, each member represents about 762,000 people, much higher than any other democracy in the world; by comparison, the British Parliament and German Bundestag are larger than our House even with populations only 20-25% of ours.[39]

Conclusion:

As Nikki Haley, former Governor of South Carolina and United Nations ambassador, noted in announcing her bid for the 2024 Republican presidential nomination, the GOP has lost the popular vote in seven of the last eight presidential elections. As a result, many Republican officeholders and activists have abandoned any pretense of trying to win the majority vote. They have opened up new ways to win minority rule, such as by limiting voting on college campuses and tightening rules for voter registration and mail ballots.[40] All of these place democracy at risk. The chapters to follow will deal with the threat of minority rule during the election campaigns leading up to the 2024 elections.

References:

1. Stiglitz, JE. *People, Power, and Profits: Progressive Capitalism for an Age of Discontent,* 2019, p. 332.
2. Rubenstein, DM. *The American Experiment: Dialogues on a Dream.* New York. *Simon & Schuster,* 2021, p. 7.
3. Clemente, F. Billionaires by the numbers. *Americans for Tax Fairness & The Institute for Policy Studies Inequality Program,* July 15, 2020.
4. Nader, R. "Polarized" political parties work together against the public interest. *The Progressive Populist,* November 1, 2021, p. 19.
5. Reich, R. $32 million to 147 Republican members of Congress—guess which ones? *Inequality Media Civic Action,* June 23, 2022.
6. Corasaniti, N, Epstein, RI, Johnston, T et al. How maps reshape American politics. *New York Times,* November 12, 2021, A 18.
7. Harrison, V.UPS and other major companies bankrolling far-right legislation. *Common Cause,* December 19, 2022.
8. Wines, M. Process of redrawing congressional districts is coming to an end. *New York Times,* June 7, 2022: 16.
9. Walter, A. The Cook Political Report. (https://cookpolitical.com/redistricting).
10. Redden, M. Large corporations spent millions in support of GOP election deniers. *HuffPost,* November 10, 2022.
11. Barragan, J, Livingston, A, Astudillo, C. Texas reduced Black and Hispanic majority congressional districts in proposed map, despite people of color fueling population growth. *Texas Tribune,* September 27, 2021.
12. Pierce, CP. No one can pretend that Wisconsin is a republic. *Esquire,* November 10, 2022.
13. Marley, P. Wisconsin Supreme Court adopts legislative maps drawn by Republicans. *Milwaukee Journal Sentinel,* April 16, 2022.
14. Roberts, J. As quoted by Bouie, J. Madison saw something in the Constitution we should open our eyes to. *New York Times,* November 12, 2021. (*CHECK REFS, 2 0FF)*
15. Yu, I. Wisconsin Supreme Court swings to left with new Justice. *Wall Street Journal,* August 4, 2023, A:5.
16. Cochrane, E. Judges rebuke Alabama over latest map. *New York Times,* September 6, 2023, A:1.
17. Bravin, J. Court tosses Alabama map in rebuke. *Wall Street Journal,* September 6, 2023, A:3.

18. Firestone, D. Opinion. Alabama cherishes its history of defying the federal courts. *New York Times*, September 8, 2023, A:22.
19. Corasaniti, N. The battle to protect the rights of voters. *New York Times*, November 23, 2023, A:18.
20. Vaillancourt, W. Trump supporters bombard election officials with threats and abuse. *Rolling Stone*, December 30, 2021.
21. Under the radar, right-wing push to tighten voting laws persists. *New York Times*, May 8, 2023.
22. Public Citizen. Corporate America's contributions to voter suppression bills in 12 states. Washington, D.C.
23. Reich, R. Trump's Big Lie supporters are trying to take over our elections. *Inequality Media Civic Action*, May 10, 2022.
24. Stancil, K. 'You will be executed': Arizona poll workers endure right-wing midterm threats. *Common Dreams*, November 7, 2022.
25. Easley, J. Republicans just tried to not count tens of thousands of Detroit votes but a judge said no. *Politicus USA*, November 7, 2022.
26. Vigdor, N. Some GOP-led states leaving bipartisan group that tends to voter rolls. *New York Times*, March 8, 2023: A: 17.
27. Wegman, J. Do Republicans really care about election integrity? *New York Times*, Opinion, June 7, 2023: A:18.
28. Ibid # 12.
29. Thomas, J. Analysis: 18% of the U. S. population elects 52% of the country's senators. *The Intellectualist*, February 6, 2020.
30. Siddiqui, S, Tracy, R. AI's growth imperils 2024 campaigns. *Wall Street Journal*, June 6, 2023, A:4.
31. Minkoff-Zern, J. Regulating artificial intelligence. *Public Citizen News*, November/December, 2023, p. 16.
32. Weisman, R. Candidates must pledge not to use A. I. or deepfakes to deceive voters. *Public Citizen*, May 15 2023.
33. Rosen, D. Electoral Count Reform Act helps Trump-proof future presidential elections. *Public Citizen News* 43(2), March/April 2023, p. 7.
34. Kornacki, S. As quoted by the *Progressive Turnout Project*, GOP gerrymandering. November 18, 2022.
35. Liptak, A. In turnabout, Court rules map denied Black voters. *New York Times,* June 9, 2023, A:1. 24. Siddiqui, S, Tracy, R. AI's growth imperils 2024 campaigns. *Wall Street Journal*, June 6, 2023, A:4.
36. Dionne, EJ, Jr, Rapoport, M. It's time for universal voting. *The American Prospect*, August, 2022, pp. 27, 2022.
37. Jackson, J. Automatic voter registration a sensible first step. *The Progressive Populist*, March 15, 2023, p. 14.
38. Reich, R. How do we get democracy back into presidential elections? *The Progressive Populist*, March 15, 2023, p. 13.
39. Allen, D. Opinion: The House was supposed to grow with population. It didn't. Let's fix that. *The Washington Post*, February 28, 2023.
40. Bouie, J. Republicans are changing the rules. *New York Times*, April 30, 2023, Commentary p. 3.

PART IV

THE BATTLE AHEAD: DEMOCRACY UNDER ATTACK AND AT RISK

We are in a bad spot. It isn't just that we have to contend with plutocrats. It's that we have divorced property ownership from caretaking itself. Our industrial supply chains are fragile, concentrated and full of dangerous and hidden risks. . . Democracies are falling globally, in part because people understand that the formal mechanisms of voting do not matter when decisions about political economy are reserved to a coddled elite. But we can fight back.

—Matt Stoller, author of *Goliath: The 100-Year-War Between Monopoly Power and Democracy.*[1]

America has not stood so clearly at a fork in the road since the 1860s. The route laid out by our nation's founders is clearly marked. The other road, of which they warned, has danger signs flashing all along the way, and yet many Americans are tugging at the steering wheel to yank us in that dangerous direction. They must be outvoted. It is trite but true: We have a rendezvous with destiny once again to see if our government of all the people, by all the people, and for all the people shall perish from the earth.[2]

—John Dean, counsel for President Richard Nixon from 1970 to 1973, well known for his key Congressional testimony that led to Nixon's resignation

A half century ago, when America had a large and growing middle class, those on the "left" wanted stronger social safety nets and more public investment in schools, roads, and research. Those on the "right" sought greater reliance on the free market. But as power and wealth moved to the top, everyone else—whether on the old right or the old left—has become disempowered and less secure. Today the great divide is not between right and left. It's between democracy and oligarchy.[3]

—Robert Reich, Professor of Public Policy, University of California Berkeley, founding editor of *The American Prospect,* and author of *The System: Who Rigged It, How We Fix It.*

References:

1. Stoller, M. *Goliath: The 100-Year-War Between Monopoly Power and Democracy*, 2020, p. 454.
2. Dean, JW, Altemeyer, B. *Authoritarian Nightmare: Trump and His Followers.* Brooklyn, New York. *Melville House*, 2020, p. 284.
3. Reich, R. *The System: Who Rigged It, How We Fix It.* New York. *Alfred A. Knopf*, 2020, p. 18.

CHAPTER 11

HOW OLIGARCHY, AUTHORITARIANISM AND FASCISM THREATEN DEMOCRACY TODAY

One consequence of the neoliberal social-economic policies is collapse of the social order, yielding a breeding ground for extremism, violence, hatred, search for scapegoats—and fertile terrain for authoritarian figures who can posture as the savior. And we're on the road to a form of neo-fascism.[1]

— Noam Chomsky, Ph.D., Professor Emeritus of Linguistics the Massachusetts Institute of Technology and co-author of the new book, with C. J. Polychroniou, *Illegitimate Authority: Facing the Challenges of Our Time*

We saw in the chapters of Part I how the corporate state, elitism and oligarchy enveloped America over the last 60 years or so. Then in Parts II and III, we saw how oligarchs defend their power and threaten fair elections. Here we have three goals: (1) to describe how oligarchy, authoritarianism and fascism threaten our democracy; (2) to describe twin threats to democracy going forward; and (3) to consider what is and can be done to reverse the problems brought about by the unrestrained growth of oligarchy and the corporate state.

I. How Oligarchy, Authoritarianism and Fascism Pose a Threat to Our Democracy

1. Our votes are stolen.

Most, if not all of us, would agree that former-President Trump is an authoritarian. During his time in office, he pressured the U. S. Census Bureau to add a citizenship question to its process. His racist policies led to a higher than usual undercount in 2020 among Latinos, which more than tripled compared to 2020. Overall, the 2020 census undercounted 19 million minorities while overcounting Whites, thereby reducing voting power among minorities in districts across the country.[2]

Other ways that our votes can and do get stolen, as we saw in the last chapter, include gerrymandering, voter suppression, and opposing the Voting Rights Act. All of this is to be expected with today's Republican Party's far right stance. Professor Ruth Ben-Ghiat, Professor of History at New York University, whom we met in the Preface (page 1), writes in her 2021 book, *Strongmen: Mussolini to the Present*:

> *Whether or not Trump runs for office in 2024, the time-tested methods of autocracy—electoral manipulation, voter suppression, the criminalization of protest, political violence, and disinformation—are now part of the way the GOP conducts its business as a far-right party. After January 6, nothing is off the table: extremists might well view the failed coup as a trial run.*[3]

As Common Cause reports, more than 170 election deniers were elected to federal or state office by the 2022 midterms, and will continue to promote the Big Lie, new voter suppression laws, and election sabotage tactics. They will be active in coordinating voter suppression efforts at all levels of government, including:

- prohibiting states from using automatic voter registration systems;
- prohibiting states from providing absentee ballots to many voters;
- restricting the use of drop boxes for absentee ballots;
- blocking many Americans from no-excuse absentee voting; and
- preventing most individuals from voting at a polling place during an early voting period.[4]

2. Our elections are corrupted.

Our system of campaign finance relies almost entirely on private money, which corrupts our election process in several ways:

- During the 2020 election cycle, more than $14 billion was spent by the ultra-wealthy for federal candidates, party committees, and Super Pacs, double the $ 7 billion doled out in the 2016 cycle.[5]
- By its uneven playing field—the average cost of running and winning a seat in the U. S. House of Representatives is now $1.6 million, while winning a Senate seat averages almost $10.6 million.
- According to the Center for Responsive Politics, the highest spending candidate wins in 90 percent of House elections and 80 percent of Senate races.
- The Republican State Leadership Committee, a dark money group largely funded by the Judicial Crisis Network, spent $2 million for TV ads in the closing weeks of the 2022 midterms to control redistricting in Ohio, a swing state.[6]
- Billionaire Richard Uihlein, who was the single biggest Republican donor in the 2022 midterms, also gave $20 million to right-wing election deniers and anti-abortion groups in the 12 months following the January 6 insurrection attack on the Capitol.[7]
- "Moms for America," a deceptively named far right extremist group funded by ultra-wealthy donors and designated as anti-government by the Southern Poverty Law Center, pushes voter suppression and election denialism.[8]
- Rulings by the U. S. Supreme Court have fostered this high level of corruption of elections by large amounts of money. In 1976, the Supreme Court ruled that campaign spending limits and limits on the spending of a candidate's own money were unconstitutional *(Buckley v. Valeo);* in 2004, Justice Scalia co-signed that "The mere possession of monopoly power, and the concomitant charging of monopoly prices, is not only not unlawful, it is an important element of the free market system;"[9] and in 2010 *(Citizens United),* it ruled that

campaign spending by corporations should be protected as free speech without restrictions.[10]

3. *Legislators and legislation are compromised by conflicts of interest.*

According to a recent *New York Times* report, 183 current members of the U. S. Senate and House of Representatives (and their family members) traded stock or another financial asset between 2019 and 2021, with more than one-half of them having conflicts of interest by sitting on committees that gave them direct insight into those companies and stocks.[11] The wealth of Senate Majority Leader Mitch McConnell has grown from $3 million in 2004 to $34 million in 2018, an increase of 1,000%.[12] Joe Manchin (D-WV) is the # 1 recipient of oil and gas campaign money, especially from the Next Era and the Mountain Valley Pipeline, as he stood in the way of major Democratic legislation.[13]

4. *Corporate greed contributes to inflation.*

A panel of the U. S. House Committee on Oversight and Reform recently reported that "certain corporations are using the cover of inflation to raise prices excessively, resulting in record profits and profit margins" at the expense of consumers.[14] That report was based on an analysis by the House Subcommittee on Economic and Consumer Policy, which included these findings between 2019 and 2021:

- Three of the largest public companies in the shipping industry had profits rise by 29,965%;
- Profits for the two largest public companies in the rental car industry increased by 597%.
- Studies by the Economic Policy Institute and the Roosevelt Institute have demonstrated that profits contributed more to price growth in the U. S. from mid-2020 through the end of 2021 than at any other point from 1979 to the present, especially in highly concentrated industries, and continue to contribute markedly today.[15]
- The average American household pays $5,000 a year more for the necessities of life than the average Canadian or European household.[16]
- Prices in the U. S. over the last 17 years have increased by more than 15 percent compared to Europe.[17]

- Monopolized U. S. hospitals charge 10 to 20 times the rates of hospitals in France for less quality and efficiency of service, with bills here including capital costs of mergers and costs of equipment without any regulation of prices.[18]

As Congresswoman Katie Porter (D-CA) has recently pointed out, 54% of our current inflation is actually the result of corporate price gouging of American consumers.[19] Thomas Philippon, Professor of Finance at the Stern School of Business, New York University and author of the 2019 book, *The Great Reversal: How America Gave Up on Free Markets*, has written:

> *Over and over, we have seen that the way oligopolies maintain high prices and avoid outrage and crackdowns is by hiding their fees. That is true of banks, credit card companies, pharmaceutical companies, hospitals, insurers, and internet platforms.*[20]

Figure 11.1 illustrates this long-standing problem of corporate greed driving considerable price gouging and inflation.

Figure 11.1

CORPORATE GREED INFLATION

Source: John Darkow Reprinted with permission

As Thom Hartmann observes:

> *The most important takeaway from today's inflation crisis is that we must get our corporations back under control if we're to have an economy that works for us instead of just for the billionaires.*[21]

Ralph Nader adds:

> *Establishing inferior legal status for corporations within our political economy is essential . . . It is time to rein in unaccountable, cost shifting, autocratic, hierarchical "Frankenstein monsters" that create their own out of control engines.*[22]

5. *The labor movement is opposed.*

Conservative forces and corporate consolidation since the 1970s have led to loss of union power in the U. S. Today, only 6% of the private sector labor force are union members.[23] Although Amazon's first-ever labor union was formed at the JFK8 fulfillment center in 2022, Amazon has not only ramped up its union-busting behavior at other warehouses, but also refused to even come to the negotiating table with the union.[24]

Union busting has become common in recent years as workers across the country organize for fair pay, benefits and scheduling. As one example, workers at 329 Starbucks stores in 39 states have voted to unionize since December 2021. Starbucks has refused to come to the negotiating table while the company registered $4.1 billion in profits in 2021. It also illegally fired union organizers and intimidated workers. As Senator Bernie Sanders has said:

> *Starbucks is waging the most aggressive and illegal union busting campaign in modern history.* [25]

In his 2020 book, *Evil Geniuses: The Unmaking of America: A Recent History*, Kurt Andersen notes how other rich countries have been able to maintain powerful unionized labor forces while also dealing with increased automation and international competition. He raises the key, not yet answered question about the future outcomes of automation on labor and jobs in a new global economy—what happens when the two basic directions clash—the drive of large corporations for maximal profits through automation and smaller human workforces vs. the availability of good jobs for Americans in a competitive global economy? As he notes:

> *As for when and how many particular jobs will be taken over by machines, either disembodied A.I. or robots, the estimates range widely, but pre-pandemic most predicted that between 15 and 30 percent of current jobs in the United States and the rest of the developed world will be eliminated during the next ten to twenty years, with many more at risk.*

And further:

> *Without effective counterweights to the power of big business and the rich, the United States will continue morphing into a super-automated plutocracy, and that how people work and get paid needs to become a primary subject of our politics.*[25]

While it is still too early to know the impacts of A.I. on jobs and the workplace, we can learn from well informed projections of others. The 2021 book, *The Age of AI and Our Human Future* by Henry Kissinger, Eric Schmidt and Daniel Huttenlocher has this to say on the matter:

> *As A.I. transforms the nature of work, it may jeopardize many people's sense of identity, fulfillment, and financial security. Those most affected by such change and potential dislocation will likely hold blue-collar and middle management jobs that require specific training as well as professional jobs involving review or interpretation of data or drafting of documents in standard forms . . . . Whatever A.I.'s long-term effects prove to be, in the short-term, the technology will revolutionize certain economic segments, professions, and identities. Societies need to be ready to supply the displaced not only with alternative sources of income but also with alternative sources of fulfillment.*[26]

6. Public dollars are diverted from the common good.

U. S. corporations are raking in record profits—annual profits in 2021 of $2.8 trillion, up by 25% from the previous year [27] and in 2022 the highest profit margin in more than 70 years. Despite those profits, they continued to ask that Congress give them a new round of tax breaks before the end of the year. At the same time, as multinational corporations, they were taking in billions of dollars a year by shifting profits to overseas tax havens to avoid paying taxes in the U. S.[28] Those dollars could have gone a long way toward alleviating essential costs of living for many Americans struggling under the burden of corporate-induced inflation.

In their book, *The Privatization of Everything*, which we referenced in Chapter 3, Donald Cohen and Allen Mikaelian show how these huge corporate profits at the expense of the common good could be more usefully applied to societal needs in this country:

> *If we take back control of our public goods—if we reject what political philosopher Michael Sandel calls "a market society"—we will gain an incredible opportunity to build instead a society based on public values and a commitment to ensuring that public goods are available to all. And as we increase access to public goods, we strengthen our ties to each other. We're better off when we limit privatization and market competition over things that we need—things including public health, key infrastructure, water, education, and democracy itself.* [29]

7. Fair and true reporting by news media is threatened.

Corporate media have increasingly controlled what is presented to the public as unbiased news and supposedly as truth, but the truth and lack of bias must increasingly be questioned. The recent cancellation of the CNN program, *Reliable Sources*, and firing of Brian Stelter and his staff, is a case in point. That show has been a reliable source of truth in news and criticism of Fox News and right-wing media. On his last show, Stelter said:

It's not partisan to stand up for decency and democracy and dialogue. It's not partisan to stand up to demagogues. It's required. It's patriotic. We must make sure we don't give platforms to those who are lying to our faces.[30]

The back story is revealing. Stelter had long been a critic of the American right's embrace of disinformation. John Malone, a billionaire cable magnate and the most powerful investor in Warner Brothers Discovery, Inc., as the new owner of CNN has said that he wished that CNN was more like Fox News, which had "actual journalism." CNN's new CEO had previously met with Republican lawmakers to assure them that "We want to win back your trust."[31]

Dan Rather, well known journalist over many years, brings us this perspective about fairness in reporting by the news media:

Fairness means looking at the truth without blinking, and right now, the Republican Party is embracing a leader who vocally and unabashedly conveys that if reelected, he will try to end American democracy as we know it. His party is working at every level of government to entrench minority rule, tear apart the norms that have allowed our nation to function, and sow the seeds of autocracy.[32]

Jennifer Rubin, columnist for the *Washington Post*, brings us another observation after covering a rally by Trump for Ohio Republican candidates in September 2022, where QAnon symbol one-armed salutes were elicited, a resemblance to the Nazi salute. She calls out the mainstream political media for disguising the political reality we face—for refusing to use the words for Republican conduct as "fascist" or "racist", but instead as "conservatives."[33] Figure 11.2 illustrates the continuing grievances of racism, anti-semitism, and white supremacy that former President Trump promoted instead of draining the swamp.[34]

Figure 11.2

DRAINING THE SWAMP

Source: Reprinted with permission from Nick Anderson

Along the way, the largely corporate controlled media have instilled in us the idea that the Dow Jones stock exchange numbers are a direct measure of the state of the U. S. economy. By that specious measure, if the Dow is doing well (with all its corporate price gouging), the economy must be in good shape; if it has fallen markedly, we must be in recession.

8. The rule of law is threatened.

As we saw in Chapter 6, corporate interests with strong backing by the GOP over many years have stacked the U. S. Supreme Court with a conservative majority that has already handed down rulings against human rights, such as women's reproductive rights, and the public interest, such as gun control. It has hardly been an entirely democratic process that has allowed such a political shift to the right of the High Court. The 52 senators who approved Clarence Thomas' nomination in 1991 represented a minority of Americans. Trump's three appointments to the Supreme Court happened after he had lost the popular vote.

Rulings of the current Court continue to magnify the disconnect between public opinion and government policy by overruling Congress on such issues as reproductive rights, in the same way that earlier Courts did with voting rights and campaign finance. The North Carolina case, pending hearing by the Court, poses an extreme risk to the right to vote should it agree that the Constitution gives the state legislature (which gerrymandered itself into power) the authority to oversee federal elections, thereby bypassing state courts for other bodies.

The Court's need for a code of ethics is shown by the failure of Justice Clarence Thomas to recuse himself in a case related to the January 6 insurrection after his wife, Ginny Thomas, had been shown to have sent text messages to the former White House chief of staff concerning plans for that criminal conspiracy.[34]

9. Epidemic gun violence

There are far more guns in circulation in the U. S. than anywhere else in the world, with more than 50 people killed each day by a firearm. In each of the last three years, there have been more than 600 mass shootings, each with four or more people killed. About 80% of all homicides in the U. S. are gun-related, compared to 40% in Canada, and 4% in England and Wales.[35] Gun violence is the leading cause of death among children and teenagers in this country.

The AR-15, in use by the military since the 1950s, became the weapon of choice in many of the increasing numbers of mass shootings. Its rapid growth in the market was fueled by private equity investors as millions of Americans saw it as the epitome of violent dysfunction in a gun-obsessed country.[36]

Figure 11.3 shows how mass shootings in this country have increased over the last ten years. A recent report by the Anti-Defamation League found that white supremacists committed more than 80% of mass shootings in 2022, accounting for the highest number of deaths from assault in the world. As Adrienne LaFrance concludes in her excellent recent article on anarchy in *The Atlantic*:

> *We face a new phase of domestic terror, one characterized by radicalized individuals with shape-shifting ideologies willing to kill their political enemies.*[37]

Figure 11.3

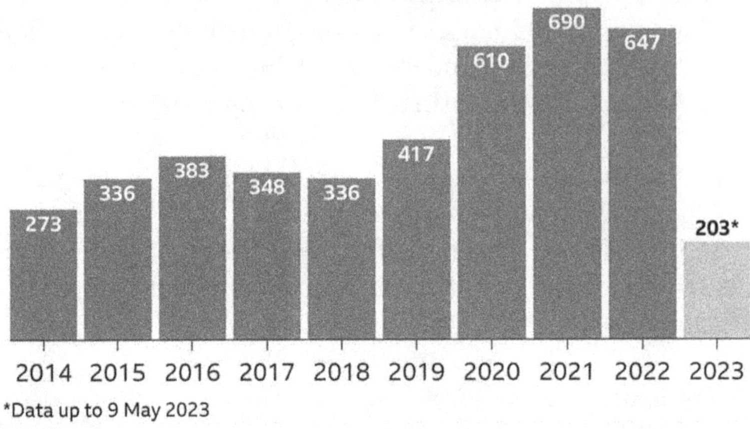

Source: BBC

II. Twin Threats to American Democracy Going Forward

A recent extensive article by Pulitzer Prize winning *New York Times* journalist David Leonhardt sees "American democracy facing two distinct threats, which together represent the most serious challenge to the country's governing ideals in decades:"

1. *As an acute threat, based on "a growing movement within the Republican Party to refuse to accept defeat in an election," and*
2. *as a chronic but growing threat, that "the power to set government policy is becoming increasingly disconnected from public opinion."*

The acute threat is very concerning based on these factors:

- Hundreds of Republican election deniers, claiming that the 2020 elections were rigged, ran for statewide offices in 2022, with many possibly positioned to overturn election results in 2024 or later.
- Figure 11.4 shows the shares of Republican state legislators, as of May 2022, who took steps to discredit or overturn the results of the 2020 presidential elections.[39]

FIGURE 11.4

STATE LEGISLATORS AND ELECTION LIES

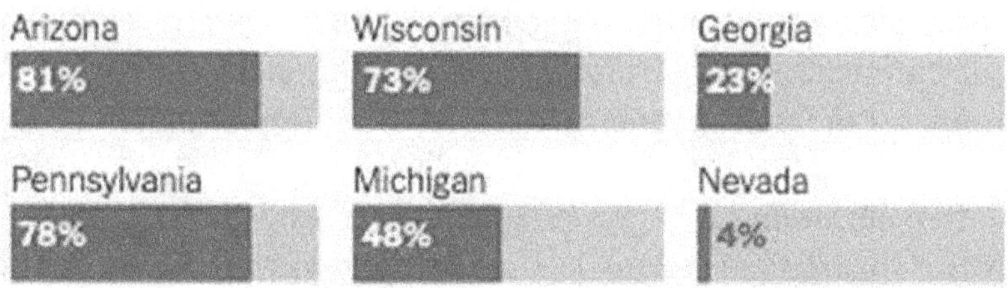

Percentage of Republican state legislators that took steps to discredit or overturn the 2020 presidential election results

Source: The *New York Times* analysis of legistlative votes, May 2022

- The rise of authoritarian sentiment, or acceptance of it, often becomes part of the acute threat among many voters based on these kinds of circumstances—slow-growing living standards for the American working class and middle class; cultural fears, especially among Whites, that what they have known is being transformed into a new country.[38]
- Infiltration by extremists into local law enforcement through the Constitutional Sheriffs and Peace Officers Association (CSPOA), an anti-government group based on the premise that the county sheriff is the ultimate authority in a county, able to halt enforcement of any federal or state law or measure they deem unconstitutional.[40]
- The authoritarianism shown by Ron DeSantis as Governor of Florida and 2024 GOP presidential candidate, with the takeover of the progressive New College of Florida, together with the banning of history books telling the story of America's racist past, are clear examples of fascism emerging in this country.[41]

Heather Cox Richardson, Professor of History at Boston College and author of the 2023 book, *Democracy Awakening: Notes on the State of America*, brings this historical perspective to the teaching of critical race theory ("CRT") in public schools:

> *Republican-dominated legislatures passed laws forbidding teachers from teaching critical race theory or any lesson suggesting that the American system might ever have had systemic inequalities . . . A history that looks back to a mythologized past as the country's perfect time is a key tool of authoritarians. It allows them to characterize anyone who opposes them as an enemy of the country's great destiny.*[42]

Jamelle Bouie, *New York Times* columnist, makes a strong case that the threat to freedom is increasingly coming from the states. These are several examples raised to support that premise:

- Millions of women losing their right to bodily autonomy and right to make their own decisions about reproductive health.
- Barriers placed for women's travel to get an abortion.
- States reneging the right to free and fair elections. [43]

The chronic threat has taken rise based on these kinds of impediments to voters' decisions and public opinion—gerrymandering, increasing use of the filibuster in Congress, and anti-democratic decisions by the U. S. Supreme Court, as we saw in Chapter 6. The chronic threat also has these roots in the U. S. Constitution:

- Residents of the more populous states have less voting power than those in small states; the differences are marked—California has 68 times as many residents as Wyoming, but the electoral college for the two states is equal.
- Geographic sorting with changing population patterns has resulted in large states having more minority voters while small states are disproportionately White.
- Even with Senate seats in the U. S. Congress split 50-50, the 50 Democratic senators represent 186 million Americans while the 50 Republican senators represent 145 million, so that Democrats need to win considerably more than half of the nationwide votes to gain control of the Senate.

- Because of this kind of sorting and differences of states' electoral results in presidential and congressional elections, the disconnect from the popular vote gives Republicans an advantage in shaping the membership of the U. S. Supreme Court. Although Democrats have won the popular vote in 7 of the 9 past presidential elections and the presidency in 5 of the 9, the High Court is dominated by a six-member conservative majority.[44]

Taken together, the acute and chronic threats to democracy in this country bring this overall challenge, as viewed by Steven Levitsky and Daniel Ziblatt, Professors of Government at Harvard University and co-authors of the 2018 book, *How Democracies Die*:

> *The fundamental problem facing American democracy remains extreme partisan division—one fueled not just by policy differences but by deeper sources of resentment, including racial and religious differences. America's great polarization preceded the Trump presidency, and is very likely to endure beyond it. . . Few societies in history have managed to be both multiracial and genuinely democratic. That is our challenge. It is also our opportunity. If we meet it, America will truly be exceptional.*[45]

III. Can Wall Street and the Corporate State Be Reined In?

Based on patterns of corporate monopolization, its political leverage and deep pockets exerting strong influence on legislators and political campaigns, and the outcomes of the 2022 midterms whereby Republicans gained control of the House of Representatives, the prospects for reform in the near future are poor. A recent report by Public Citizen and Groundwork Collaborative found that corporations opposed to anti-price gouging and profiteering bills were responsible for more than 2,600 lobbyist engagements on Capitol Hill compared to fewer than 300 by supporters of the legislation. Dark money and the U. S. Chamber of Commerce funded 1,300 of those engagements.[46] Beyond that, Yascha Mounk, expert on liberal democracies and Associate Professor of the Practice of

International Affairs at Johns Hopkins University, gives us the worst case if election denial continues as a major part of the Republican party:

> *There is the possibility, for the first time in American history, that a legitimately elected president will not be able to take office.*[47]

On the positive side, however, there are many signs for optimism *if* enough pushback to today's entirely unacceptable and undemocratic, corporate dominated non-system can be countered. These are components of an action plan for legislation in Congress going forward, as delineated by Public Citizen[47] and other groups:

- The DISCLOSE Act, which would outlaw dark money.
- The Freedom to Vote Act.
- The Electoral Count Reform Act.
- The Government by the People Act (in the House).
- The Fair Elections Now Act (in the Senate).
- Ending Corporate Greed Act.
- Workplace Mobility Act.
- Stop Wall Street Looting Act.
- Prohibiting Anticompetitive Mergers Act.
- The George Floyd Justice in Policing Act.
- Protecting the Right to Organize (PRO) Act.
- Reward Work Act.

Political action groups involved in advocacy for progressive legislative reforms include:

- Fight Corporate Monopolies (FCM), promoting its Corporate Power Agenda with 19 policy recommendations focusing on making life more affordable for Americans, protecting small businesses from monopolization, and strengthening antitrust enforcement.[49]
- Citizen and advocacy groups for public financing of elections include American Promise, Common Cause, the Brennan Center for Justice, Democracy Initiative, Demos, Equal Citizens, Move to Amend, Represent Us, and others.
- Universal Civic Duty Voting (Working Group on Universal Voting, under auspices of the Brookings Institution and the Ash Center for Democratic Governance and Innovation at Harvard's Kennedy School.)

- National Popular Vote Compact; 15 states and the District of Columbia have already signed on to agree to assign their electors to the winner of the national popular vote in presidential races, thereby avoiding the need to amend the Constitution if just a few more states so decide.[50]

Other components of an action agenda for the Biden administration:

- Implement legal protections for election workers against threats and intimidation.
- Complete the January 6 Select Committee Report and demand accountability and prosecution of former President Donald Trump.
- Impose a windfall profits tax on the Big Oil industry.
- Force large corporations that receive government contracts to disclose their political spending.
- Raise the corporate income tax rate and close offshore corporate tax loopholes.[51]

Another potential encouraging sign toward reining in corporate abuses against the public interest is the recent bipartisan bill being proposed by Senators Lindsey Graham (R-SC) and Elizabeth Warren (D-MA), the Digital Consumer Protection Commission Act, which would create an independent, bipartisan regulator charged with licensing and policing the country's Big Tech companies such as Meta, Google and Amazon.[52]

National polls document public support for many of the reforms being considered in these areas:

- More than 80% of Americans say they oppose the Citizens United ruling that allows unlimited corporate spending.
- Over 75% of Americans believe there should be limits on the amount of money individuals and groups can spend on campaigns.
- 69% of Americans believe that SuperPacs should be illegal.
- 52% of respondents say they "strongly" support public financing of campaigns (Clean Elections)
- A majority of Americans across party lines believe that corporate greed and price gouging are major drivers of inflation.[53]

Conclusion:

The negative impacts of rule by the powerful, very rich few in the American oligarchy and its associated authoritarianism have been blighting the American Dream. They represent problems to be resolved going forward as this challenge before us remains:

> *The United States of America inarguably has a multiracial population. The task of the moment, the urgency of the hour, the fight we are engaged in, is to win a centuries-old Civil War and forge a multi-racial democracy in which everyone can thrive. It is a fight we can and should win. And once we win this Civil War, once we defeat white supremacy for good, we can write a new social contract for the kind of country where we really want to live.*[54]
>
> —Steve Phillips, author of, *How We Win the Civil War: Securing a Multiracial Democracy and Ending White Supremacy for Good* and *Brown Is the New White*

Yale University Professor of History Tim Snyder, whom we met in Part I (p.3), further warns us of the high risks of the 2024 elections:

> *We're looking almost certainly at an attempt in 2024 to take power without the election. The antidemocratic actions of Republican-controlled state legislatures are all working toward that scenario in 2024 when they lose by 10 million votes but they still appoint their guy. Republicans are digging themselves ever deeper into becoming a party which only wins by keeping other people from voting, and that's a downward spiral.*[55]

With that, it is time to move to the next chapter to see what can be learned from the 2022 midterms as they portend to the crucially important 2024 elections.

References:

1. Chomsky, N. as quoted by Polychroniou, CJ. Noam Chomsky: "We're on the road to a form of neofascism. *Truthout*, December 8, 2022.
2. Easley, J. Trump's 2020 census undercounted 19 million minorities and over-counted white people. *PoliticusUSA*, March 10, 2022.
3. Ben-Ghiat, R. Strongmen: Mussolini to the Present. New York. *W. W. Norton & Company*, Inc, 2021, p. 271.
4. Flynn, KH. Post 2022 midterms report from *Common Cause*.
5. Reich, R. The connection between neofascism and capitalism. robertreich@ substack.com).
6. McCarter, J. Dark money swoops in to steal state supreme courts for the right, *Daily Kos*, October 4, 2022.
7. Inside the billionaire-backed 'hub for election denial', *Daily Beast*, November 28, 2022.
8. Bowen, A. A Jan. 6 "Moms" group funded by big lie donors is stoking voter suppression. *Truthout*, July 9, 2023.
9. Scalia, A. As quoted by Stoller, M. The 100-Year War between Monopoly Power and Democracy. New York. *Simon & Schuster*, 2019, p. 423.
10. Amy, DJ. Second-rate democracy: Seventeen ways America is less democratic that other major western countries and how we can do better. An ongoing web project.
11. Kelly, K, Playford, A, Parlapiano, A. Stock trades reported by nearly a fifth of Congress show possible conflicts. *New York Times*, September 13, 2022.
12. Stock trades are CORRUPTING Congress's decisions. We have proof. *More Perfect Union*, February 10, 2022.
13. Hightower, J. The people vs. robber baron Manchin. *Hightower Lowdown* 24 (9): October/November 2022.
14. Corbett, J. 'Drowning out democracy': U. S. billionaires have pumped nearly $900,000,000 into midterms, *Common Dreams*, November 4, 2022.
15. Power and Profiteering: How Certain Industries Hike Prices and Drove Inflation. Analysis by the House Subcommittee on Economic and *Consumer Policy*. September 2022.
16. Hartmann, T. Is most of America's inflation due to monopolies, price-gouging & oil barons fleecing us? *The Progressive Populist*, December 1, 2022.
17. Philippon, T. *The Great Reversal: How America Gave Up on Free Markets*, Cambridge, MA. Belknap Press of *Harvard University Press*, 2019, p. 122.
18. Kuttner, R. Hospital billing is a crime against American patients. *The American Prospect*, November 22, 2022.
19. Porter, K. As quoted by Ibid # 10.
20. Ibid # 17, p. 296.
21. Ibid # 16.

22. Nader, R. Rescue our democratic society: Constitutionally render corporations unequal to humans. In the Public Interest. *The Progressive Populist,* March 15, 2023, p. 19.
23. Phillips-Fein, K. I wouldn't bet on the kind of democracy big business is selling us. *New York Times*, December 1, 2022.
24. Tell Amazon: Come to the table with Amazon Labor Union! *Amazon Labor Union*, February 26, 2022.
25. Andersen, K. Evil Geniuses: *The Unmaking of America: A Recent History,* New York. *Random House*, 2020, pp. 353, 330.
26. Kissinger, HA, Schmidt, E, Huttenlocher, D. *The Age of AI and Our Human Future*, New York. *Little, Brown and Company,* 2021, pp 183-184.
27. Clemente, F. Congress should raise, not cut, corporate taxes during lame-duck session. *Americans for Tax Fairness*, November 17, 2022.
28. Johnson, J. Secrecy enabled by rich countries lets corporations dodge $90 billion in taxes per year. *Common Dreams*, November 15, 2022.
29. Cohen, D, Mikaelian, A. *The Privatization of Everything: How the Plunder of Public Goods Transformed America and How We Can Fight Back.* New York. *The New Press*, 2021, p. 283.
30. Stelter, B. As quoted by Reich, R. Why CNN cancelled Brian Stelter. Follow the money. substack.com. August 23, 2022.
31. Dispatches. Brian Stelter, Reliable Sources out, staffers anxious as CNN moves right. *The Progressive Populist,* September 15, 2022, p. 5.
32. Rather, D, Kirschner, E. It's not "Congress" or "Washington." Steady by Dan Rather, October 6, 2023.
33. Rubin, K. Opinion: Trump's frightening rally in Ohio shows the media still doesn't get it. *The Washington Post*, September 19, 2022.
34. Easley, J. Text messages bust Ginny Thomas in plot to overturn the election. *PoliticusUSA*, March 24, 2022.
35. How many U. S. mass shootings have there been in 2023? BBC, May 26, 2023.
36. McWhirter, C, Elinson, Z. The selling of America's most controversial gun. *Wall Street Journal*, September 23-24, 2023, C:1.
37. LaFrance, A. Anarchy. *The Atlantic*, April, 2023, p. 25.
38. Corasaniti, N, Yourish, K Collins, K How Trump's 2020 elecction lies have gripped state legislatures, *New York Times*, May 22, 2022.
39. Kuttner, R. Will America be a democracy next July 4th? *The American Prospect*, July 4, 2022.
40. The Constitutional Sheriffs and Peace Officers Association (CSPOA) and Richard Mack: How Extremists Are Successfully Infiltrating Law Enforcement, the *Anti-Defamation League*, September 20, 2021.
41. Giroux, HA. U. S. fascism is spreading under the guise of "patriotic education." *Truthout*, April 10, 2023.
42. Richardson, HC. Democracy Awakening: Notes on the State of America. New York. Viking. 2023, p. 251.

43. Bouie, J. The threat to freedom is coming from the states. Columns and Commentary, *New York Times*, May 28, 2023.
44. Leonhardt, D. 'A crisis coming': The twin threats to American democracy. *New York Times*, September 21, 2022, p. 23.
45. Levitsky, S, Ziblatt, D. *How Democracies Die*. New York. *Broadway Books*, 2018, pp. 220, 231.
46. Feng, R. Protecting the profiteer. *Public Citizen News*, November/December 2022, p. 12.
47. Mounk, Y. As quoted by Leonhardt, D. 'A crisis coming': The twin threats to American democracy. *New York Times*, September 21, 2022, p. 2.
48. Weissman, R. Editorial. Assessing November's election. *Public Citizen News,* November/December 2022, p. 3.
49. Fight Corporate Monopolies, Groundwork Collaborative, Unrig Our Economy, July 26, 2022.
50. Reich, R. Stop letting candidates who lose the popular vote win the presidency. Inequality *Media Civic Action*, July 10, 2022.
51. Wilkins, B. As corporations enjoy record-high profits, experts urge Congress to 'rein them in.' *Nation of Change*, December 1, 2022.
52. Graham, L, Warren, E. We have a way for Congress to rein in Big Tech. Opinion. *New York Times*, July 27, 2023, A:22.
53. Johnson, J. Poll shows majority of U. S. voters blame corporate profiteering for inflation. *Common Dreams*, February 28, 2022.
54. Phillips, S. How We Win the Civil War: Securing a Multiracial Democracy and Ending White Supremacy for Good,2022. New York. *The New Press*. 2022, p. 324.
55. Snyder, T. As quoted by Milbank, D. T*he Destructionists: The Twenty-Five Year Crack-Up of the Republican Party.* New York. *Doubleday*, 2022, p. 308.

CHAPTER 12

LESSONS FROM THE 2022 MIDTERMS FOR THE 2024 ELECTIONS

Previous efforts to build a multiracial democracy in America have failed . . . It is only in the twenty-first century that a solid majority has embraced the principles of diversity and racial equality . . . But this majority alone isn't enough to save our democracy, because in America majorities do not really rule. Not only have steps toward a more inclusive politics triggered a fierce backlash among an authoritarian minority, but our institutions have amplified the power of that minority. The acute constitutional crisis triggered by the Trump presidency might have passed, but rather than regarding those four years as an exception, we should regard them as a warning. The conditions that gave rise to the Trump presidency—a radicalized party empowered by a pre-democratic constitution—remain in place.

We stand at a crossroads: either America will be a multiracial democracy or it will not be a democracy at all.[1]

—Steven Levitsky and Daniel Ziblatt, professors of government at Harvard University and authors of *How Democracies Die* and *Tyranny of the Minority*

The real battle for America isn't between the left and the right, or even between Republicans and Democrats. It's between the oligarchy—corporate and Wall Street monied interests—and everybody else.[2]

—Robert Reich, author of *The System: Who Rigged It, and How We Fix It.*

Having seen in the last chapter how authoritarianism has become such a serious threat to American democracy, it is now especially pertinent to consider what we can learn from the 2022 midterms to avoid such a threat. This chapter has three goals: (1) to discuss what we can learn from the 2022 midterms; (2) to describe how the opposing forces have collided in the runup to the 2024 elections; and (3) to review what developments have happened since the midterms that will relate to the 2024 elections.

I. Lessons From the 2022 Midterms

Although the 2020 elections had a record-breaking turnout with almost 60% of potential voters participating, one-third of potential voters were still left on the sidelines. Turnouts in past elections (since 1789) in the U. S. have been lower than most might think—about 57% in presidential elections and 41% in midterm elections.[3] As E. J. Dionne, Jr. and Miles Rapoport tell us in their 2022 book, *100% Democracy: The Case for Universal Voting*, in a close election with 60 percent turnout, the winner receives votes from only about 30% of the population theoretically eligible to vote.[4]

While acknowledging that the 2022 midterms fell short of a majority of eligible voters participating, we can draw these conclusions about the process and results:

1. Despite the many millions of dollars poured into the midterms by wealthy Republicans, (including more than $16 million by large corporations which earlier had suspended donations to members of Congress who objected to certification of the 2020 election)[5], the vaunted Red Wave never happened.
2. Independent voters tended to lean away from GOP.[6]
3. Younger voters favored Democratic candidates(Figure 12.1).[7]
4. The election process was fair and without Trumpian claims of election fraud.[8]
5. Election denialism remains common as GOP infighting and flawed candidates turned off many moderate marginal GOP voters. [9]
6. Inflation, closely followed by abortion, with major differences between the two parties, were the most important issues driving midterm voting, according to national exit polling.[10] (Figure 12.2)
7. Reproductive rights were strongly supported by voters in a politically diverse mix of states, including those that had ballot measures on abortion in Michigan, California, Vermont and Kentucky.[11]

8. On the other hand, almost half of states banning abortion would also oppose expansion of Medicaid, thereby increasing further stressing the safety net and increasing human need. Of the 15 states with the strictest abortion laws, 10 rank in the bottom quartile for cash assistance available to poor families.[12] (Figure 12.3)

FIGURE 12.1

YOUNGER VOTERS FAVORED DEMOCRATS IN THE 2022 MIDTERMS

Source: Catalist, by the *New York Times*

FIGURE 12.2

NATIONAL EXIT POLL: ISSUES BY PARTY

Which issue mattered most in deciding how to vote

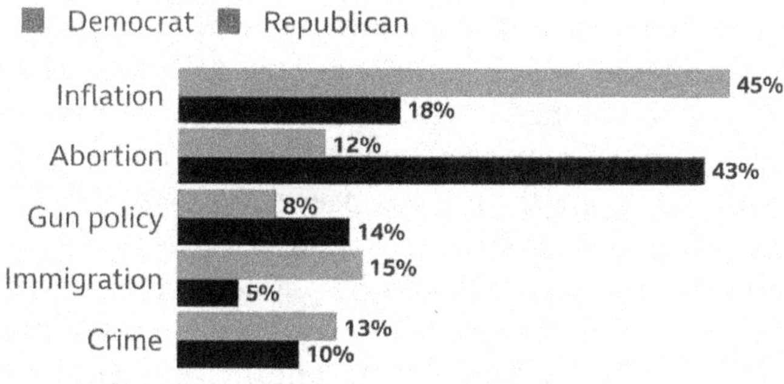

Sample size: 4,636 respondents.
Figures may not sum to 100 and all figures have a margin of error

Source: Edison Research/NEP via Reuters.

FIGURE 12.3

STATES BANNING ABORTION AND EXPANSION OF MEDICAID

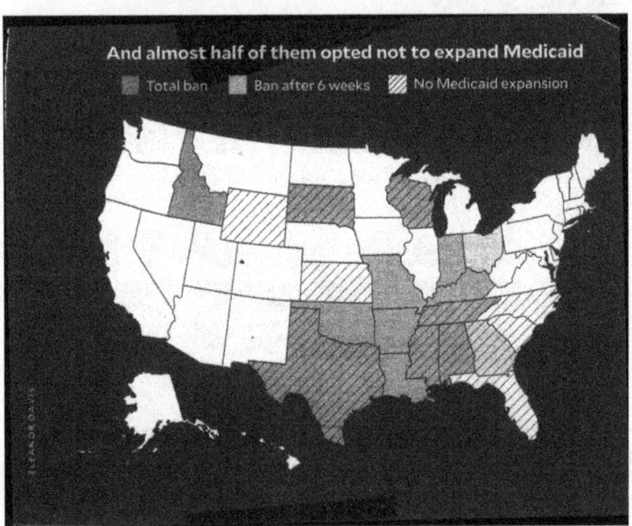

Source: Kaiser Family Foundation, June 29, 2022 and July 7, 2022

9. Democrats have been losing support in rural counties for some years, especially in the upper Midwest, where White working-class counties favored Trump by a margin of over 51 points in 2016. The enemy in rural America is often giant companies that won't allow farmers to repair their own tractors and hedge funds that buy up farmland and outbid locals. Democrats could do much better in rural counties if they campaign more actively there and recognize that while rural voters may be more conservative on such issues as guns, they are more progressive on such issues as increasing taxes on corporations and allowing Medicare to negotiate drug prices.[13] In bright red Nebraska, for example, almost 60% of the electorate voted for a $15 minimum wage.[14]
10. Voters' concerns about the future of U. S. democracy after the midterms were extraordinarily high with more than two-thirds thinking that democracy was somewhat or very threatened.[15] (Figure 12.4).

FIGURE 12.4

VIEWS OF THREAT TO DEMOCRACY

Do you think democracy in the US today is:

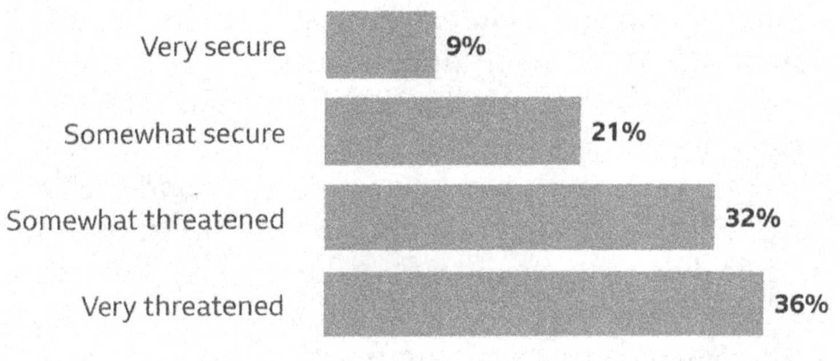

Sample size: 4,238 respondents.
Figures may not sum to 100 and all figures have a margin of error

Source: Edison Research/NEP via Reuters.

II. How the Forces Collided in the Run-up to the 2024 Elections

1. Internal battle within the GOP

What happened with Trumpism?

Although more than 210 election deniers won congressional seats, governor, secretary of state, or attorney general seats in 2022 elections,[16] the MAGA wave was but a ripple. Many Republicans blamed Trump for their poor showing in the midterms. When he announced his 2024 presidential candidacy, the response was lack-luster at best as his potential supporters heard him continue to claim "fake news." Dana Milbank, political columnist for *The Washington Post*, noted:

> *. . . angry man singing a song of himself.* [17] *The magic was missing —instead of the audience singing, it was just one.*

Trump talked about getting rid of the Constitution in this way:

> *A Massive Fraud of this type and magnitude allows for the termination of all rules, regulations, and articles, even those found in the Constitution . . . UNPRECEDENTED FRAUD REQURES UNPRECEDENTED CURE!* [18]

Trump's "platform," as in previous years, continues to wallow in a swamp, which he can never drain of grievance, conspiracy theory, racism, and white supremacy. But he still seems to have solid support of the conservative base and holds the GOP's front-runner position as challengers run against him and are polling poorly. Even the civil case that he lost for sexual assault didn't change his poll numbers. He had a field day with countless lies during CNN's gift of coverage for the live, prime-time New Hampshire Town Hall featuring a biased GOP attendance and Trump's continuous lies going virtually unchallenged. CNN came under fire afterwards for its departure from truth-seeking journalism as it sought increased ratings and viewership from the beleaguered Fox News, while giving an already twice impeached and indicted cult leader an open microphone without accountability. [19]

When the Republicans took control of the House of Representatives during the first week of January 2023, the battle for Speaker of the House made clear that they were not prepared or even interested in governing. A faction of 15 extremists, the MAGA Freedom Caucus, dominated the proceedings as votes for Speaker went to 15 ballots—for the first time in 100 years—before Rep. Kevin McCarthy was finally elected Speaker. That was after he had given away whatever power he would need to lead in the House. The concessions to the hard right members even included their ability to remove McCarthy at any time by just one of them calling for another vote to vacate the chair of the Speaker.[21]

The editors of the *Wall Street Journal* were moved to say this about the GOP's chaos caucus:

> *House Republicans have won two years in the majority to show the electorate they can govern better than Democrats and President Biden. They're getting off to the kind of start that will persuade even their own voters to send them back to the minority in short order.*[22]

As Trump the demagogue campaigns for the GOP presidential nomination, his rhetoric continues with lies well described by novelist and civil rights activist Toni Morrison this way:

> *At its core, his language: actively thwarts the intellect, stalls conscience, suppresses human potential . . . It cannot form or tolerate new ideas, shape other thoughts, tell another story, fill baffling silences . . . It is the language that drinks blood, laps vulnerabilities, tucks its fascist boots under crinolines of respectability and patriotism as it moves relentlessly toward the bottom line and the bottomed-out mind.* [23]

As a predictable result, death threats and violence and the odds of political violence have increased as the campaign moves along.

The GOP lacks its own policy agenda, and is just there to obstruct the dealings of necessary government to meet the nation's needs. The right-wing extremists of the House Freedom caucus have initiated investigations of the Bidens, the Select January 6 Committee, the FBI and others.

The recent release of the almost 1,000 page "Project 2025" handbook by the very conservative Heritage Foundation and its allies reveals the extent of the destructive plan of the Trump campaign should it win the 2024 election. Among its goals, it would gut the "administrative state" from within, fire as many as 50,000 federal workers, reclassify tens of thousands of the 2 million federal employees as at will workers who could more easily be fired, curb the independence of the Department of Justice, end FBI efforts to combat the spread of misinformation, and increase prosecution of those providing or distributing abortion pills by mail. It would greatly increase powers of the presidency over every part of the federal government, including revival of the practice of "impounding" funds, whereby the president can refuse to spend money appropriated by Congress for programs the president doesn't like.[24] He would use his office to attack his political enemies, telling his MAGA supporters that:

> *I am your warrior. I am your justice. And for those who have been wronged and betrayed, I am your retribution.*[25]

As Michael Tomasky warned in his signature piece in *The New Republic* in June 2023:

> *Donald Trump loves an America of his twisted imagination. He hates—and fears—the America that actually exists. And if he gets back to the White House . . . look out.* [26]

2. Realignment of the two major political parties

Big changes in the two parties have led Paul Starr to this analysis:

> *. . . the Democrats becoming the party of racial and cultural transformation, while the Republicans became the across-the-board party of backlash even as they remained the party of business, and then: the collapse of the center-right, the takeover of the Republican party by its ethnonationalist right wing, and the resulting uncertainty as to whether it can still be counted on to follow the basic rules of democratic government, like giving up power after losing an election.*[27]

Robert Reich describes four phases in the descent of the Republican Party to its present state of confusion and irrelevance:

1. *Half century ago: Party of limited government, overlooked corporate power, resisted civil rights, for lower taxes and against Democratic attempts to enlarge scope of federal power.*
2. *1990s: Cultural conservatism—against abortion, contraception, gay marriage, voting rights, immigration, and teaching of America's history of racism.*
3. *Resentment and authoritarianism—associated with decline of middle class, blockage of upward mobility, disappearing good-paying union jobs.*
4. *Epicenter of emerging anti-democratic movement fueled by hate and Trump.*[28]

Figure 12.5 brings us a graphic view of the devolution of the Republican Party.[29]

FIGURE 12.5

DE-EVOLUTION OF THE G.O.P.

Source: Permission by Molton Cartoons, Mountain Express

III. Developments Since the Midterms that Relate to 2024 Elections

1. The battle over abortion

The ruling by a Texas judge in April, 2023 to suspend the FDA's approval of mifepristone, an essential drug for medication abortion, challenged the FDA's authority and threatened to impose a nationwide ban on its use. In less than an hour, another federal judge in Washington State issued a ruling that directly contradicted the Texas ruling.[30] The DOJ also promptly moved to invalidate the Texas judge's ruling as the battle over abortion entered a new phase.[31, 32]

In the Republican-friendly gerrymandered state of Wisconsin, the State's supreme court saw a critical election break an evenly divided impasse in Democrats' favor. The liberal candidate, Janet Protasiewicz, won election by 11 percentage points, while the defeated right-wing judge refused to concede his loss.[33] That win is good news for likely reversal of Wisconsin's ban on abortion dating back to 1849 as well as overturning Republican friendly legislative maps.[34]

Abortion was a top issue energizing women and Democratic voters in the 2022 midterms. As a result, Republican congressional candidates won the U. S. House by a smaller- than-expected margin while also failing to win the Senate. A Gallup poll in mid-2023 found that support for abortion in the first trimester has reached a record high of 69%.[35] Gathering stories of the dangerous situations encountered by pregnant women in states with abortion bans added support to an energized pro-choice movement. A national Kaiser Family Foundation survey found that 69% of practicing obstetricians reported that abortion bans worsen their ability to safely manage pregnancy in such states, further warning that pregnancy-related mortality would increase, together with increased racial and ethnic inequities in maternal health (70%).[36] In response to restrictive state abortion laws and hostile state legislatures, physicians caring for high-risk pregnancies are leaving what were already considered maternity care deserts, such as Idaho, Oklahoma, and Tennessee.[37]

It is therefore likely that the abortion issue will be a major, even defining issue in the 2024 elections. Fortunately, however, the Supreme Court's threat to contraception has been nullified by the recent approval by the F.D.A. of Opill, an effective over-the-counter daily contraceptive to become available in early 2024.[38]

2. Supreme Court: Originalism vs. Evolving with Times

Today's U. S. Supreme Court, dominated by five conservative ideologues, including three appointed during the Trump administration, is wedded to the past and tone-deaf to current politics and needs. In a 2022 article, Bill Blum, a Los Angeles attorney and former State of California administrative law judge, describes the current situation:

> *Originalism has led the court to enter a legal fantasy world in which the answers to contemporary questions about matters such as voting rights and gerrymandering, union organizing, the death penalty, abortion, and gun control are to be found solely in the meaning that the Constitution had for the Founding Fathers. For originalists, this meaning is forever fixed, and can only be altered by Constitutional amendments.* [39]

The Supreme Court's past rulings have been made worse by its lack of an enforceable ethical code of conduct. The Senate Judiciary Committee recently held a hearing looking into its ethical standards and pressing Chief Justice Roberts to investigate the long-standing relationship of Justice Clarence Thomas with Harlan Crow, a Texas real estate billionaire.[31] But even as more brazen undisclosed conflicts of interest and evidence of corruption involving several Justices and their families continued to emerge, Chief Justice Roberts refused to appear before that Committee.[40]

3. *What did the GOP do with its new control of the House*

The McCarthy battle for the House Speakership was a farce from start to finish, during which he ceded virtually all of his potential authority to the other members of the Freedom Caucus. He could be voted out by them at any time over any issue. Despite that beginning, however, those extreme House members continued to pursue an extremist, anti-life, anti-freedom and anti-American agenda as they sought to criminalize abortion, refused to deal with gun violence, and attempted to force cuts in Social Security and Medicare (created in 1935 and 1965, respectively) and various safety net programs. On April 26, 2023, they barely passed their Debt Reduction Act by one vote in their caucus. That deciding vote was cast by Rep. George Santos (D-NY), well known for his widespread lying that resulted in federal prosecutors in New York filing multiple criminal charges against him.[41]

The extreme GOP House members showed their true anti-democratic and anti-American colors in dealing with the debt ceiling crisis, attempting to hold President Biden and much of Congress hostage unless they acceded to draconian spending cuts and not raising the debt limit. As Treasury Secretary Janet Yellen warned of economic disaster here and around the world if that limit was not raised by June 1, a game of chicken ensued as McCarthy showed little knowledge about the issue or concern about its consequences. He seemed unaware that the debt limit had been raised three times without preconditions during the Trump administration (2017, 2018, and 2019), for which he had voted![42] The debt ceiling had also been extended or revised 78 separate times since 1960, 49 under Republican administrations and 29 under Democratic presidents.[43] Moreover, the Trump administration added $7.8 trillion to the national debt, more than any president before him, including the 2017 GOP tax cut with 83% of the benefits going to the wealthiest 1%.[44]

After intense and prolonged partisan wrangling over the debt limit, a bipartisan deal was finally struck to raise the debt limit for two years—past the 2024 elections to January of 2025— and capping some government spending. Although the Republican Freedom Caucus and many progressives were unhappy with the outcome, it passed in the House by a bipartisan 314-117 vote.[45] Default on the debt was averted at the last moment as the bill soon passed the Senate (63-36). Instead of a recession through debt default, President Biden could take credit for his deal-making prowess. [46]

But that was not to last, as predicted by Katrina Vanden Heuvel, editorial director and publisher of *The Nation:*

> *The debt ceiling is not repealed; it is simply kicked down the road to after the election. The bill does little to reduce federal budget deficits but succeeds in once more elevating and distorting the importance of debt and deficits, at a time when the dollar is still strong, and the country faces far more pressing challenges. . . At a time of obscene inequality, nothing is done to reverse the perverse tax cuts handed out to the rich and corporations over the past decades.*[47]

The next crisis was just three months down the road, threatening government shutdown by October 1, 2023. Five far-right members of the Freedom Caucus refused to allow a bipartisan Pentagon spending bill to come up for debate just days before the September 30 deadline. [48] Another big fight with MAGA House extremists pushing for deep spending cuts forcing government shutdown culminated with Speaker McCarthy caving to them and using Democratic votes to pass a 45-day continuing resolution to keep the government open until November 17th. That CR was immediately passed by a vote of 335-91 in the House, by 88 to 9 in the Senate (including 39 Republican senators), and signed by President Biden just under the wire.

Crises resumed days later when McCarthy's position was vacated by a vote of 216 to 210 in response to a motion put forward by far-right Matt Gaetz (R-FL) of the Freedom Caucus. Eight GOP hard-liners joined Democrats to remove McCarthy from the Speakership, the first such occurrence in U. S. history, leaving the House chamber in chaos and showing how the GOP was unable to govern.[49] The House was shut down for almost four weeks as potential candidates fought it out before another GOP House vote to name his replacement. Figure 12.6 illustrates how far from a realistic view of the needs of the country the House GOP had fallen.

FIGURE 12.6

THE OTHER VACATED REPUBLICAN SEAT

Source: Reprinted with permission from Nick Anderson

As the House Speaker's position continued unfilled over the next consecutive weeks in October, and while the new Israel-Hamas war destabilized the Middle East, the editorial board of the *New York Times* drew this conclusion:

> *The U. S. Capitol may be perched on a hill, but it is understandable why so many Americans look down upon it. One of the main reasons is that their Congress, which ought to be a global beacon of liberal values, continues to succumb to self-inflicted paralysis. How else can it be that fewer than a dozen lawmakers from the outer fringes of the Republican Party are holding one of the world's democracies hostage to their wildest whims?* [50]

After three weeks of infighting among the House Republicans, Rep. Mike Johnson (R-LA) was elected House Speaker in a 220-209 vote, becoming the 56th Speaker of the House of Representatives just three weeks before the November 17 government funding deadline. As an election denier and hard-right religious conservative, he had been an early and active supporter of Trump's scheme to overturn the 2020 election results and is opposed to abortion rights, homosexuality and gay marriage.[51] He is also a strong supporter of cuts to Social Security, Medicare, and Medicaid. He is ranked almost at the bottom among 435 lawmakers for bipartisanship on a 2021 bipartisan index, but unlike McCarthy, will have the support of the Freedom Caucus on the House floor.[52]

Jennifer Rubin of *The Washington Post* drew this conclusion from all these circumstances:

> *The pandemonium surrounding the selection of a House Speaker points to the party's inability to govern itself, let alone the country. We can expect plenty of other MAGA outbursts and mayhem with this faction's nihilistic approach to politics—including, for example, the baseless impeachment effort against Biden—between now and the 2024 elections. Biden would have no trouble making the case against agents of anarchy, destruction and dysfunction. It should not surprise us that a party that embraces conspiracy theories, spews propaganda and seeks to empower a candidate with authoritarian impulses is incapable of governess.*[53]

The Brennan Center for Justice warns us of Speaker Johnson's election-denying background, his push to decertify 2020 election results in key states, and his support for the independent state legislature theory whereby state legislators can control the process and results of federal elections in their states. Trump immediately gave him his full support, labelling him MAGA Mike.[54] True to form, with the first bill that he brought to the House floor as Speaker for a vote, the House voted to claw back billions of dollars in IRS funding that has allowed the agency to crack down on wealthy and corporate tax cheats.[55]

Then, with a government shutdown facing the country unless the debt limit was extended by November 17, 2023, the House finally passed, by a bipartisan vote of 336 to 95, a bill funding federal agencies at current funding levels with two different expiration dates—January 19 and February 2, 2024. It took 209 Democrats to rescue a plan opposed by many Republicans, once again showing that the House Republicans were not prepared to govern.[56] That bill went on to pass the Senate and be signed by President Biden by the deadline, but future House battles before the 2024 expiration dates could be expected, such as over spending cuts to the departments of Justice, State and Commerce Departments, including budget cuts for the F.B.I.[57]

While a tentative bipartisan agreement was reached for an overall top line of $1.59 trillion by the end of the Christmas/New Year break, later difficult negotiations could still be expected by the January 19 deadline over such issues ranging from support for the Ukraine war and U.S. border security.

3. *What has happened to the rule of law?*

There have been so many investigations of Donald J. Trump's nefarious business and political activities in recent years that it is difficult to keep track of them. Figure 12.7 summarizes the status of criminal cases involving the former president as of August 3, 2023.[58]

FIGURE 12.7

STATUS OF CRIMINAL CASES AGAINST TRUMP

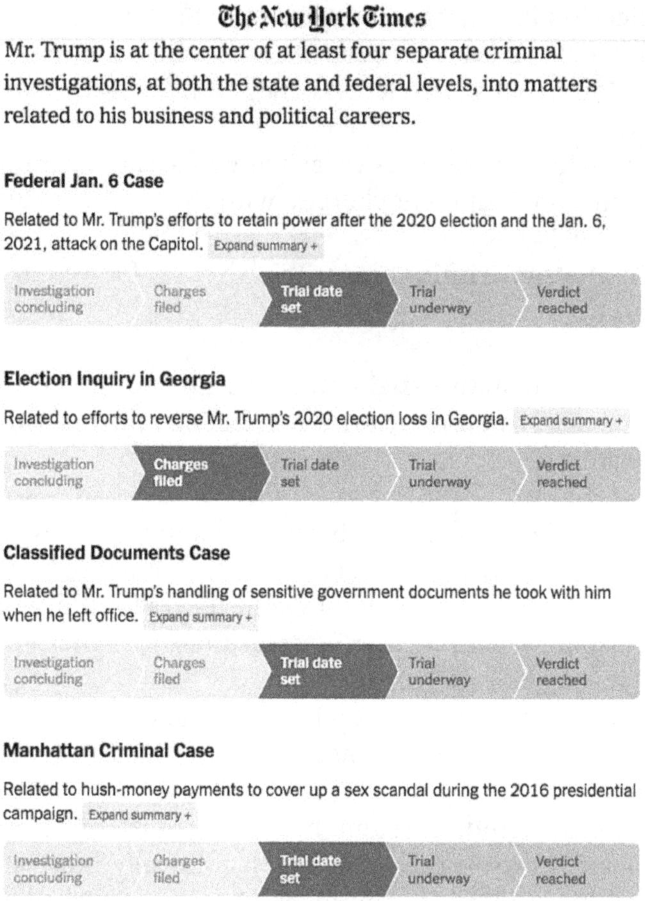

The New York Times

Mr. Trump is at the center of at least four separate criminal investigations, at both the state and federal levels, into matters related to his business and political careers.

Federal Jan. 6 Case

Related to Mr. Trump's efforts to retain power after the 2020 election and the Jan. 6, 2021, attack on the Capitol. Expand summary +

Investigation concluding | Charges filed | **Trial date set** | Trial underway | Verdict reached

Election Inquiry in Georgia

Related to efforts to reverse Mr. Trump's 2020 election loss in Georgia. Expand summary +

Investigation concluding | **Charges filed** | Trial date set | Trial underway | Verdict reached

Classified Documents Case

Related to Mr. Trump's handling of sensitive government documents he took with him when he left office. Expand summary +

Investigation concluding | Charges filed | **Trial date set** | Trial underway | Verdict reached

Manhattan Criminal Case

Related to hush-money payments to cover up a sex scandal during the 2016 presidential campaign. Expand summary +

Investigation concluding | Charges filed | **Trial date set** | Trial underway | Verdict reached

Source: *The New York Times*

Since then, as this book goes to press, the following updates have occurred in each of the four major criminal cases:

- **Federal Jan. 6 and 2020 election inquiry:** Judge Tanya S. Chutkan rejected Trump's request for a trial date in 2026 as she set it for March 4, 2024, citing the need to meet the public interest well before the 2024 Elections; she further ruled that "Former Presidents enjoy no special conditions on their federal criminality. Defendant may be subject to federal investigation, indictment, prosecution, conviction, and punishment for any criminal acts undertaken while in office."[59]
- **Election inquiry in Georgia:** As of September 1, 2023, a trial date had not yet been set as sparring continued with Fulton County District Attorney Fani Willis involving 19 defendants.[60]
- **Classified documents case:** Trump faces 40 criminal counts on 7 different charges, with the trial scheduled in May 2024.[61]
- **Manhattan criminal case:** Trial date set for March 25, 2024.

All of these tentative trial dates are in flux as Trump's appeals and delaying actions play out, with March 2024 the most likely earliest such date.[62]

Already, the rule of law has been upheld in these ways:

- January 6 investigations have resulted in upholding rule of law with accountability—4 Oathkeepers for seditious conspiracy, with further investigations of higher ups re- planning and coordination. [63]
- Trump indicted for sexually abusing and defaming E. Jean Carroll. $5 million payments. [64]

On the other hand, as Trump has appeared in courts in his own defense to avoid prison time, his angry politically motivated rhetoric has led to an increasing number of armed attacks by MAGA lone wolves against public officials in Congress, statehouses and local offices across the country. This pattern has been called weaponization of the 2nd amendment and stochastic terrorism. Polls have found that one in three respondents now believe that political violence against the Wisconsin governor can be excused on that basis.[65]

Even more worrisome in Trump's escalating rhetoric was this Hitler-like pledge declared at his November 11, 2023 Veterans Day speech in Claremont, New Hampshire:

> *If he's elected in 2024, declaring to "root out" the "radical left thugs that live like vermin within the confines of our country", declaring further that "We are a failing nation. We are a nation in serious decline."* And also: *The real threat is not from the radical right; the real threat is from the radical left, and it's growing every day, every single day.*[67]

5. What has happened with inflation?

Inflation rose as the economy rebounded from the COVID pandemic during supply chain disruptions and labor shortages. The Federal Reserve tries to keep the consumer price index (CPI) under control through periodic interest rate increases. The Fed has raised interest rates nine times over the last year with the intent to cool the economy and tame inflation, but that seems to be the only approach in its toolkit.[68]

Consumers and voters evaluate the administration and candidates for the next election on the basis of the prices they find for such items as groceries, gasoline, utilities and medical care. Meanwhile, as we saw in Chapter 2, corporate monopolies and price gouging are the main drivers of inflation in our economy, avoiding control and not well covered by the mainstream media. Instead, the public hears from the media that recession is just around the corner. As one current example, Big Food corporations hiked their prices to gain combined net earnings in the first quarter of 2023 by 51% over the year 2022 to a combined $3.47 billion. As that was taking place, at least 34 million people live in food-insecure households, according to the U. S. Department of Agriculture.[69]

A new report from the progressive watchdog group Accountable. US has drawn these conclusions about corporate drivers of inflation:

> *It is clear that the corporate profiteering epidemic will persist no matter how many times the Fed doubles down . . . Corporate greed is a stubborn thing and required serious action from Congress.*[70]

6. Coordinated assault on democracy

The several years since the 2020 elections have seen unprecedented fascist behavior by GOP state governments in a number of red states across the country, including:

- Florida, where GOP presidential candidate Governor Ron DeSantis has imposed the tightest immigration measures by any state in more than 10 years, new voter restrictions; banning of books in school libraries that record the country's racist past, and open carry gun policies even down to age 18. [71]
- Virginia, where a Jim Crow-era voting law is being re-applied that disproportionately impacts Black voters.
- Tennessee, where conservatives in the State House expelled duly elected Black legislators and continue to disregard the urgent need to rein in gun violence.
- Mississippi, where state conservatives are instituting legislation that removes power from Black Mississippians in Jackson.
- Alabama, where a GOP bill has been introduced whereby the state is granted the authority to arrest and charge women with murder if they willfully terminate their pregnancies.[72]

As these kinds of anti-democratic actions take place around the country, the words 'oligarchy' and 'fascism' have become part of our everyday language, as exemplified by the January/February 2024 issues of *The Atlantic*, (*If Trump Wins*) and of *Mother Jones*, (*American Oligarchy*).

Eric Holder, Jr., former Attorney General in the Obama administration, had this to say about these actions:

> *These brazen actions are part of a years-long effort by conservative extremists to stifle the voice of the people and exert anti-democratic control over our nation's ideals and infrastructures.* [73]
>
> —Eric Holder, 82nd Attorney General of the United States

The above post-2022 midterm developments would have to be dealt with in the 2024 elections. It is helpful to recall these classic words by Dr. Martin Luther King, Jr., which are ever so important today:

> *We are all caught in an inescapable network of mutuality, tied in a single garment of destiny. Whatever affects one directly affects all indirectly.*[74]
>
> — King, ML Jr. Legendary civil rights leader and political philosopher

New York Times columnist David Brooks adds his voice to the 2024 elections representing a continuing battle for the soul of America:

> *The contest between Biden and Trumpism is less Democrat versus Republican or liberal versus conservative than it is between an essentially moral vision and an essentially amoral one, a contest between decency and the opposite.* [75]

CONCLUSION:

The status of Donald Trump remains unclear as this book goes to press—whether or not he will be further indicted and face prison time as a result of one or more of his criminal convictions. Whenever the January 6 investigation is closed, however, famed Harvard constitutional law professor Lawrence Tribe has already called for Attorney General Merrick Garland to prosecute Trump for seditious conspiracy. He further believes that Special Counsel Jack Smith will likely indict him on additional counts, and that the Republic will be "in grave danger if Trump is not held accountable under the rule of law." [76] Whatever the circumstances are as the election campaigns wind up to November of 2024, the voters will decide, in probably the most important election in our history, the future of American democracy.

References:

1. Levitsky, S, Ziblatt, D. *Tyranny of the Minority*. New York. *Crown Publishing Company*, 2023, p. 225.
2. Reich, R. *The System: Who Rigged It, How We Fix It*. New York. *Alfred A. Knopf*, 2020, p. 18.
3. United States Election Project. National General Election VEP Turnout Rates, 1789-Present. (http://www.electproject.org/national-1789-present.)

4. Dionne, E. J. Jr. and Rapoport, M. 100% *Democracy: The Case for Universal Voting*. New York. *The New Press*, 2022, p. xxii.
5. Reich, R. Corporations said they'd stop. They have not. *Inequality Media Civic Action*, October 2, 2022.
6. Zitner, A, McCormick, J. Turnout, swing voters aided Democrats. *Wall Street Journal*, November 10, 2022: A 6.
7. Leonhardt, D. Younger voters are turning out more than ever, and they're leaning left. *New York Times,* June 6, 2023.
8. Kuttner, R. Did we just save democracy? *The American Prospect*, November 11, 2022.
9. Scherer, M, Dawsey, J, Knowles, H et al. How Trump, infighting and flawed candidates limited Republican gains. *The Washington Post*, November 10, 2022.
10. Data journalism team. U. S. midterm elections results: How the parties did in maps and charts. *BBC News*, November 24, 2022.
11. Kusisto, L, Calfas, J. Abortion-rights measures prevail, indicating a post-Roe backlash. *Wall Street Journal*, November 10, 2022: D 7.
12. Murphy, T, Democracy was on the ballot. It won the chance to stay there. *Mother Jones*, November/December 2022.
13. Kuttner, R. The rural turnaround. *The Progressive Populist*, 28 (22), December 15, 2022, pp. 1, 8.
14. Hightower, J. Lessons from midterm elections. *The Progressive Populist* 28 (22), December 15, 2022, p. 2.
15. Reich, R. Keeping the Senate! Woo-hoo! (almost). (substack.com), November 14, 2022.
16. Stancil, K. 210+ GOP candidates who spread doubt and lies about 2020 election won their races. *Common Dreams*, November 9, 2022.
17. Milbank, D. At Trump's angry announcement, the magic is gone. *The Progressive Populist* 28 (22), December 15, 2022.
18. Trump, D.J. As quoted by Demirjian, K, Olorunnipa, T. White House rebukes Trump's suggestion to suspend Constitution over 2020 election. *The Washington Post*, December 3, 2022.
19. Grynbaum, MM, Mullin, B. CNN asserts Trump event was service to the public. *New York Times*, May 12, 2023.
20. Morrison, T, as quoted by Giroux, HA. Mouths full of blood: Trump and his backers spread lies, violence and fascism. *Truthout*, September 23, 2023.
21. Edmondson, C. House approves rules as Speaker sways holdouts: Concessions at issue. *New York Times*, January 10, 2023.
22. Review and Outlook. The GOP's chaos caucus returns. *Wall Street Journal*, January 4, 2023.
23. Mascaro, L. Conservatives aim to restructure U. S. government and replace it with Trump's vision. PBS News Hour. *Associated Press*, August 29, 2023.
24. Swan, J, Savage, C, Haberman, M. Trump and allies forge plans to increase presidential power in 2025. *New York Times*, July 28, 2023.
25. Trump, DJ. As quoted by Tomasky, M. Donald Trump against America. *The New Republic*, June 2023, p. 19.
26. Tomasky, M. Donald Trump against America. *The New Republic*, June 2023, p. 12.

27. Starr, P. How American politics turned deadly: The explosive consequences of the realignment of the two major parties. *The American Prospect*, August 2022, p. 57.
28. Reich, R. The party's over. The end of the GOP. *Substack*, January 3, 2023.
29. Reich, R. The GOP's death cycle. December 7, 2023. <robertreich@substack.com
30. Belluck, P. Judge invalidates F.D.A. approval of the abortion pill mifepristone. *New York Times*, April 7, 2023.
31. Kusisto, L, Whyte, LE. DOJ files appeal to keep abortion pill legal. *Wall Street Journal*, April 11, 2023, A:1.
32. Jewett, C, Belluck, P. Abortion drug ruling could bring 'chaos' to F.D.A.'s authority. *New York Times*, April 10, 2023 A: 13.1.
33. Epstein, RJ. Post-Roe lift in Wisconsin fuels the left. *New York Times*, April 6, 2023: A:1.
34. Conley, J. Defeated right-wing judge refuses to concede to victor he deems not 'worthy'. *Common Dreams*, April 5, 2023.
35. Kusisto, L. Abortion battle scrambles politics. *Wall Street Journal*, June 24-25, 2023: A: 1.
36. Rubin, J. Opinion. A year after Dobbs, the pro-choice movement has never been stronger. *The Washington Post*, June 26, 2023.
37. Stolberg, SG. Help for risky pregnancies drops as doctors flee abortion limits. *New York Times*, September 7, 2023, A:1.
38. Belluck, P. F.D.A. approves selling of pill over counter. *New York Times*, July 14, 2023, A:1.
39. Blum, B. The new era of rightwing judicial supremacy. *The Progressive Magazine*, August 1, 2022.
40. Hulse, C. Senate Judiciary Committee promises hearing into ethics of Supreme Court. *New York Times*, April 11, 2023, A:17.
41. Gold M, Rashbaum, WK, Ashford, G. George Santos is charged by federal prosecutors in New York. *New York Times*, May 9, 2023.
42. Jayshi D. Did GOP vote to raise debt ceiling 3 times with no preconditions during Trump era? *Snopes*, May 3, 2023.
43. Kass, D. There aren't just two choices on the debt ceiling crisis. *Americans for Tax Fairness*, May 13, 2023.
44. Stancil, K. House Dems unveil hail Mary plan to defuse GOP's debt ceiling 'ticking time bomb.' *Common Dreams*, May 2, 2023.
45. Hughes, S, Andrews, N. House passes debt-ceiling, spending deal, *Wall Street Journal*, June 1, 2023, A:1.
46. Rubin, J. Opinion: Biden's underrated deal-making prowess strikes again, *The Washington Post*, May 30, 2023.
47. Vanden Heuvel, K. Once more, the Washington debt ceiling ritual ends in a lousy deal. *The Progressive Populist*, July 1-15, 2023, p. 12.
48. Hulse, C. 5 far-right G.O.P. members frustrate McCarthy on Pentagon spending bill. *New York Times*, September 20, 2023, A:18.
49. Edmondson, C, Hulse, C, Parlapiano, A. House Republicans push deep cuts to spending bills they rarely back. *New York Times*, July 3, 2023, A:14.

50. Editorial Board. America deserves better than a government held hostage by extremists. *New York Times*, October 5, 2023, A:22.
51. Edmonson, C. G.O.P. elects Speaker, ending bitter feud. *New York Times*, October 26, 2023, A:1.
52. Gillum, J, Peterson, K, Ball, M. Social conservative, a Trump ally, takes helm. *Wall Street Journal*, October 26, 2023, A:4.
53. Rubin, J. Opinion. Democrats' all-purpose message for 2024: Defeat MAGA chaos. *The Washington Post*, October 30, 2023.
54. Team DASS. Democratic Association of Secretaries of State, November 2, 2023.
55. The IRS plans to crack down on 1,600 millionaires to collect millions of dollars in back taxes. *Associated Press*, September 8, 2023.
56. Edmondson, C. House passes Johnson's plan to avert shutdown in bipartisan vote. *New York Times*, November 14, 2023.
57. Firestone, D. The fight many House Republicans really want. Opinion. *New York Times*, November 17, 2023, A:22.
58. Smart, C, Gamio, L, Escobar, MC, et al. The Trump investigations. Keeping track of the criminal cases. *New York Times National*, August 3, 2023, A:14.
59. Feuer, A, Thrush, G. Trial for Trump is set for March in federal case. *New York Times*, August 29, 2023, A:1.
60. Chutkan, TS, as quoted by Rubin, J. Trump's biggest loss yet: No immunity. *The Washington Post*, December 4, 2023.
61. Hakim, D, Fausset, R. Trump pleads not guilty in Georgia case as he waives his arraignment. *New York Times National*, September 1, 2023, A:15.
62. Gregorian, D, Reiss, A. Trump on trial: What to expect in 2024. *NBC News*, December 28, 2023.
63. Gurman, S, Acosta, D. Smith seeks January trial for Trump vote case. *Wall Street Journal*, August 11, 2023, A:4.
64. Wilkens, B Jury case finds Trump sexually abused defamed E. Jean Carroll in civil case. *Common Dreams*, May 9, 2023.
65. Wallace, N. Deadline White House MSNBC show on October 5, 2023.
66. Levenson, M. Armed man seeking Wisconsin governor posts bail and returns with rifle. *New York Times*, October 5, 2023.
67. Johnson, J. Trump issues sinister threat to 'root out' leftists if elected in 2024. *Common Dreams*, November 12, 2023.
68. Guilford, G, Timiraos, N. U. S. inflation eased to 5% in March, *Wall Street Journal*, April 12, 2023.
69. Corbett, J. Big food raking in huge profits from price hikes as U. S. hunger persists: Analysis. *Common Dreams*, May 10, 2023.
70. Johnson, J. Top U.S. companies admit to hiking prices to pad their profits: analysis. *Common Dreams*, June 13, 2023.
71. Jordan, M. DeSantis seeks tightest clamp on immigration in the country. *New York Times*, April 11, 2023: A:1.
72. Walker, C. Alabama GOP bill aims to charge people who get an abortion with murder. *Truthout*, May 12, 2023.
73. Holder, EH. This is a deliberate and coordinate assault on our democracy. *All On the Line*, April 11, 2023.

74. King, ML Jr. As quoted by Senator Raphael Warnock, January 16, 2023.
75. Brooks, D. Biden and the struggle for America's soul. Op-Ed. *New York Times*, April 28, 2023, A:23.
76. Luttig, JM, Tribe, LH. The Constitution prohibits Trump from ever becoming president again. *The Atlantic*, August 19, 2023.

CHAPTER 13

THE 2024 ELECTIONS: THE SURVIVAL OF OUR DEMOCRACY IS ON THE BALLOT

For over 30 years, the American public has been reared on a neoliberal dystopian vision that legitimates itself through the largely unchallenged claim that there are no alternatives to a market-driven society, that economic growth should not be constrained by considerations of social costs or moral responsibility and that democracy and capitalism were virtually synonymous. At the heart of this market rationality is an egocentric philosophy and culture of cruelty that sold off public goods and services to the highest bidders in the corporate and private sectors, while simultaneously dismantling those public spheres, social protections and institutions serving the public good.[1]

—Professor Henry Giroux, Professor of English and Cultural Studies at McMaster University in Canada

The true story of American democracy is that it is never finished. It is the story of people who have honored the idea that a nation can be based not in land or religion or race or hierarchies, but rather in the concept of human equality.[2]

—Heather Cox Richardson, Professor of History at Boston College and author of *Democracy Awakening*

So now let us see where we are in "serving the public good" as the 2024 elections draw nigh in our divided and polarized country. The goals of this final chapter are: (1) to bring some brief perspective to policies of neoliberalism that have come to threaten democracy in this country; (2) to briefly describe the dangerous circumstances as the two major political parties proceed toward the 2024 elections; (3) to discuss some useful steps for the road ahead toward renewed democracy; and (4) to consider why we can be guardedly optimistic that democracy can be rejuvenated in this country.

I. The Havoc of Neoliberalism

Challenging times that we are in today are no accident. They are the predictable end result of what Ronald Reagan intended when he took office as President 41 years ago. He saw government as the problem as he promised to end the American experiment of pluralistic liberal democracy. Thom Hartmann, author of *The Hidden History of American Oligarchy*, asks and answers the question of what the final stage of Reaganism would look like:

> ***We're there. Reaganism brought us:***
> - *the collapse of the middle class;*
> - *student and medical debt that's impossible to climb out of;*
> - *an explosion of predation of health insurance companies and for-profit hospitals;*
> - *political manipulation by corporations and billionaires;*
> - *an explosion of homelessness and untreated mental illness;*
> - *and turned our elementary schools into killing fields.*
>
> ***As further examples, he cites:***
> - *violence toward women and minorities has exploded.*
> - *armed militias tried to assassinate the Vice President and Speaker of the House in an attempted coup directed by the Republican President of the United States;*
> - *they tried to kidnap and murder the Democratic governor of Michigan;*
> - *they're blowing up power substations from Oregon to the Carolinas;*
> - *they've embedded themselves in DHS, police departments, and our military;*
> - *they're coordinating with fascists overseas.*[3]

Income and wealth inequality among Americans is greater than at any time in our history. A recent report by Oxfam International found that two thirds of all new wealth in the world has flowed into the hands of the top 1% since 2020. For every $1 gained by a person in the bottom 90 percent by wealth since 2020, a billionaire acquired $1.7 million. This decade is being described as the best yet for billionaires— a roaring '20s boom for the world's richest.[4] Recent decades have proven that tax cuts for the rich do not result in their wealth 'trickling down' to everybody else, with 81 billionaires now owning more wealth than the bottom one-half of humanity.[5] Figure 13.1 shows the adverse impacts of economic and tax policies on our society that were brought in by the Reagan Revolution.[6]

FIGURE 13.1

INCOME GROWTH AFTER TAXES AND BENEFITS BY INCOME GROUP

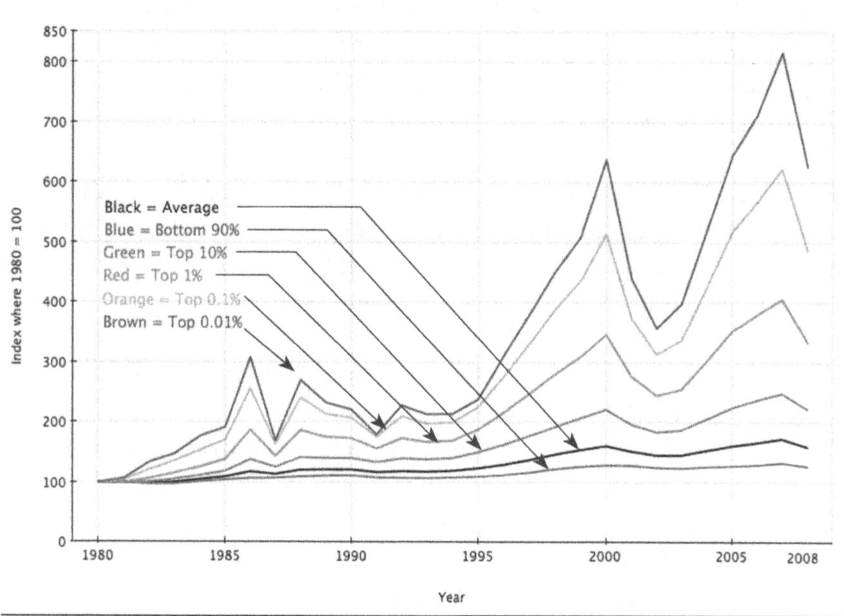

Source: Piketty and Seaz, World Top Incomes Database

Other experts from different vantage points draw these useful conclusions as to how we have come to this place. Robert Kuttner, well-known economist, co-founder of *The American Prospect* and author of *Everything for Sale: The Virtues and Limits of Markets and Can Democracy Survive Global Capitalism?*, observes:

> *The era since 1981 has been one of turning away from public remediation, toward tax cuts, limited social spending, deregulation, and privatization. None of this has worked well, except for the very top. For everyone else, the shift to conservative policies generated more economic insecurity.* [7]
>
> —Robert Kuttner

Chris Lehmann, D.C. Bureau Chief for *The Nation Magazine*, notes:

> *Republicans remain committed to promoting the interests of the wealthy in government . . . By focusing on the abuses of oligarchy—the rampant migration of top- heavy economic power into political life—Democrats can build on the outcome of the 2022 midterms to make an argument for expanding provisional, pandemic era commitments to social democratic justice into the broader spheres of working life and civil society.*[8]

So now, almost three years after Trump's failed attempt to overthrow our way of government and democracy, Public Citizen reminds us that this infamous event was the product of years of democratic backsliding in these kinds of ways:

- The lies, racism and propaganda of Fox News and the far-right media ecosystem;
- Years-long efforts by Republicans to disenfranchise voters of color;
- Big corporation dominance of our politics and economy that has left many voters alienated and hurting;
- Extreme racial and partisan gerrymandering that has led to the election of far right extremists that traffic in conspiracy and fascism;
- Trump and the Trump cult's embrace of authoritarianism.[9]

II. What Each Party Brings to the 2024 Elections

1. Who are the candidates at the top of the ticket for the two major parties?"

For the Democrats, President Joe Biden, again with his vice president running mate, Kamala Harris, filed their candidacies early, on April 26, 2023, with a virtual lock to again win his party's nomination. As he embarked on this second presidential campaign, he called attention to his first term's accomplishments, including the Inflation Reduction Act, the American Rescue Plan, and the CHIPS Act. He summarized his achievements as working to save democracy and the soul of America, and that now he had to "finish the job."[7] He framed his platform as a fight for freedom, with voting rights and abortion access as examples of freedoms under serious threat. Vice President Kamala Harris, once again his running mate, warned especially against "Maga extremists."[11]

For the Republicans, the GOP ticket is more difficult to explain. Former President Donald Trump, acting as cult leader for the Make America Great Again (MAGA) movement, soaks up almost all of the news surrounding the election. He frames his candidacy as saving the country under the guise of White Christian Nationalism, clearly racist in itself.[12] He remains the front runner as this book goes to press, despite his continuing to spread the Big Lie, his multiple indictments and anti-democratic views, including the January 6 attempted coup against the U. S. Capitol. He talks about the January 6 insurrection attack as "a beautiful day," denies that there was any danger to his vice president, Mike Pence, and says that if elected he would pardon many of those involved in the attacks. [13]

In openly fascist and civil insurrection kind of talk, Trump frames the 2024 election as "the final battle to save our dying country." Together with a well-funded network of conservative groups, he plans a sweeping expansion of presidential power, concentrating greater authority in his own hands, bringing independent government agencies under direct presidential control and getting rid of tens of thousands of career civil servants.[14] If elected, he would pursue criminal cases against President Biden and his political adversaries, weaponize the DOJ and FBI for that purpose, and expand the powers of the National Guard and state officials to arrest and deport people.[15]

In his 2020 book, *How Fascism Works: The Politics of Us and Them,* Jason Stanley, Professor of Philosophy at Yale University, brings us this perspective:

> *We can think of fascist politics as a politics of hierarchy (for example, in the United States, white supremacy demands and implies a perpetual hierarchy), and to realize that hierarchy, we can think of it as the displacement of reality by power.*[16]

As Trump maintains strong support from the Republican base and as his legal problems mount, *New York Times* columnist Charles Blow observes:

> *His primary standing is because he is making a political militia of the Republican Party itself, with its core voters activated to defend him no matter what . . . He has been unflinchingly loyal to them, and his followers are simply reciprocating . . . They don't worry about Trump torching the country if he's re-elected, because they believe that they will frolic in the ashes. They believe that whatever benefits Trump will eventually benefit them. Trump has deceived his people into believing trickle down tyranny.*[17]

Cartoonist John Darkow has a field day in picturing what would have happened had Abraham Lincoln been Trump in Civil War times (Figure 13.2).

FIGURE 13.2

IF LINCOLN HAD BEEN TRUMP

Source: CABLE CARTOONS, Reprinted with permission

As he skips GOP debates with his opponents, candidate Trump talks about retribution against those who cross him, and already asserts that it would be voter fraud if he were to lose the 2024 election.[18] In fact, nonpartisan pro-democracy groups are already tracking 185 bills introduced or passed in 38 states that would put election administrators in an "untenable position" and make it easier for partisans to manipulate 2024 election results.[19]

Trump is clearly dangerous and a serious threat to the survival of democracy in this country. However, as a former public official who has engaged in insurrection, he would be disqualified from ever holding public office again if Section 3 of the 14th Amendment to the U. S. Constitution were ever to be enforced.[20] If he were ever to be elected despite multiple indictments and all of his negative baggage, he would be barred by the Constitution from using the pardon power to prevent his own impeachment and removal from office.[21]

Remarkably, although about 10 candidates had initially filed their intent to oppose Trump, most did not take him on directly. Some dropped out of the race, and the primary debates, which Trump avoided altogether, did not alter his frontrunner position. Even after Special Counsel Jack Smith unsealed his 49-page federal indictment against Trump with 7 charges and 37 counts, his GOP rivals tended to defend him while labeling the indictment a gross injustice.[22]

2. How do the political parties compare in public polling and voter perceptions?

For the Democrats:

They bring to the table impressive legislative achievements during Biden's first term, including trying to curb prescription drug prices, rebuilding the nation's infrastructure, expanding health benefits for veterans, and slowing climate change. Biden reversed the attacks on our government and its institutions by the preceding Trump administration. The Biden administration also strengthened our foreign policy, strengthened the European Union, helped defend against the Soviet invasion of Ukraine, and supported Israel in defending itself after the October 7, 2023 attacks by Hamas. Biden called early on for a cease fire to enable humanitarian relief for the many thousands of people bearing the brunt of the Israeli ground invasion. When Prime Minister Netanyahu persisted in carrying the war beyond military targets to the point of war crimes as viewed here and abroad, Biden strongly urged Prime Minister Netanyahu to desist, but that was too late to avoid understandable polling backlash in this country.

Biden's 2024 spending proposal sheds further light on his platform and policy priorities:

- 3.2% increase for Defense, compared to the preceding year's budget enacted by Congress;
- Increased funding for health care, including Medicare, Medicaid, and the Veterans Administration, as well as increases for Social Security, law enforcement, immigration, and energy/environment.
- Raising the corporate tax rate from 21% to 28%, taxing top earners' capital gains at higher rates, and increasing taxes on U. S. companies' foreign profits from 10.5% to 21%.[23]
- Initiated planning for a price negotiation program to cut the costs of 10 very expensive medications, despite the strong opposition of Big PhRMA.[24]

Despite its legislative achievements and steadying influence after the disruptions caused by his predecessor, Biden's second term candidacy is hobbled by an approval rating of just under 40%, a lower reading than any president in 75 years of polling except for Trump and Reagan (who was dealing with a deep recession at this stage of his candidacy). At year's end of 2023, NBC polling found that Biden had a 40% approval rating vs. 57% disapproval, with Trump having a 2-point advantage, while 68% of voters were seeing the outcomes of Trump's legal matters as of major or moderate concerns for them.[25]

Despite those polling results, Biden can make a strong case against a Trump candidacy (assuming he's not in jail after his multiple future indictments!) by making the 2024 campaign a marked choice between the two parties, not a referendum on his own first term.[26] He can point to the proven case of GOP incompetency to govern after the avoidable threat of government shutdown over the debt ceiling and failure to advance needed legislation in Congress, in glaring contrast to his own steady hand over a long career in public service.

For the Republicans:

As pointed out in the last chapter, the GOP, as illustrated by the Freedom Caucus (aptly named the Chaos Caucus) in the House, has no policy agenda except to fight against any legislation by the Democrats and to regain control of Congress and the presidency. The

McCarthy led House passed a spending bill that would cut domestic spending by 22%, a bill that could not be passed in the Senate or avoid a presidential veto. That showed a lack of concern for the impacts of cuts ranging from Medicare, Social Security, education, safety net programs, child care, and food safety to clean air and water, railsafety and border security. That gave Biden an opportunity to ramp up his anti-Trump argument about adverse impacts on so many societal needs as well as a threat to democracy. Figure 13.3 shows the GOP platform in terms of authoritarian anti-democratic overreaching.

Figure 13.3

OVERREACHING OR JUST RANK AUTHORITARIANISM?

Source: Reprinted with permission from Nick Anderson

A CBS News poll taken April 27-29, 2023 asking likely GOP voters their preferences for the candidate for the 2024 Republican presidential nomination found these top answers for likely GOP voters: [27]

• Challenges woke ideas	85%
• Opposes any gun restrictions	66%
• Says Trump won in 2020	61%
• Makes liberals angry	57%

"No Labels" Party

This is a so-called party pretending to be a "centrist" eyeing a third party run in 2024. As a dark money group, it has pledged $70 million to support a third-party candidate who could draw enough votes from President Biden to return Trump to the presidency. As a front group for Trump, it is funded by pro-GOP billionaires and large corporations invested in maintaining the status quo and securing a GOP win that would continue current tax policies to their benefit. When we consider that just 44,000 votes out of more than 10 million cast in Arizona, Georgia and Wisconsin in 2020 were the difference between the Biden presidency and an Electoral College tie, the possibility of that risk becomes especially worrisome.

Although polling can be misleading and meaningless a year before the 2024 elections, some polls have found that one in five voters in six battleground states dislike the leading presidential candidates in both parties.[28] Robert F. Kennedy, Jr., has thrown his hat into the no labels ring, while Senator Joe Manchin, the bane of the Democrats in past years, is exploring doing so.[29] The potential risk for the Democrats would be the loss of some Biden votes and increasing the odds of a GOP win.

3. Where are the two parties on inflation and the economy?

As we saw in Chapter 2, corporate monopolies and price gouging are key drivers of inflation in our economy, typically resistant to control by either party. Yet consumers evaluate the administration and candidates for the next election on the basis of the prices they find for such items as groceries, gasoline, utilities and medical care. The Federal Reserve tries to keep the consumer price index (CPI) under control through periodic interest rate increases, but pays little attention to corporate price gouging.

Inflation rose as the economy rebounded from the pandemic during supply chain disruptions and labor shortages. The Biden administration gets little credit for what has happened to the economy and inflation from what he inherited from the Trump years and `the COVID pandemic. The CPI rose 5% in March, 2023, the smallest gain since in 2021 and still elevated compared to the 2.1% average in the three years before the pandemic. In June, 2023, the CPI rose just 3% for the year through that month, just one-third of the 9% peak in the summer of 2022.[30] According to comparative international measures, the U. S. has had the strongest recovery in the advanced world with the lowest inflation rate among major economies.[31]

Figure 13.4 shows how the U. S. economy has recovered from the pandemic-era losses, both in terms of employment and the G.D.P.[32] Figure 13.5 shows the marked drop in forecasted consumer-price index as of November 2023. Austan Goolsbee, Chicago Fed President, observed:

Figure 13.4

THE U. S. ECONOMY HAS RECOVERED FROM PANDEMIC-ERA LOSSES

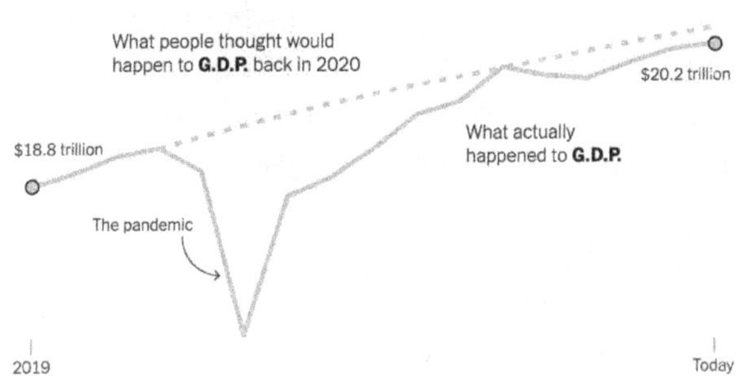

Source: Bureau of Labor Statistics, Congressional Budget Office

FIGURE 13.5

CONSUMER PRICE-INDEX WELL CONTROLLED

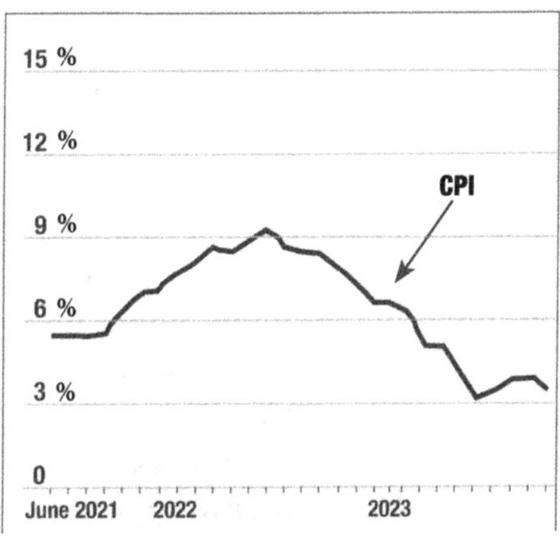

Source: Adapted from *Wall Street Journal* and the Labor Department

We may have brought down inflation as fast as it has ever come down, and we did this without starting a recession.[33]

Considerable disinformation surrounds the subject of inflation as the GOP keeps denying the progress by the Biden administration in bringing back jobs in a stabilized economy and heralding inflation as a problem owned by Democrats. The collapse of the Silicon Valley Bank, following the weakness of some regional banks, led Robert Kuttner to these important observations:

The economy is still doing well, but a weakened banking system, coupled with a Fed that is hawkish on rates but kind and gentle on financial regulation, could be the economy's undoing . . . When the histories are written about this economy and Fed policy, they should observe that the Fed's priorities of loose regulation and tight money were exactly backwards.[34]

According to the Bureau of Labor Statistics, the U. S. added 336,000 jobs in September 2023, together with an unemployment rate of 3.8%. Economists saw that as confirming the labor market's vitality and overall hardiness of an economy facing a variety of forces.[35] The GOP, however, has continued to dismiss positive economic data from the Biden administration as fake, leading Paul Krugman to deny that conspiracy theory in these words:

A recession might eventually happen,
but it isn't happening now.[36]

III. Steps to Rebuild Democracy

With wide and growing consensus across the country that democracy is on line in the 2024 elections, these are some of the major directions to rebuild democracy in this country. While they won't be positively considered in the current 118th Congress with its House "leadership" under Freedom Caucus control, these steps can provide a framework for planning legislation, Democratic campaigning, and future governing.

As we consider these steps, we should remind ourselves of how John Adams, as one of our Founding Fathers, saw the role of government:

> *Government is instituted for the common good; for the protection, safety, prosperity, and happiness of the people; and not for the profit, honor, or private interest of any one man, family, or class of men; therefore, the people alone have an incontestable, unalienable, and indefeasible right to institute government; and to reform, alter, or totally change the same, when their protection, safety, prosperity, and happiness require it.*[37]

1. Pass the Voting Rights Act

Passage of the John Lewis Voting Rights Act in the Democrat-controlled Congress after successful campaigns and the 2024 elections—is target #1 to restore the democratic process and re-establish our democracy.

2. Codify Roe v. Wade

This has the support of almost two-thirds of respondents to national polls and is essential to ensure that American girls and women have full rights to their own bodies and reproductive health. Given the draconian laws against abortion in a number of states, even including medication abortion, federal legislation is clearly needed at the highest priority to restore those rights established by the Court's Roe v. Wade ruling in 1973.

3. Reform the Supreme Court

The GOP under Trump set up today's 6-3 conservative Court as part of a long-term effort over many years, including blocking the appointment of Democrat nominees. The U. S. Supreme Court as presently constituted is anti-democratic with its 6-3 politicized conservative membership blocking progress toward renewing our democracy. They often interpret the Constitution without regard to changes in the country since the late 1700s. Some of their rulings have been seen as more political than judicial.[38] Moreover, they increasingly come to their decisions by a "shadow docket"—decisions that are unseen, unsigned and almost always unexplained.[39] Reform could well include expansion of its numbers, setting of term limits, and enforcement of a new ethical code of conduct.

Whether it likes it or not, the Supreme Court finds itself at the center of a legal storm that has everything to do with whether our republic and democracy will survive the 2024 elections.[40] Pivotal questions have become urgent for the 2024 elections, including whether Trump as former President is immune from prosecution for the January 6 insurrection attack on the Capitol and his efforts to overturn the results of the 2020 election. Colorado's highest court recently barred Trump from its primary ballot, ruling that Trump is disqualified from being president again for that reason.[42]

Another major question is whether or not we will end up with federal election laws vs. a patchwork non-system with each state having its own election laws.[43] Maine soon became the second state to rule that Trump isn't fit for its primary ballot,[44] which increases the pressure on the Supreme Court to make a definitive ruling that settles that matter.[45]

4. Reject Citizens United

The Citizens United ruling 13 years ago by the U. S. Supreme Court opened the floodgates to unlimited amounts of campaign cash to be spent on elections. The billionaire class has turned its wealth into political power. Figure 13.6 shows this striking impact by midterm cycle. Billionaires spent $1 billion in the 2022 midterms, 300 times what they spent on elections prior to passage of Citizens United. [46]

5. Get rid of the Electoral College

Our present Electoral College system has led to 5 presidents being elected after losing the popular vote. The January 6 insurrection shows how this has became a danger to democracy and the American people. Sixty-three percent of Americans support a popular vote method for electing our presidents, according to the Pew Research Center.[47] The Electoral Count Reform Act was passed by both houses of Congress in December 2022 as part of an omnibus spending package, but will require a constitutional amendment to be implemented.[48]

6. Implement gun control

There are more guns than people in the U. S., the most armed country on the planet. The 2022 Midterm Voter Election Poll found that 68% of all 2022 voters supported banning AR-15 assault rifles.[49]

Figure 13.6

BILLIONAIRE CAMPAIGN CONTRIBUTIONS BY MIDTERM CYCLE, 2010-2022

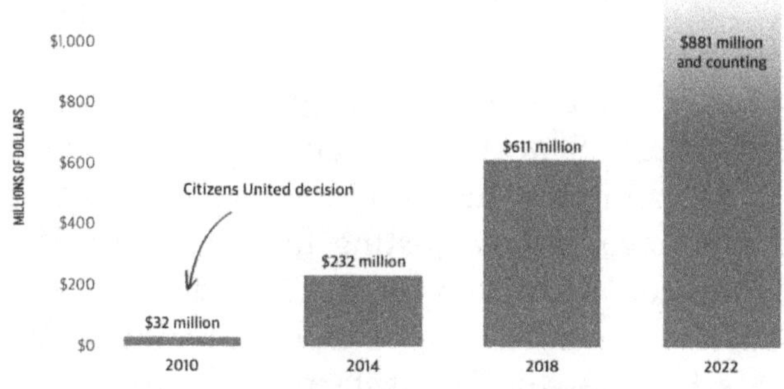

Source: ATF Analysis of Open Secrets contributions data and FEC receipts data

Yet there were more than 600 mass shootings in that year and 39 mass shootings in the first 24 days of 2023. Senator Diane Feinstein (D-CA) took the lead on this issue by introducing two bills on the first legislative day in the 2023 U. S. Senate—an Assault Weapons ban and the Age 21 Act, which would raise the minimum age to purchase assault weapons from 18 to 21.[50]

7. *Simplify and reform the tax code*

Words in the U. S. tax code have grown from 409,000 in 1955 to 4 million in 2021. It is overly complex, favors the wealthy, and disadvantages the majority of Americans. Loopholes for the rich should be closed and corporate tax rates increased to similar levels during the Eisenhower years. Scott Galloway, Professor of Marketing at NYU's Stern School of Business and author of the 2022 book *Adrift: America in 100 Charts*, recommends eliminating itemized deductions in favor of higher standard deductions for households, and stopping favorable tax treatment given to income earned by the sale of assets.[51]

8. *Rebuild regulatory apparatus*

Regulatory systems are underfunded with regulators outnumbered by corporate lobbyists; as one example, Amazon has more full-time lobbyists than there are sitting U.S. senators.[52] The Biden administration, however, has taken on the goal of ramping up guidelines, regulations, and enforcement through the FTC to counter monopolies and encourage competition.[53] Progress on that front includes a recent suit by the DOJ against Google to break up its business brokering digital advertising across much of the internet.[54]

9. *Raise minimum wage to a living wage.*

One third of the U. S. work force—almost 52 million workers—earn less than $15 an hour; the average worker makes $54 a week less than 50 years ago, after adjusting for inflation.[55] We have a long way to go to correct this problem. The federal minimal wage increased from $7.25 an hour to $9.50 an hour on July 1, 2023.[56] On the positive side, however, the FTC is starting the process of banning non-compete clauses in labor agreements whereby employers can sue former employees who go to work for another company in the same industry. If and when adopted, the FTC estimates that it would open up new job opportunities for 30 million Americans and raise wages by some $300 billion a year.[57]

10. *Overhaul the debt limit.*

The near disaster that occurred in the recent debate in Congress between an uninformed and irresponsible House Freedom Caucus and the rest of the House highlighted the vulnerability of the U. S. (and the world) over this issue. Democrats in the House and Senate have fortunately shown the way forward by their recent introduction of the Debt Ceiling Reform Act. It would empower the Treasury Department to continue paying the nation's bills for its existing obligations, but afford Congress 30 days to pass a veto-proof disapproval resolution.[58]

11. *Prevent disinformation from the use of A.I. during election campaigns.*

We have seen in earlier chapters the downsides of A.I., which could well become a serious problem in election campaigns. Public Citizen has already called attention to the likelihood that it may soon become impossible, even for experts, to distinguish so-called "deepfakes" from audio and video recordings that are real. As such, this could pose a threat to truth and democracy.

Today, there is no federal law that would stop political candidates or their parties from using deepfakes to willfully deceive voters.[59]

12. Counter the GOP's anti-woke campaign against DEI

DEI (diversity, equity and inclusiveness) as combined in a rhetorical assertion of "being woke," assert the positive principles of DEI. As Jim Hightower observes:

> *The GOP's crusade against being woke is against America itself, for we are a nation united under the essential principal of e pluribus unum. As affirmed by the egalitarian principles of the Declaration of Independence, the 14th amendment, the Statue of Liberty—and our kindergarten teachings of sharing and fairness—ours is a country rooted in diversification, expanding equality, and the democratic idea every voice ought to be included. Our country needs more of all three!* [60]

IV. Reasons for Guarded Optimism

With unprecedented levels of inequality of income and wealth, increased polarization across our country, decline of the middle class, increased political violence, corporate greed-induced inflation, and other basic problems impacting the American people, how can we maintain some sense of optimism about the future of our country?

Collectively, these are some of the reasons that we can be optimistic about the eventual success of our country in rejuvenating its claimed democracy for the good of all Americans:

1. An extensive 2020 Harris poll showed results supporting the American Dream, as reported by David Rubenstein in his 2021 book, *The American Experiment: Dialogues on a Dream*:

- 69% of Americans think America is the best country in the world.
- 57% of Americans think that America's best days are ahead.
- 59% of Americans expect to achieve the American Dream.
- A majority of Americans agree on two qualities distinctive of America: freedom of speech and free and fair elections.

- More than one-half of Americans would risk their lives for Freedom of Speech and/or the Right to Equal Justice.
- Three in five Americans believe that the country is still impacted by the fact that it was founded while sanctioning slavery.
- Three in four Americans believe that America is moving farther away from the ideals of the Founding Fathers.[61]

2. Attacks on 'wokeness' by GOP candidates in their primaries are not carrying as much political potency as they had hoped.[62]
3. In response to today's wide wealth inequality, more Americans on the right are looking left with growing support for major changes in our economic system.[63]
4. With abortion a major issue in this coming election, it will be a losing issue for the GOP as the number of abortions increased in the first half of 2023 compared to 2020 as women traveled out of state and access to abortion pills expanded.[64] Moreover, the November 7, 2023 elections showed that voters came to the polls to defend abortion rights in both red and purple states, including Ohio, Kentucky, Pennsylvania and Virginia.[65] And furthermore, abortion rights activists are seeking to put the issue on the ballot in numerous states in 2024.[66]
5. If the GOP Freedom Caucus (misnamed since it's not about freedom!) ends up showing its incapacity for governance by letting the federal debt proceed to government shutdown, a majority of voters may well favor the party with a record of governance.
6. If the race is so close as to come down to electoral college votes in the battleground states, recent state polls and surveys by *the New York Times* and Siena College have shown President Biden to be running as well or better in the battlegrounds as nationwide.[67]
7. And if the GOP sticks with Trump as its nominee with multiple indictments and perhaps convictions, and if he were to win the 2024 election, the Constitution specifically bars the president from using pardon power of the office to prevent his or her own impeachment and removal.[68]
8. The Rule of Law is being tested, and these are positive signs that it will be upheld and that no one is above the law:

- the $1.6 million fine of the Trump Organization as the first ever criminal conviction of a former President's companies for defrauding tax authorities in New York.[69]
- a $1 million fine on Trump and his attorney for filing a frivolous lawsuit alleging a political conspiracy during the 2016 election.[70]
- Four of the Oath Keepers actively involved in the January 6 insurrection attack on the Capitol have been convicted of seditious conspiracy and will face up to 20 years' jail time; [71] four more members of the far-right Oath Keepers militia were found guilty of seditious conspiracy for trying to keep Donald Trump in power;[72] Stewart Rhodes, the Oath Keepers' founder, Yale Law School graduate and former Army paratrooper, has been sentenced to 18 years in prison for seditious conspiracy.[73]
- the guilty verdict with $5 million in payments due from Trump to E. Jean Carroll in her defamation and sexual assault lawsuit.[74]
- Special Counsel Jack Smith's comprehensive and fully documented indictment of Trump.[75]

9. Younger voters will become a major force in 2024 and in later years. Millennials (born 1981-1996) and Gen Z (those born since 1997) will together comprise almost one half of the voting population (48.5%) in 2024 and in 2026 will become the first majority nonwhite generation. Researchers have found that these generations are more interested in policy than political parties. They have low levels of trust in Congress (20%) and large corporations (11%).[76] The latest data from the General Social Survey, conducted by the National Opinion Research Center at the University of Chicago finds that younger voters are tilting left and staying there.[77]

The 2024 general elections will present voters with two widely divergent options for the future—a progressive vision for America with a competent and concerned government rebuilding the middle class and unifying the country within a multiracial, multicultural democracy vs. a dysfunctional GOP committed to extending its own political power, authoritarianism (even dictatorship and fascism if Trump were to win), deregulation, and further dissolution of long-established government agencies. David Rothkopf, political affairs analyst and commentator, brings us this serious view of the stakes of these elections:

> *After decades of promoting minority rule—but dressing up their intentions with a fig leaf of respect for America's history, values, and tradition—the GOP has now dropped any pretense of caring about our Constitution or the principles upon which the United States was founded . . . State-level GOP legislators are actively trying to overturn the will of the people. The new Speaker is a far-right extremist. And Trump sounds more like Hitler every day.*[78]

Robert Kuttner sees the outcome favorable to Democrats in 2024:

> *The ouster of the former House Speaker by a tiny fraction of nihilists does serious damage to Republican chances of holding the House in 2024. Republican candidates, not just the GOP incumbents in the 18 districts that voted for Biden in 2020, can reasonably be charged by Democrats as a party that cannot be trusted to govern. This will also spill over into the contests for the presidency and control of the Senate.*[79]

Despite all the bad news and the continued disintegration of the Grand Old Party, Dana Milbank, author of the 2022 book, *The Destructionists: The Twenty-Five-Year Crack-up of the Republican Party,* brings us this good long-term prediction:

> *Things will get better in the long run with the rise to political dominance of the millennials and Gen Z, who have grown up in, and overwhelmingly favor, a multicultural America. The source of political rage, the older white backlash as the United States becomes majority-minority, will in the long run be quashed because there is no stopping that demographic transition. The transition to a white minority country is inevitable.* [80]

Joseph E. Stiglitz, Ph.D., Nobel Laureate in Economics, former chief economist at the World Bank and author of the 2012 book, *The Price of Inequality: How Today's Divided Society Endangers Our Future*, brings us hope that today's corporate dominance of our culture can be reined in for the common good.

The well-being of our citizens—and even our economic growth, especially if properly measured—will be much higher than what we can achieve if our society remains deeply divided. I believe that it is still not too late for this country to change course, and to recover the fundamental principles of fairness and opportunity on which it was founded. Time, however, may be running out. [81]

The 2024 elections are likely to be the closest in a generation at all three levels of national elected office—the House, Senate and White House. Figure 13.7 shows how these are up for grabs as of early November 2023.[82]

Figure 13.7

2024 ELECTIONS ARE UP FOR GRABS

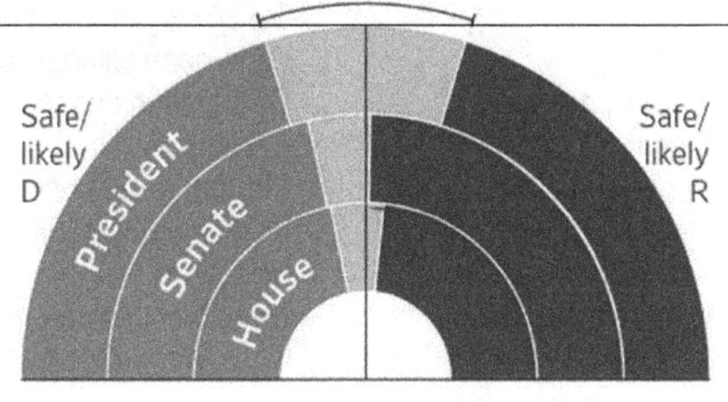

Source: ATF Analysis of Open Secrets contributions data and FEC receipts data

Effective comparisons of the Democratic and Republican Parties will be essential in addition to competition between individual candidates.

Drawing from his 2018 book, *The Common Good*, and what has happened since then, Robert Reich adds this timely hope for the outcome of the 2024 elections:

Hopefully, democracy will survive the 2024 election. The longer-term challenge for America will be to respond to the anger, despair, and suspicions of those who have been left behind, with hope rather than neofascism. We must assert a common good based on democracy, the rule of law, and a system that works for the good of all. [83]

Table 13.1 shows the high stakes involved with contrasting outcomes of the 2024 elections.

Table 13.1

CONTRASTING OUTCOMES AFTER 2024 ELECTIONS:

DEMOCRATIC PRESIDENT WITH CONTROL OF CONGRESS	REPUBLICAN PRESIDENT WITH CONTROL OF CONGRESS
Democracy lives	Oligarchy and authoritarianism
Fair elections	Big Money restricting voting rights
Rule of law upheld	Wide open without rule of law
Corporations more accountable	Corporations unaccountable
Antitrust regulation in progress	Unregulated
Small business prospers again	Minimal small business
Multicultural society possible	Increased inequality and inequities
Supreme Court reformed	No reform
Media open based on truth	Untruth with controlled media
American Dream possible	No longer possible

Conclusion:

So there you have it—the big issues are right in front of us as we go forward to the 2024 elections, when democracy will once again be on the ballot. A January 2024 special issue of *The Atlantic*, 'January 6 Was Practice', details the existential threat to our democracy, essentially democracy vs. authoritarianism and fascism, if Trump were to be elected.[84]

These two observations are especially relevant to how the future can, and will unfold:

Midnight is the darkest moment of the day, everywhere in the world. But it is also the most hopeful, because everything that comes after holds the promise of light. America has a genius for reinvention, and we must use it. As Lincoln said, we must "disenthrall ourselves" to save our country. From the same forces of bigotry that divided and nearly defeated the country in the Civil War, yes, without a doubt, but from something new to the American landscape as well, from a dangerous experimentation with a uniquely American brand of authoritarianism. We must all play our part. We must confront the question
—Why should I? [85]

—Rep Adam Schiff (D- CA), member of the House Select Committee Investigating the January 6 insurrection, and author of *Midnight in Washington: How We Almost Lost Our Democracy and Still Could*

The arc of the moral universe is long, but it bends toward justice. [86]

—Theodore Parker, Massachusetts abolitionist minister in 1853, as often paraphrased in later years by Dr. Martin Luther King Jr.

As the foregoing in this book makes clear, corporate monopoly power has enveloped the economic, social and political life of our country over so many years as to become normalized. Corporate power is focused on itself, not the national interests. The far-right extremism of the Republican party, as illustrated by the former Trump presidency and the GOP House in Congress today, shows how corporate power has corrupted elections and pushed governing away from the public interest.

We need to come together in the 2024 elections to get us on track to reclaim our democracy and sense of community. The stakes are the highest in our history. Wake up and get engaged, America!

References:

1. Giroux, HA, A society consumed by locusts: Youth in the age of moral and political plagues. *Truthout*, April 5, 2020.
2. Richardson, HC. The fight for our America. *The New Republic,* November, 2023, p. 17.
3. Hartmann, T. What the final stage of Reaganism looks like. *The Progressive Populist*, February 1, 2023, p. 12.
4. Zhang, S. For every $1 gained by a bottom 90 percenter since 2000, a billionaire got $1.7 million. *Truthout*, January 17, 2023.
5. Leonhardt, D. Argument over economic policy will shape GOP in post-Trump era. *New York Times*, August 7, 2023, A:17.
6. Ibid # 4.
7. Kuttner, R. Conservatives mugged by reality. *The American Prospect*, July/August, 2014, p. 5.
8. Lehmann, C. American Oligarchy. *The Nation*, December 19, 2022.
9. Weissman, R. Marking two years since the Jan. 6 attack on the U. S. Capitol. *Public Citizen News*, January/February, p. 3.
10. Weisman, J, Baker, P. Biden declares 2024 bid. *New York Times*, April 26, 2023: A:1.
11. Lucey, C, Thomas, K. Biden opens re-election bid. *Wall Street Journal,* April 26, 2023, A: 1.
12. Reich, R. True patriotism is the opposite of Trump's White Christian Nationalism. <robertreich@substack.com>
13. Goldmacher, S, Swan, J, Haberman, M, Lai, S. Trump lays out 2nd-term vision: Wrecking norms. *New York Times,* May 12 2023, A :1.
14. Swan, J, Savage, C, Haberman, M. Trump and allies forge plans to increase presidential power in 2025. *New York Times*, July 17, 2023.
15. Reich, R. What is Trump planning if he gets a second term? Chaos and consolidation. November 10, 2023. <robertreich@substack.com
16. Stanley, J. How Fascism Works: The Politics of Us and Them. New York. Random House, 2020, p. 13.
17. Hagerman, M, Goldmacher, S. Trump vow of 'retribution' foretells a 2nd term of spite. *New York Times*, March 8, 2023, A: 17.
18. Ludwig, M. A 2023 wave of "election subversion" bills threatens 2024 results. *Truthout*, June 11, 2023.
19. Reich, R. How we can stop Donald Trump's campaign. Right now. *Inequality Media Civic Action*, May 18, 2023.
20. Blow, CM. Trump's 'people' means his people. New York Times, September 28, 2023, A:27.
21. Rubin, J. Opinion. Trump has it all wrong: He needs someone else to be president. T*he Washington Post*, June 22, 2023.
22. Goldmacher, S. An uneasy task for GOP rivals: Defend the man leading in the polls. New York Times, June 10, 2023, A:14.

23. Rubin, GT, What's in the President's 2024 spending proposal. *Wall Street Journal*, March 10, 2023. 22. Reich, R. Biden's State of the Union, and the paradox at the center of his presidency. robertreich@substack.com, February 7, 2023.
24. Stolberg, SG, Robbins, R. U. S. announces first drugs picked for Medicare price negotiations. *New York Times*, August 29, 2023.
25. Howe,
26. Reich, R. We should be very, very concerned about this. Inequality *Media Civic Action*, September 14, 2023.
27. Last, JVl. The just-say-stuff party. The Bulwark, May 2, 2023.
28. Epstein, RJ, Igielnik, R, Baker, C. voters dreading a 2024 rematch give independents another look. *New York Times*, November 8, 2023, A:14.
29. Broadwater, L. In blow to Senate democrats, Manchin will not run again. *New York Times*, November 10, 2023, A:1.
30. Smialek, J. Inflation cools sharply in June, good news for consumers and the Fed. *New York Times*, July 12, 2023.
31. Krugman, P. The secret of America's strong economic recovery. *New York Times*, October 28, 2023, A:28.
32. Guilford, G, Timiraos, N. U. S. inflation eased to 5% in March, *Wall Street Journal*, April 12, 2023.
33. Timiraos, N, Omeokwe, A. Inflation cools, market soars. *Wall Street Journal*, November 15, 2023, A:1.
34. Kuttner, R. The economy is still doing well. *Kuttner on Tap*, April 28, 2023.
35. DePillis, L, Nerkar, S. U. S. payrolls grew by 199,000 in November. *Bureau of Labor Statistics*, December 8, 2023.
36. Krugman, P. No, the economic data isn't being faked. *New York Times*, July 9, 2023
37. Adams, J, as quoted by Potter, W and Penniman, N in Nation on the Take: How Big Money Corrupts Our Democracy, New York. *Bloomsbury Press*, 2016, p. 229.
39. Vladeck, S. *The Shadow Docket: How the Supreme Court Uses Stealth Rulings to Amass Power and Undermine the Republic.* New York. *Basic Books*, 2023, pp. 12-13.
40. Feuer, A. Trump cases may reshape '24 election. *New York Times*, December 21, 2023, A:1.
41. Wolfe, J, Timms, M. Colorado's ban on Trump forces high court into political thicket. *New York Times*, December 21, 2023, A:1.
42. Bouie, J. Red state-blue state divide tells America's future. *New York Times*, Opinion, December 28, 2023, A:19.
43. Russell, J, Anstead, A, Cromwell, S. Alarm and applause in Maine as Trump is pushed off the ballot. *New York Times*, December 30, 2023, A:12.
44. Liptak, A. Both sides ask justices to rule if Trump is fit to be on the ballot. New York Times, December 29, 2023, A:15.
45. Liptak, A. Justices to decide whether Trump is eligible for Colorado ballot. *New York Times*, January 5, 2024.

46. Kass, D. How Clarence Thomas's billionaire benefactor is using his wealth to influence elections. *Americans for Tax Fairness*. November 16, 2023.
47. Salzer, R, Kiley, J. Majority of Americans continue to favor moving away from Electoral College. *Pew Research Center*, August 5, 2022.
48. Walker, C. Jamie Raskin says it's time to end the electoral college. *Truthout*, December 28, 2022.
49. Sanchez, GR, Bennett, C. Voters want Congress to address gun violence and mass shootings, *Brookings*, January 23, 2023.
50. Feinstein, D. Introducing an assault weapons ban is more important than ever. (contact @fundforthemajority.com)
51. Galloway, S. *Adrift: America in 100 Charts*, New York. *Penguin Random House*, 2022, p. 228.
52. Ibid # 51, pp. 230.
53. Dayen, D. A pitched battle on corporate power. *The American Prospect*, January 25, 2023.
54. Kruppa, M, Schechner, S, Michaels, D/ DOJ sues Google, seeking to break up online advertising business. *Wall Street Journal*, January 24, 2023.
55. Sanders, B. The state of the working class in America. info@berniesanders.com.
56. Nassauer, S. Walmart to raise starting hourly wages to $14. *Wall Street Journal*, January 25, 2023: B1.
57. Shakir, F. Building power for working people. *More Perfect Union*, January 25, 2023.
58. Wise, L. Democrats press to overhaul debt limit. *Wall Street Journal*, June 10-11, 2023, A:6.
59. *Public Citizen*. Candidates must pledge not to use A.I. or deepfakes to deceive voters, May 15, 2023.
60. Hightower, J. True "wokeism" is a core American value—stand up for it!. *Jim Hightower's Radio Lowdown*, June 15, 2023.
61. Penn, M, Gerzema, J, Broughton, A. in Rubenstein, D. T*he American Experiment: Dialogues on a Dream*. New York. *Simon & Schuster*, 2021, pp. 427-437.
62. Weisman, J. Attacks on 'wokeness' falling flat with GOP voters. *New York Times*, August 7, 2023, A:14.
63. Smith, TJ. Wealth gap has some on the right looking left. *New York Times*, September 6, 2023, A:1.
64. Walker, AS, McCann, A. Despite state restrictions, abortions in U. S. increase as overall access improves. *New York Times*, September 11, 2023, A:11.
65. Zitner, A, Kusisto, L. Elections lay bare GOP's abortion liability. *Wall Street Journal*, November 9, 2023, A:1.
66. Kusisto, L, Vielkind, J. Abortion rights backers move to expand ballot push in 2024. *Wall Street Journal*, November 11-12, 2023, A:1.
67. Cohn, N. Trump's teetering electoral college edge. *New York Times*, September 14, 2023, A:14.

68. Tribe, LH, Painter, R, Eisen, N. *The Washington Post*, 2017.) REF?
69. Corporate Crime Reporter 37 (3), January 16, 2023, p. 10. COMPLETE
70. Tau, B. Trump fined for suit deemed frivolous. *Wall Street Journal*, January 21-22, 2023, A:12.
71. Wolfe, J, Barber, CR. Four Oath Keepers guilty. *Wall Street Journal*, January 24, 2023.
72. Montague, Z. Four more Oath Keepers members convicted of sedition in second trial. *New York Times*, January 23, 2023.
73. Barber, CR. Oath keepers founder Stewart Rhodes sentenced to 18 years for seditious conspiracy. *Wall Street Journal,* May 25, 2023.1
74. Weiser, B, Fadulu, L, Christobek, K. Donald Trump sexually abused and defamed E. Jean Carroll, Jury finds. *New York Times*, May 9, 2023.
75. Viswanatha, A, Gurman, S, Barber, CR. Trump indictment unsealed. *New York Times*, June 10-11, 2023, A:1.
76. Smith, C. How much could younger voters affect future election outcomes? *Governing*, April 10, 2023.
77. Bouie, J. Younger voters are tilting left and staying there. *New York Times*, October 25, 2023, A:23.
78. Rothkopf, D. Republicans are fighting a war on democracy all over America. *The Daily Beast*, November 14, 2023.
79. Kuttner, R. The House GOP's self-immolation. Today on Tap. *The American Prospect*, October 4, 2023.
80. Milbank, D. *The Destructionists: The Twenty-Five-Year Crack-up of the Republican Party,* New York. *Doubleday*, 2022, p. 309.
81. Stiglitz, JE. *The Price of Inequality: How Todays Divided Society Endangers Our Future*. New York. *W. W. Norton & Company, Inc*, 2012, pp. 289-290.
82. Yelp, R. The 2024 election could be the closest in a generation. *Wall Street Journal*, November 8, 2023, A:4.
83. Reich, R. Why have so many Americans succumbed to Trumpism? robertreich@substack.com, September 8, 2023.
84. Gellman, B. January was practice. *The Atlantic*, January, 2023.
85. Schiff, A. *Midnight in Washington: How We Almost Lost Our Democracy and Still Could*. New York. *Penguin Random House*, 2021, xvi.
86. Parker, T, as quoted by Dr. Martin Luther King, Jr. in Hartmann, T., America is being exhausted by the fear-and hate-mongers. T*he Progressive Populist,* June 1, 2023, p. 13.

SOME PENDING, STILL UNANSWERED QUESTIONS

This book has addressed, in an evidence-based way, the historical and present circumstances that this country now faces in terms of governance, professed values, and the future of its democracy. I hope that this has been helpful to you, dear reader, in sorting through the serious threats to our country and the crucial importance of the coming 2024 elections. A recent article in *The Economist* entitled, *Donald Trump Poses the Biggest Danger to the World in 2024*, put the stakes of the 2024 elections in this country as:

> *A second Trump term would be a watershed in a way the first was not. Victory would confirm his most destructive instincts about power. His plans would encounter less resistance. And because America will have voted him in while knowing the worst, its moral authority would decline. The election will be decided by tens of thousands of voters in just a handful of states. In 2024 the fate of the world will depend on their ballots.*

These are pending, still unanswered questions as this book goes to press, and will have much to do with the survival of democracy in America:

1. Will former-president Donald Trump be held accountable under the rule of law for the four pending criminal prosecutions against him?
2. Who will be the final presidential candidates for the Republican, Democratic and No Label parties?
3. To what extent will hate speech and disinformation be controlled during the buildup to the 2024 elections? One example—far right legislators and activists are recasting the January 6 insurrection as a benign event that should exonerate the participants.[1]
4. What has been blocking reform of the Electoral College and not supporting a national popular vote system that would guarantee the presidency to the candidate receiving the most popular votes nationwide?

5. With 36 House lawmakers in the House (in both parties) giving notice that they will retire[2], how will that affect the outcome of House control after the 2024 elections?
6. If the need arises, can the new ethics code of the U. S. Supreme Court be enforceable?

My hope is that this book has helped to equip you, as voters in November, to preserve our democracy.

—John Geyman, M.D.

References:

1. Broadwater, L, Feuer, A, Fichera, A. Right is using Jan. 6 footage to distort past. *New York Times*, November 24, 2023: A:1.
2. Hughes, S. Departure plans surge in Congress after GOP House Speaker drama. *Wall Street Journal*, November 24, 2023: A:4.

Index

A

C

F

G

I

J

K

L

M

N

T

W

Y

Z

About the Author

John Geyman, M.D. is professor emeritus of family medicine at the University of Washington School of Medicine in Seattle, where he served as Chair of the Department of Family Medicine from 1976 to 1990. As a family physician with over 21 years in academic medicine, he also practiced in rural communities for 13 years. He was the founding editor of *The Journal of Family Practice* (1973 to 1990) and the editor of *The Journal of the American Board of Family Medicine* from 1990 to 2003. Since 1990 he has been involved with research and writing on health policy and health care reform.More recently, he has shifted his interest to national politics, the increasing polarization across our country, and the imminent threat to American democracy as the 2024 elections approach.

His most recent book is *Are We the UNITED States of America? Can We Hold Together As One Country?* (2022) Earlier books include: *The Future of U.S. Health Care: Corporate Power vs. the Common Good,* (2022), *Transformation of U.S. Health Care, 1960-2020: One Family Physician's Journey* (2022), *America's Mighty Medical-Industrial Complex: Negative Impacts and Positive Solutions* (2021), *Profiteering, Corruption and Fraud in U.S. Health Care* (2020), *Long Term Care In America: The Crisis All Of Us Will Face In Our Lifetimes* (2020), *Struggling and Dying Under Trumpcare* (2019), *TrumpCare: Lies, Broken Promises, How It Is Failing, and What Should Be Done?*

(2018), *Crisis in U.S. Health Care: Corporate Power vs. the Common Good* (2017), *The Human Face of ObamaCare: Promises vs. Reality and What Comes Next* (2016), *How Obamacare Is Unsustainable: Why We Need a Single-Payer Solution For All Americans* (2015), *Souls on a Walk: An Enduring Love Story Unbroken by Alzheimer's* (2013), *Health Care Wars: How Market Ideology and Corporate Power Are Killing Americans* (2012), *Breaking Point: How the Primary Care Crisis Threatens the Lives of Americans* (2011), *Hijacked: The Road to Single Payer in the Aftermath of Stolen Health Care Reform* (2010), *The Cancer Generation: Baby Boomers Facing a Perfect Storm* (2009), *Do Not Resuscitate: Why the Health Insurance Industry Is Dying* (2008), *The Corrosion of Medicine: Can the Profession Reclaim Its Moral Legacy* (2008), *Shredding the Social Contract: The Privatization of Medicare* (2006), *Falling Through the Safety Net: Americans Without Health Insurance* (2005), *The Corporate Transformation of Health Care: Can the Public Interest Still Be Served?* (2004), *Health Care in America: Can Our Ailing System Be Healed?* (2002), *Family Practice: Foundation of Changing Health Care* (1985), and *The Modern Family Doctor and Changing Medical Practice* (1971).

John has also published five pamphlets following the approach of Thomas Paine in 1775-1776: *Common Sense About Health Care Reform in America* (2017), *Common Sense: U.S. Health Care at a Crossroads in the 2018 Congress* (2018), *Common Sense: The Case For and Against Medicare For All. Leading Issue in the 2020 Elections* (2019), *Common Sense: Medicare For All: Foundation for a 'New Normal' In U.S. Health Care* (2020), and *Common Sense: Medicare For All: What Will It Mean For Me?* (2021)

He also served as the president of Physicians for a National Health Program from 2005 to 2007, and is a member of the National Academy of Medicine.

Printed in the USA
CPSIA information can be obtained
at www.ICGtesting.com
CBHW030305120324
5206CB00003B/5